NEW JERSEY
AQUATIC PLANTS

A Guide to the Garden State's Floating, Submersed & Floating-leaved Flora

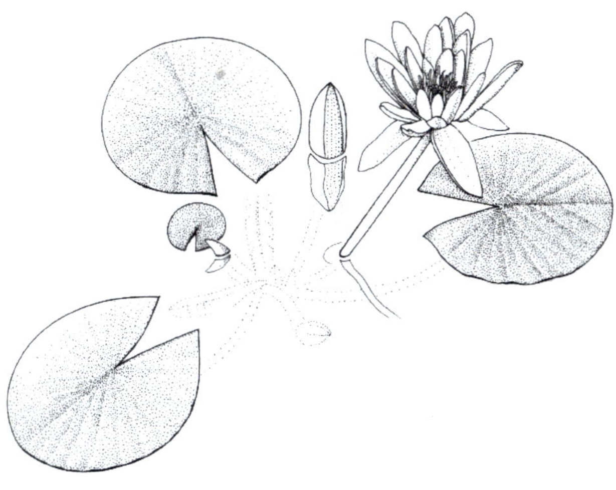

Donald J. Padgett

NEW JERSEY AQUATIC PLANTS
A Guide to the Garden State's Floating, Submersed & Floating-leaved Flora

Donald J. Padgett

Spatterdock Press
Middleboro, Massachusetts

Printed in USA by KDP, An Amazon.com Company

ISBN: 979-8-218-36319-2 (paperback)
ISBN: 979-8-218-36560-8 (hardcover)

"The water of the Pine Barrens is soft and pure,
and there is so much of it that, like the forest above it,
it is an incongruity in place and time."

John McPhee, 1978

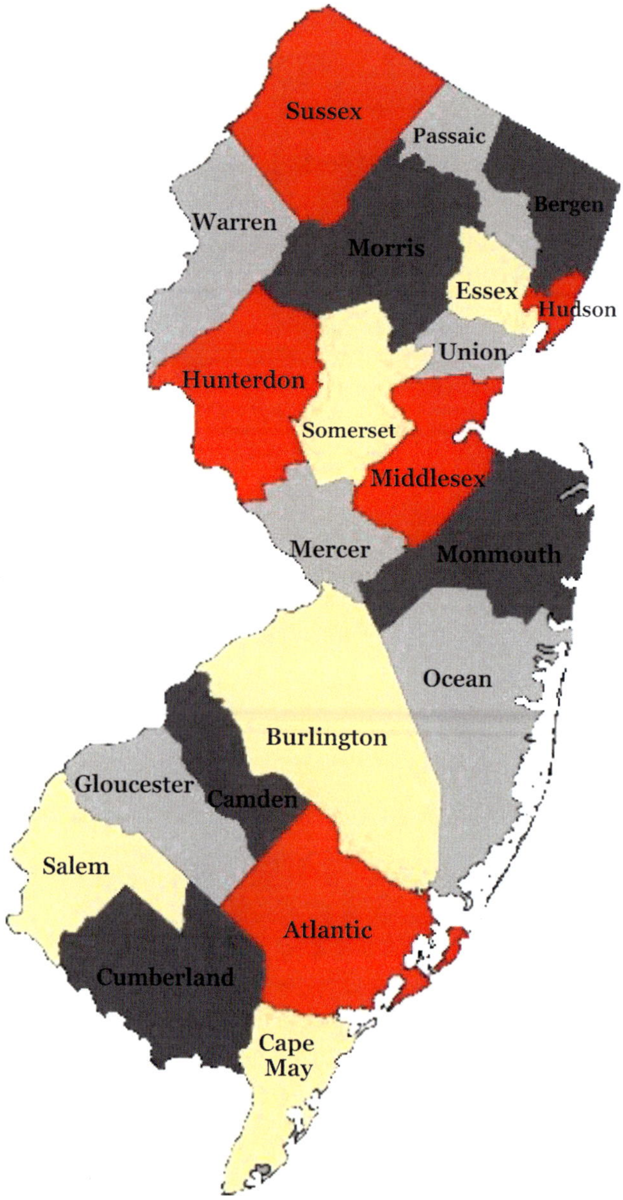
Sussex
Passaic
Warren
Bergen
Morris
Essex
Hudson
Union
Hunterdon
Somerset
Middlesex
Mercer
Monmouth
Ocean
Burlington
Gloucester
Camden
Salem
Atlantic
Cumberland
Cape
May

CONTENTS

Preface vii
Acknowledgments ix
Introduction 1

How to use this book 3

- Format 3
- Use of keys 3
- Plant names 3
- Species descriptions 3
- Illustrations & Photographs 4

Aquatic Plants of New Jersey 5

- Composition 5
- Geographic distribution 5
- Features of aquatic plants 6
- Aquatic Bryophytes 10
- Macrophytic algae 11

Keys to Genera 12

- Synopsis of Keys 12
- Submersed plants 12
- Floating & floating-leaved plants 16
- Plants with some leaves or stem portions extending above the water surface 19

Keys to Species & Descriptions 23

References 243
Illustration & Photograph Credits 244
Glossary 249
Index 251
About the Author 256
Notes 257
Ruler 258

PREFACE

This book was developed following a series of identification guides dedicated to the aquatic plants of the New England states. Like that of its predecessors, the impetus to construct this book arose from teaching about aquatic plants and their role in assessing waterbodies and the frustration of locating an appropriate field manual for students. While there are excellent field guides on aquatic plant identification for this region, most either use terminology far too advanced for novices or are overly simplistic, always embrace too broad a geographic coverage which unnecessarily adds many species to the mix for consideration, and exclude telling photographs. So, like my other guides, this book was constructed as a quasi-technical—yet comprehensive—identification resource devoted to all the fully aquatic macrophytes in New Jersey. It offers dichotomous keys to identify species, illustrations, color photographs, basic distribution maps, and general descriptive accounts of each species. I hope that it will be of use to anyone with professional or amateur interests in the hydrophytes of this region and surrounding areas.

DJP

ACKNOWLEDGEMENTS

I am always grateful to those who helped advance my career interests in aquatic plants, particularly Garrett Crow, Barre Hellquist, Jack Holt, Don Les, and Tom Philbrick. Appreciation is given to Elaine Padgett and Jennifer Moran for support and encouragement, and special attention to all those who granted use of their photographs, especially Katy Chayka and Peter Dziuk (minnesotawildflowers.info), Michael Graziano, Roger Hammer (rogerlhammer.com), Barre Hellquist, Steve Turner (Missouriplants.com), and Bob Wernerehl. I thank Kathleen McCauley for providing technical assistance with some species distribution data. As always, I am thankful to Bridgewater State University for ongoing support of my work. Lastly, a note of love to Shannon, Morgan, Sullivan, and my pups Ali and Whiskey.

Brasenia schreberi

INTRODUCTION

New Jersey Aquatic Plants summarizes the distribution, habitat, and biology of plants that grow in fresh, brackish, or saline waters of the Garden State. It is intended to foster an appreciation of this fascinating group of plants and assist users in identifying them to species. This guide aims to update and bridge the gap between the more technical manuals and the overly simple field guides of the region, with a focus on the floating, submersed, and floating-leaved flora. Consequently, advanced botanical terminology is used at a minimum, with simpler descriptive words or phrases used as a substitute.

I included all truly aquatic plant species (of angiosperms, ferns, and fern-allies) considered native or introduced in New Jersey that one may encounter in ponds, lakes, pools, rivers, streams, and marshes. Truly aquatic (or "fully" aquatic) species are defined here as those with most of their cycle spent floating on, or submerged in, fresh, brackish, or saline water. Native or indigenous plants are those which occur naturally in New Jersey. Introduced species entered the flora from other geographic regions either by intentional or accidental means. To make the book as comprehensive as possible, both common and rare species are included. While less likely to be encountered in the field, the rare and endangered species were combined with the more common ones so that their place in the region's rich aquatic diversity may be fully appreciated, and with the hope that new occurrences may be discovered and protected.

While 152 species are described in detail, 33 additional species are discussed for comparison purposes or represented in various ways.

What This Book Does Not Cover

While this guide covers the 152 "true" aquatic plants of New Jersey, there are still many plants (or plant-like relatives) which occur in or around aquatic habitats that are not included in this book. Notably, this guide excludes the many "emergent" species—unless such species can also be found as a distinctive submersed growth form (e.g., *Gratiola aurea*). Emergent or wetland plants grow in shallow or damp areas typically along the edges of marshes, ponds, lakes, and rivers. Unlike true aquatic vegetation, emergent species are rooted in the ground with most of their stems, leaves, and flowers held above the water surface [e.g., Cattails (*Typha*), Wild rice (*Zizania*), sedges (*Carex*), etc.]. In cases where genera contain aquatic as well as common emergent species (e.g., *Sagittaria*, *Sparganium*), the emergent species are noted in the descriptive account of the genus. Likewise, any aquatic plant that is known to be an interspecific hybrid (e.g., hybrids in *Potamogeton* and

Isoëtes) is not detailed here outside of sometimes noting within the parental species accounts a hybrid is known.

Lastly, also for the sake of brevity, the coverage of aquatic bryophytes (i.e., non-vascular plants) and macrophytic freshwater algae has been kept to a minimum. General descriptions of some of these species can be found on pages 10-11. All macrophytic marine algae (i.e., seaweeds, kelps) are excluded from this guide.

Pine Barrens

HOW TO USE THIS BOOK

Format. The book is arranged into an easy-to-use format. If the common name (e.g., Eurasian water-milfoil) of a plant is known, a quick check in the index can direct you to the page number for the species description. If the scientific generic (genus) name is known (e.g., *Myriophyllum*), flip through the descriptive text pages to locate the page for that plant(s). The descriptive pages for plants arc arranged alphabetically by genus name, and then by species within the genus. Another method would be to thumb through the book and look for an illustration or photo of a plant like the one you are trying to identify. If the plant in question is completely unknown to you, or if you are not completely certain of its identity using the preceding methods, the plant can be identified using the taxonomic keys in the book.

Use of keys. Identification keys were constructed to facilitate the identification of species. They consist of a series of numbered couplets, with a choice of contrasting statements. After a choice is made, a number at the end of the statement directs you to either to the next couplet or a plant name. Two sets of keys are provided to help sort out this large group of plants: 1) keys to genera, and 2) keys to species within a genus. Once a genus is identified in the key, locate the genus descriptive page. If there are more than one species in the genus, each descriptive entry begins with an overview of the group and ends with a key to the various species.

Plant names. The scientific plant names in this book generally agree with Crow and Hellquist (2023). To make the book useful to a wide audience, the plants are referred to by common names in addition to their scientific names (except for keys). If a species has more than one popular common name, alternate common names are provided within the text.

Species descriptions. At the top of each species descriptive page the **common name** and accepted **scientific name** and author (who named the species) is given. The family name in scientific form is included if the species is the only one for the genus and there is no genus descriptive page.

A description of the species is then provided with features useful for its identification emphasized. Descriptions are organized with a sequence of plant type, stems, leaves, flower clusters, flowers, and then fruits, and are based on the feature's appearance during the active growing season. If a feature is not especially useful for identifying a plant (e.g., anther number), it is not mentioned. **Habitat & Distribution** indicates native status, provides the common habitat types the species occupies, and its general range with an attempt to characterize its abundance in New Jersey. If the species is listed as rare in the state this information is noted here. **Notes** provides information regarding any specific environmental conditions the plant requires or offers, its role in a community, and similarity to other plant species.

A **map** shows the distribution of each species as documented within the counties of New Jersey and includes known introductions or invasions. A county is shaded in which the species is known to occur. In some cases, distributions may include historic occurrences. The maps differentiate by color between native (green) and introduced (red) occurrences.

Illustrations and photographs. Each species account is supplemented with photographs and or illustrations. Attributable credits of each illustration or photo are found on Page 244.

Hydrocharis morsus-ranae

AQUATIC PLANTS OF NEW JERSEY

Composition

Nearly 16% (or 1368 sq. miles) of New Jersey is permanently covered by water. Collectively, the 10,900 lakes, ponds, and reservoirs and 8600 miles of freshwater streams host a diverse assemblage of aquatic plants. The geographic position of this state places the region at the intersection of major bioregions (exerting northern, southern, coastal influences). This convergence leads to great aquatic biodiversity and unique collections of species in the different areas, especially for its size. For example, some hydrophyte species in New Jersey are at the northern extent of their geographic ranges (e.g., *Eriocaulon compressum, Heteranthera multiflora, Nymphoides aquatica*), while others are at the southern limit of their ranges (e.g., *Myriophyllum sibiricum*, *Nuphar variegata*, *Potamogeton robbinsii*).

The 152 hydrophytes considered in this book include three (of four) plant life forms associated with aquatic habitats comprising 144 flowering plants, 5 quillworts, and 3 ferns. These "true", or strictly aquatic, hydrophytes range from plants that grow completely submerged to floating-leaved and free-floating species. Most species (86%) are native, but 21 are considered non-native. Plants that may grow with their roots and lower stems under water but hold a more substantial amount of their body in the air—so called *emergent* species—are important components of a state's flora but omitted from this guide. Those few emergent species (i.e., *Gratiola aurea*, *Juncus pelocarpus*, *Pontederia cordata*) that also possess a distinctive submersed growth form, however, are included.

While most of these aquatic plants may be commonly encountered, 60 species are classified as either endangered or species of concern by New Jersey's Department of Environmental Protection. Individuals of species listed in the official Endangered Plant Species List (2022) are regulated under provisions of the Endangered Plant Species Program Rules (N.J.A.C. 7:5C-1.1 et seq.). Accordingly, imperiled plants detailed in this book are indicated as "*endangered*" or, if a species of concern, as "*rare*".

Most non-native aquatic plants introduced into New Jersey are deemed invasive. Invasive aquatic plants have impacted many lakes, ponds, reservoirs and rivers and streams. Exotic species like *Hydrilla verticillata*, *Hydrocharis morsus-ranae*, *Myriophyllum spicatum*, *Najas minor*, *Potamogeton crispus*, and *Trapa natans* are infamous weeds that threaten native species and ecosystems.

Geographic Distribution

The natural occurrence of certain hydrophytes is largely regulated by chemical properties of their watery environment, as well as water depths and substrate preferences. As with all aquatic organisms, the optimal growth and survival of hydrophytes is influenced by levels of pH, alkalinity, and interactions of elements in the water. The chemical composition of most New Jersey surface waters shows regional patterns related to the underlying geology (Collins and Anderson 1994; Wolfe 1977). Low pH and alkalinity levels are typical in waters where bedrock consists of granite, sand, and gravel. Where the geologic substrate shifts (eastward and southward) from the linear belts of limestone, marble, and granite to mostly silt, clay, and sand, pH and alkalinity levels decrease. This pattern is reflected, to a degree, in the geographic distribution of many aquatic plants.

The high alkalinity, pH, and calcium levels characteristic of waterbodies in northern New Jersey (particularly the Valley & Ridge Province) support species otherwise seldom found elsewhere, like *Myriophyllum sibiricum, Rorippa aquatica, Stuckenia filiformis,* and select species of *Potamogeton* (*P. obtusifolius, P. richardsonii, P. zosterifolius*). The hard waters cause higher available nutrients. Conversely, more highly acidic waters to the south and near the coast (Coastal Plain Province) support species like *Isoëtes echinospora, Potamogeton confervoides*, *Proserpinaca pectinata*, and *Sagittaria teres*. These soft waters are nutrient-poor.

Watercourses influenced by ocean tides, dominated by Na and Cl, support *Eleocharis parvula, Eriocaulon parkeri, Lilaeopsis chinensis, Limosella australis, Sagittaria montevidensis*, and *Zannichellia palustris* in brackish conditions, and *Ruppia maritima* and *Zostera marina* in more saline conditions. Of course, numerous hydrophytes are more broadly tolerant of water chemistry. This is reflected in their more widespread distributions (e.g., *Elodea nuttallii, Nasturtium officinale, Nuphar variegata, Nymphaea odorata, Potamogeton epihydrus, P. spirillus, P. natans, P. amplifolius, Utricularia vulgaris,* and *U. purpurea*).

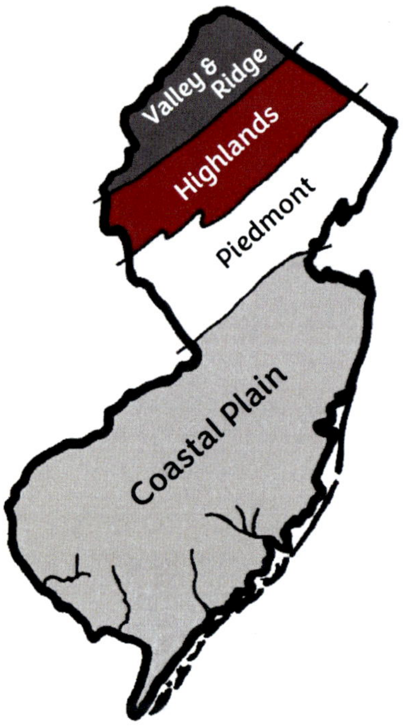

Figure 1. Physiographic provinces of NJ.

Features of Aquatic Plants

The ability to distinguish among the many kinds of aquatic plants is based foremost on a knowledge of their forms and characters. Since hydrophytes are derived from terrestrial ancestors, this group of species has developed shared features to overcome the challenges presented with life in water. It is these characteristics that we often rely on in identifying a species.

Keep in mind aquatic plants are notoriously variable in form. Local variations in water depth or flow can influence leaf size, shape, and texture, or presence of flowers or fruits which can make identification difficult—if even possible—at times.

Morphology. True aquatic macrophytes can be submersed (plant anchored to substrate or suspended), floating-leaved (plant anchored to a substrate), or free-floating on water surface (unattached to a substrate). Leaves growing submersed under water are often thin and delicate as to offer little resistance to potentially destructive water actions and to permit more light to penetrate tissues. Likewise, submersed foliage is commonly ribbon-like (Fig. 2a) or highly divided (Fig. 2c,d) in form. Submersed stems, like leaves, are often thin and supported by water, lacking strengthening agents in their tissues. Consequently, submersed stems and leaves are generally limp and collapse when held out of water. Stems and leaves of certain species are specialized to be buoyant. These organs have air trapped in swollen tissues to reach light closer to the water surface or aid in keeping flowers above water. Floating leaf blades are usually thicker, at times leathery, and capable of shedding water (Fig. 2b). Some species possess both floating and submersed leaves on the same plant (Fig. 2c).

Reproduction. As their terrestrial relatives do, aquatic plants rely on sexual reproduction via flowers (or spores outside of the angiosperms). In the majority of hydrophytes, flowers are held above water, by various means, to utilize insect pollinators or wind. The insect-pollinated flowers are often showy, colorful (yet white in many species), and sometimes fragrant. In contrast, some hydrophytes develop flowers below water and employ very unusual underwater pollination mechanisms.

Aquatic plants are noted for their ability to reproduce and spread, often aggressively, by asexual means through rapid growth, fragmentation, and or formation of dormant structures. Due to this propensity, hydrophytes are some of our most troublesome weeds (e.g., *Myriophyllum spicatum*, *Hydrilla*). Specialized overwintering, vegetative organs called turions, or "winterbuds", are prevalent among aquatic plants. These dormant, condensed shoots are found mostly in submersed and free-floating species. They are particularly common in species of *Potamogeton*, *Myriophyllum*, and *Utricularia*, and often useful for identification purposes.

Hydrilla verticillata

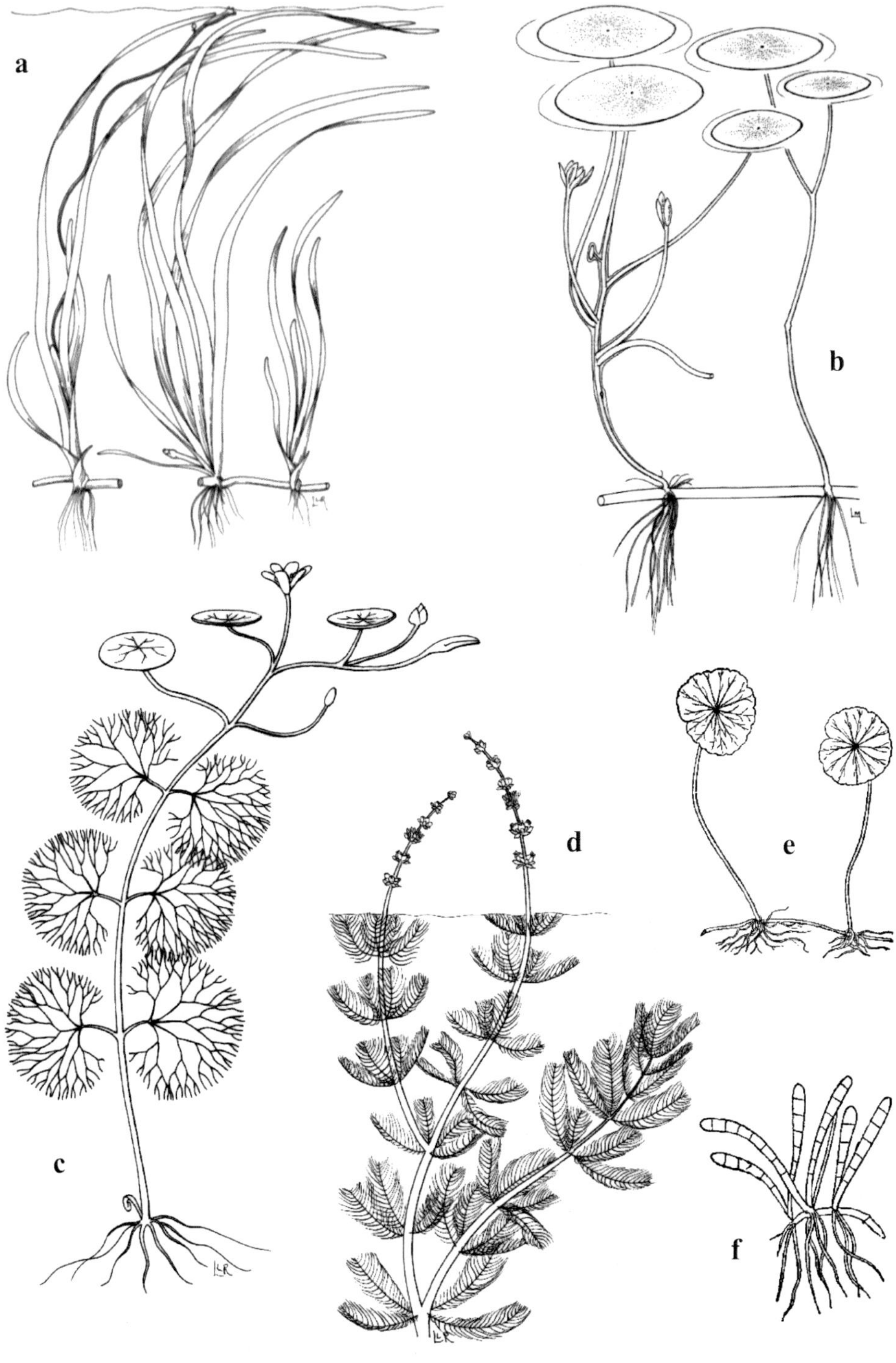

Figure 2. a. *Vallisneria*, with submersed leaves; b. *Brasenia*, with floating leaves; c. *Cabomba*, with submersed and floating leaves; d. *Myriophyllum*, submersed plant with emersed spike; e. *Hydrocotyle*, floating leaves on horizontal stems in substrate; f. *Lilaeopsis*, submersed leaves on horizontal stems in substrate.

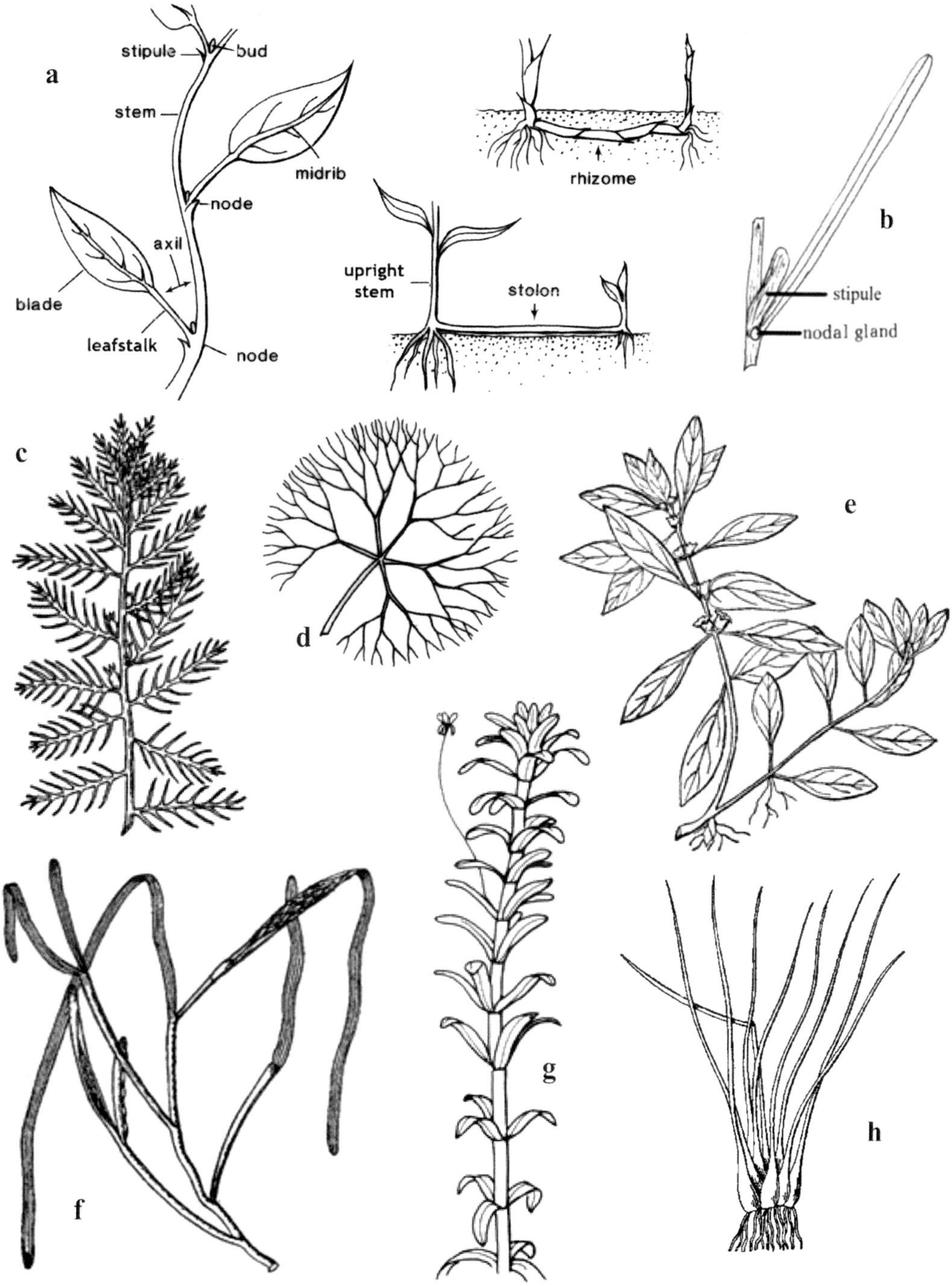

Figure 3. a. Generalized plant morphology; b. *Potamogeton*, node; c. *Proserpinaca*, pinnately divided leaves; d. *Cabomba*, palmately divided leaf; e. *Ludwigia*, undivided, opposite leaves; f. *Zostera*, ribbon-like, alternate leaves; g. *Elodea*, whorled leaves; h. *Isoëtes*, basal leaves.

Aquatic Bryophytes

There are floating or submersed Bryophytes in New Jersey waters. These lower, non-vascular plants reproduce by microscopic spores and lack the complexity and traditional leaves, stems, and roots of higher plants. Since this plant type falls outside the focus of this guide, only a limited account of these plants is offered below in case occurrences are found and in need of cursory identification.

Slender Riccia - *Riccia fluitans* L. (Ricciaceae) is one of the more common aquatic liverworts. Plants are narrow (about 4 mm wide), ribbon-like, and forked several times. They form tangled masses at or below the surface of quiet waters.

Purple-fringed Riccia - *Ricciocarpus natans* (L.) Corda (Ricciaceae) is a common aquatic liverworts in ponds or lakes. Plants are small and floating, resembling Duckweeds (*Lemna* or *Spirodela*). Bodies are fan-shaped and two-lobed. The top surface is furrowed, and the bottom is dark-scaly.

Aquatic Mosses - New Jersey hosts many mosses—both common and rare species—which occupy aquatic habitats. Aquatic moss species are too numerous and specialized for this guide (See Bowman [2017] for more a more comprehensive account). Generally, these plants grow submersed on rocks, in flowing water of streams or still waters of ponds.

New England Willow moss - *Fontinalis novae-angliae* Sull. (Fontinalaceae) is a common aquatic moss. Plants are dark green, glossy, firm, with concave leaves and wiry stems.

Macrophytic Algae

There are a few species of Charophytes—robust, plant-like, green algae—that resemble rooted, aquatic plants and can be confused with submerged flowering plants in New Jersey. These native, simplistic, macroscopic algae, which may be particularly abundant in some freshwater systems, generally have cylindrical whorls of branches coming off the main stem-like axis. Since algae fall outside the scope of this guide, a limited account is only offered here.

Muskgrass - *Chara* sp. (Characeae) is gray-green with a gritty texture, and whorls of ridged, needlelike branches that resemble leaves. They have a foul musky or garlicky odor when crushed or handled outside of water. This alga prefers hard or alkaline waters. Its gritty texture comes from the crusty calcium carbonate deposits that can form on the stems and branches.

Stoneworts – *Nitella* sp. (Characeae) is translucent green with very smooth branches which may be divided multiple times. It can be up to a meter in length and lacks the gritty texture and odor of *Chara*. *Nitella* prefers more acidic ponds or streams.

KEYS TO GENERA

SYNOPSIS OF KEYS

1\. Plants with stems and leaves entirely submersed, normally growing completely beneath the water's surface (may be temporarily exposed to air with receding water or low tides); only flowering structures may sometimes be held above water surface (fig. 2a,d)........ ....**Key I**

1\. Plants with stems or leaves exposed to air either by floating on, or held above, water surface; flowering structures may or may not also be held above water surface..2

  2\. Plants with at least some leaves floating on the water surface (fig. 2b,c)....................**Key II**

  2\. Plants with some leaves or stem portions extending above the water surface..........**Key III**

KEY I: SUBMERSED PLANTS

1\. Leaves or leaf-like stems scattered along an upright stem (fig. 2c,d).....................................2

1\. Leaves or leaf-like stems attached basally (figs. 2a, 3h) or grouped on horizontal stems in substrate (fig. 2f)...39

  2\. Leaves or leaf-like branches divided into multiple narrow segments (figs. 2d, 3c,d)......... 3

  2\. Leaf blades undivided (fig. 3e-g) 19

3\. Leaves or leaf-like branches whorled along stem (figs. 2d, 3g) 4

3\. Leaves opposite or alternate along stem (figs. 2c, 3e,f).. 9

  4\. Leaves of complicated structure, each flattened leafstalk tipped with 4–8, fine-toothed, bristles (6–8 mm long) surrounding an orbicular blade (2–3 mm long) consisting of two semicircular halves, hinged along the midrib...*Aldrovanda*

  4\. Leaves without bristles and a hinged orbicular blade at tip of leafstalk...............................5

5\. Leaf-like branches bearing small bladders at tips; flowers purple..........................*Utricularia*

5\. Plants lacking bladders at tips; flowers not purple.. 6

  6\. Leaf segments serrated with small teeth, leaves somewhat stiff; plants rootless...*Ceratophyllum*

  6\. Leaf segments without teeth, leaves soft in texture; plants rooted......................................7

7\. Submersed leaves repeatedly divided from base; flowers borne in a conspicuous, yellow, daisy-like cluster.. *Bidens*

7\. Submersed leaves feather-like, with a central axis; flowers inconspicuous................................8

  8\. Leaves crowded at top of stem; plants often with floating clusters of flowers on swollen, air-filled, spongy stalks in spring/early summer.. *Hottonia*

  8\. Leaf segments scattered along most of stem length; flowers either submersed in leaf axils or emersed on narrow spikes, throughout most of season....................... *Myriophyllum*

9\. Leaves opposite...10

9\. Leaves alternate 12

10. Submersed leaves pinnately divided, with a central axis; upper portion of stem often with a floating cluster of triangular to diamond-shaped blades and stout, spongy stalks... .... *Trapa*

10. Submersed leaves palmately divided (repeatedly divided from base); lacking a floating cluster of triangular to diamond-shaped blades.......... 11

11. Leaves with a distinct stalk (1–4 cm long); flowers white; a few inconspicuous, narrow (1–4 mm wide) floating leaves also produced at tips of stems during periods of flowering only.... .... *Cabomba*

11. Leaves stalkless (crowded and appearing whorled); flowers yellow, in a daisy-like cluster; emersed, undivided toothed leaves sometimes present.......... *Bidens*

12. Plants with leathery stems and creeping, green roots adhering to ledge, rocks, or boulders with fleshy disks; plants of rocky, fast-flowing rivers and streams...*Podostemum*

12. Plants lacking fleshy, adhesive disks; plants of lakes, ponds, or sluggish rivers and Streams. 13

13. Leaves without one central axis (midrib) 14

13. Submersed leaves each with a central axis.......... 15

14. Plants with small sac-like bladders, mostly scattered on sides of leaf-like segments; plants rootless, mostly free-floating or anchored by buried branches.......... *Utricularia*

14. Plants lacking bladders; plants rooted to substrate..........*Ranunculus*

15. Plants terminated with a floating rosette (to 50 cm diam.) of broad, triangular to diamond-shaped leaves; fruit large (2–4.5 cm wide), hard, black, and spiny.......... *Trapa*

15. Plants without a floating rosette of broad leaves; fruit smaller and without spines..........16

16. Leaf divisions of submersed leaves flattened..........17

16. Leaf divisions of submersed leaves thread-like (sometimes also flattened in *Rorippa*)..... 18

17. Leaves (2–8 cm long) becoming crowded at top of stem near water surface; flowers with 5 white petals, whorled on long (to 30 cm), emersed swollen, air-filled, flowering stems in spring/early summer.......... *Hottonia*

17. Leaves (1–4 cm long) spaced evenly along most of stem length; flowers without petals, borne in leaf axils of emergent leaves.......... *Proserpinaca*

18. Leaves crowded along stems; flowers reduced and inconspicuous, borne in axils of submersed leaves or arranged on emersed tight spikes.......... *Myriophyllum*

18. Leaves not crowded along stems; flowers conspicuous with 4 white petals, borne in emersed branching clusters.......... *Rorippa*

19. Leaves whorled along stem..........20

19. Leaves opposite or alternate.......... 23

20. Leaves linear, flaccid, toothless, 0.3–2 mm wide, in groups of 3, 4, or 6 per whorl.......... .... *Sclerolepis*

20. Leaves oblong or lance-shaped, flattened, firm, toothless or saw-toothed on edges, 2–6 mm wide, 3–8 leaves per whorl.......... 21

21. Leaves in whorls of 4–8.......... 22

21. Leaves in whorls of 3 (some leaves opposite in pairs).......... *Elodea*

22. Leaves mostly in whorls of 4, blades 15–40 mm long, margins lacking conspicuous teeth .... *Egeria*

22. Leaves in whorls of 4–8, blades 8–15 mm long, margins conspicuously saw-toothed...... .... *Hydrilla*

23. Leaves opposite..........24

23. Leaves alternate.......... 30

24. Submersed leaves linear.. 25

24. Submersed leaves lance-shaped, egg-shaped, or rounded.......... 27

25. Leaf margins with minute teeth (visible with hand lens), blades widened at base and sheathing stem.. *Najas*
25. Leaf margins without teeth; blades not widened at base.. 26
26. Submersed leaves (>1 mm wide) notched at tip; stipules lacking; plants usually with a cluster of floating egg-shaped leaves near stem tip; fruit 2-lobed.................... *Callitriche*
26. Submersed leaves (≤1 mm wide) pointed at tips; stem sheathing stipules at base of leaves; plants without floating leaves; fruit not lobed, slightly toothed on outer edge...... .... *Zannichellia*
27. Plants diminutive (usually <5 cm tall) and mat-forming...28
27. Plants larger (usually >5 cm tall) and not mat-forming..29
28. Plants somewhat fleshy and stout; leaves lance-shaped and pointed at tips; plants sterile .... *Gratiola*
28. Plants not fleshy; leaves lance-shaped, egg-shaped, or rounded, and rounded, pointed, or notched at tips; flowers borne singly in leaf axil... *Elatine*
29. Leaves small (6 mm long), rounded, and without stalks; stems flaccid and mostly unbranched; plants without flowers.. *Hypericum*
29. Leaves larger (10–50 mm long), oval to egg-shaped, and conspicuously stalked; stems many-branched and reddish; flowers borne singly in leaf axils................................ *Ludwigia*
30. Submersed leaves pinnately compound with 3–9 round to oblong blades (leaflets), leaflet at tip is usually largest.. *Nasturtium*
30. Submersed leaves simple, each with one blade...31
31. Leaves inconspicuous and reduced to minute, stubby scales (<1 mm long); stems mostly unbranched arising singly from buried rhizomes.. *Myriophyllum*
31. Leaves conspicuous (>3 cm long); stems branched 32
32. Submersed leaves linear, ribbon-like or thread-like, 0.2–12 mm wide, with or without an evident mid-vein, blades lacking a stalk; sheathing stipules present or absent at leaf base 33
32. Submersed leaves elliptic, oblong, or lance-shaped, 3–75 mm wide, with an evident mid-vein, blades with or without a stalk; sheathing stipules present at leaf base.................... .... *Potamogeton*
33. Submersed leaves flat and ribbon-like, 1–12 mm wide; stipules may or may not be present at leaf base...34
33. Submersed leaves thread-like <1 mm wide; stipules present at leaf base............................37
34. Leaves with an evident mid-vein; stipules present (2–100 mm long); plants may also have stalked floating blades; flowers and fruits borne in cylindrical spikes..........*Potamogeton*
34. Leaves without a mid-vein; stipules lacking; floating blades absent; flowers and fruits otherwise...35
35. Leaves to 10 cm long, 1–5 mm wide; flowers yellow with six petal-like lobes, borne singly; fruit an elongated capsule... *Heteranthera*
35. Leaves 30–100+ cm long, 2–12 mm wide; flowers not yellow, borne in clusters; fruit a beaked drupe...36
36. Leaves not sheathing the stem; flowers borne at or above water surface in dense, spherical clusters; plants of freshwaters. .... *Sparganium*
36. Leaves sheathing the stem; flowers submersed, enclosed within a leaf-like sheath; plants strictly marine... *Zostera*
37. Leaves 1-veined and blunt-tipped; floating blades absent; flowers and fruits borne underwater; fruits in clusters of four, each fruit on a long stalk (1–2 cm long); plants chiefly coastal in saltwater, with thread-like rhizomes.. *Ruppia*

37. Submersed leaves with 1–5 veins and sharp or blunt tips; floating blades sometimes present; flowers and fruits borne on crowded, cylindrical spikes mostly above water; plants of freshwaters, mostly lacking rhizomes...38

38. Leaves stiff, channeled, 1-veined; floating blades absent; stipules fused to leaf base for more than two-thirds of stipule length; rhizomes bearing small (1–2 cm), white tubers.... ....*Stuckenia*

38. Leaves flaccid, flat, with 1–5 veins; floating blades sometimes present; stipules free, or if fused to leaf base, then for less than half of stipule length; rhizomes lacking (or if present, not bearing tubers) .... *Potamogeton*

39. Leaves quill-like (linear and round in cross-section) and clustered into basal rosettes........40

39. Leaves (or leaf-like stems) thread-like, flattened, and/or more ribbon-like, clustered into basal rosettes or not..43

40. Roots with cross walls; flowers, if present, to 15 mm wide with 3 white petals...*Sagittaria*

40. Roots without cross walls; flowers, if present, small (3–4 mm wide) with 5 white petals, or straw-colored...41

41. Horizontal stems absent; leaves with four hollow lengthwise chambers, with a few cross-walls; flowers/fruits not produced... *Isoëtes*

41. Horizontal stems present, thread-like; leaves without four hollow chambers, with or without cross-walls; flowers may or may not be present..42

42. Leaves fleshy, without internal cross-walls, narrow at base; flowers with 5 white petals, borne singly; plants chiefly of estuarine tidal waters.. *Limosella*

42. Leaves not fleshy, with scattered internal cross-walls, widened at base; flowers straw colored and grass-like (often replaced by small bulbs), borne on multi-branched clusters; plants not restricted to tidal waters..*Juncus*

43. Leaves (or leaf-like stems) thread-like, attached singly or grouped in clusters along horizontal stems 44

43. Leaves flattened and/or more ribbon-like, clustered into basal rosettes...............................47

44. Leaves fleshy, 1–2 mm wide; flowers white.. *Limosella*

44. Leaves or leaf-like stems thread-like (<0.5 mm wide) and delicate; flowers yellow, purple, or brown...45

45. Horizontal stems thick (3–4 cm diameter)..*Juncus*

45. Horizontal stems, if present, thread-like (<2 mm diameter)...46

46. Flowers showy, yellow or purple; leaves completely or mostly hidden in substrate; plants only apparent when flowering; a few tiny (0.2–1.1 mm long) sac-like bladders may be present, also buried in substrate..*Utricularia*

46. Flowers not showy, borne in small (2–8 mm long) clusters behind overlapping brown scales; leaf-like stems upright, not hidden in substrate; plants apparent with or without flowers; bladders not produced.. *Eleocharis*

47. Leaves thin, flaccid, and ribbon-like..48

47. Leaves flattened but thicker, not ribbon-like and flaccid..50

48. Leaf blade with a 3-zone appearance (light-colored middle zone bordered by darker zone on sides); flowers small (2 mm wide) floating at surface with transparent petals; fruit a cylindrical capsule borne at end of a long, corkscrew-like stalk........... *Vallisneria*

48. Leaf blade without a 3-zone appearance; plants often sterile, but, if flowers present, larger and emersed above water; if fruit present, not borne on a long, corkscrew-like stalk..49

49. Roots with cross walls; leaves with cross veins running perpendicular to central mid-vein, blades often long (>25 cm).. *Sagittaria*

49. Roots without cross walls; leaves without cross veins, blades 6–25 cm long.........*Pontederia*

50. Plants low and small, leaves mostly 1–6 cm long..51
50. Plants larger, leaves to 35 cm long, sometimes thick and spongy.................. *Sagittaria*
51. Leaves hollow..52
51. Leaves not hollow...53
52. Leaves numerous, each with two hollow chambers in cross section; flowers conspicuous, clustered on long (>20 cm long) stalks; fruit a nodding capsule......*Lobelia*
52. Leaves 1–few, each hollow but transversely divided with 4–6 cross walls; flowers inconspicuous, and borne on stalks about as long as the leaves; fruit a nutlet with 5 corky ribs.. *Lilaeopsis*
53. Leaves attached in pairs along slender rhizomes, rounded and widest at tips; flowers borne singly on very short (0–2 mm) stalks between the leaf pairs........................*Glossostigma*
53. Leaves numerous in tufted rosettes, tapered at tips; flowers borne in clusters on longer stalks (>2.5 cm)..54
54. Roots with conspicuous cross walls; leaves widest at base and with conspicuous cross-veins; spherical whitish flower clusters borne at end of a vertically ridged stem...*Eriocaulon*
54. Roots without cross walls; leaves lance-linear in shape, without cross-vens; a few white-petaled flowers borne at end of non-ridged stem......................................*Echinodorus*

KEY II: FLOATING & FLOATING-LEAVED PLANTS

1. Whole plant is free-floating or suspended at water surface; plants either lacking roots or with roots extending into water column..2
1. Only the leaves or branches are normally floating at water surface; plants typically rooted in the substrate (fig. 2b, e) 10
2. Plants diminutive, ≤6 cm long; if present, roots unbranched; no recognizable flowers present...5
2. Plants larger; leaves 2–40 cm long, arranged in rosettes; roots branched and feathery......3
3. Leaves without stalks, light green, and velvet-hairy..*Pistia*
3. Leaves with obvious stalks, dark green, and glossy..4
4. Leaves with greatly swollen/inflated stalks, blades not spongy; flowers large (5–7 cm wide), showy, and blue or purplish-blue; roots blackened...............................*Eichhornia*
4. Leaves with stalks not inflated, blades spongy; flowers not showy, whitish; roots not black ....*Limnobium*
5. Leaves distinguished from stems, positioned in two rows along horizontal stems, blades covered in hairs..6
5. Plant body not differentiated into distinct stems and leaves; plants not covered in hairs...... 7
6. Floating blades unequally two-lobed, very small (0.5–2 mm wide); roots slender and unbranched...*Azolla*
6. Floating blades round, larger (1–1.5 cm wide); true roots lacking, but a third leaf at each node resembles a branched root.. *Salvinia*
7. Plants with roots below, extending into water; bodies flattened throughout, 1–4 mm wide.. 8
7. Plants without roots; bodies spherical, oval, linear, or boat-shaped (i.e., flattened above and rounded below), 0.5–1 mm wide... 9
8. Plants each with one root below; bodies green beneath....................................*Lemna*
8. Plants each with 7–21 roots below; bodies reddish purple beneath .... *Spirodela*

9. Plant body 0.5–1 mm long, spherical, oval, or boat-shaped (i.e., flattened above and rounded below)………………………………………………………………………………………… *Wolffia*
9. Plant body 6–8 mm long, linear and sword-shaped, curved, and hollow……………… *Wolffiella*
10. Plant with a floating rosette of noticeably inflated (swollen and spongy) leaf stalks or branches; submersed leaves finely divided with thread-like segments…………………… 11
10. Plant lacking a floating rosette of inflated branches or leaf stalks; submersed leaves, if present, not finely divided………………………………………………………………………13
11. Floating leaves or upright branches green; bladders absent on plant; flowers white…………12
11. Wheel-like rosette of whitish branches floating flat on water surface, functioning as a float for the flowering stem; numerous bladders present on submersed portion of plant; flowers yellow……………………………………………………………………………… *Utricularia*
12. Rosettes of floating leaves, with large-toothed, triangular to diamond-shaped, flat blades; flowers conspicuous; fruit large (20–45 mm wide) with stout spines………*Trapa*
12. Rosettes of erect stalks, bearing well-spaced whorls of inconspicuous flowers; fruit small (1.5–3 mm wide) lacking spines…………………………………………………*Hottonia*
13. Floating leaves linear and ribbon-like, > 10 times as long as wide, without obvious stalks, usually just tips of leaves floating……………………………………………………………14
13. Floating leaves with broad blades, not ribbon-like, with obvious leaf stalks; usually the entire blade is floating………………………………………………………………………………17
14. Leaves 10–15 mm wide, with conspicuous cross veins (short veins running perpendicular to longer veins); flowers borne either below water or on floating stems………………15
14. Leaves 2–10 mm wide, without cross veins; flowers borne above water on emergent stems………………………………………………………………………………………………16
15. Leaf with a 3-zone appearance (a light-colored middle zone bordered by a darker zone on each side), blade not widening at tip; flowers with transparent petals; fruit cylindrical (5–12 cm long), borne singly at end of a coiled stalk; roots without cross walls…………*Vallisneria*
15. Leaf without a 3-zone appearance, blade sometimes widening at tip; flowers showy, each with three white petals, borne in clusters at end of a long, usually floating, stem; fruit flattened and seed-like (to 2.5 mm long), crowded into spherical clusters; roots with cross walls……………………………………………………………………………………… *Sagittaria*
16. Leaves 15–45 cm long, dark bluish-green, with a prominent central vein; base of leaf forming a tube-like sheath around the stem; flowers and fruits in minute, narrow (1–2.5 mm wide), soft clusters……………………………………………………………………*Glyceria*
16. Leaves 50–150 cm long, green, lacking a central vein; base of leaf not tubular; flowers in spherical (5–25 mm wide) clusters developing into hard, bur-like fruit clusters ……………………………………………………………………………………………… *Sparganium*
17. Leaf stalks centrally attached to underside of floating leaf blade………………………………18
17. Leaf stalks attached at the edge of floating leaf blade……………………………………… 20
18. Leaf blades are broadly oval; submerged portions of plant covered in a clear, jelly-like coating; stems flexible and buoyant; flowers red purple, borne singly……………*Brasenia*
18. Leaf blades are circular; submerged portions of plant not covered in a jelly-like coating; stems creeping on substrate; flowers yellow, whitish, or pink, borne singly or in clusters ………………………………………………………………………………………………19
19. Plants typically massive with large (to 60 cm wide), blue-green, leaf blades attached to long (to 2 m) stout stalks; flowers large (10–20 cm wide), yellow or pink, and borne singly……… ………………………………………………………………………………………… *Nelumbo*
19. Plants with smaller (1–7.7 cm wide), green, leaf blades attached to shorter (to 25 cm) stalks; flowers minute, whitish, and borne in clusters of 15–35…………………………… *Hydrocotyle*
20. Leaves are all basal, arising from base of plant close to substrate…………………………21
20. Leaves attached along an upright or floating stem in the water column ………………….29

21. Floating leaves divided into segments or deeply lobed along sides.................................22
21. Floating leaves neither divided into segments nor lobed along sides (blades may have a basal sinus).. 24
22. Floating leaf comprised of 4 triangular segments (each 7–21 mm long, 6–19 mm wide), resembling a four-leaf clover; reproductive structures (not flowers) submersed, hairy, pea-shaped (5 mm), near base of leaf stalks... *Marsilea*
22. Floating leaf simple, blade deeply lobed and divided into 3–7 main segments; yellow or white flowers in clusters, emersed above water 23
23. Flowers whitish or greenish, borne in clusters (umbels) of 4–10 flowers where all flowers are attached to same point at end of a 1–6 cm long, hairless stalk, one cluster per node; floating stems solid, sending out numerous long roots at nodes...................... *Hydrocotyle*
23. Flowers yellow, numerous, borne on hairy branching clusters; floating stems hollow.......... .... *Ranunculus*
24. Floating blades blue green, parallel-veined, oblong to elliptical, without a sinus; flowers minute, without petals, and borne in dense clusters at end of thick, white stalks.......... ....*Orontium*
24. Floating blades green to purplish, veins centrally radiating and /or branching, generally round or heart-shaped, with a deep sinus; flowers conspicuous, with petals, not borne on thick, white stalks...25
25. Plants also with submersed, linear, phyllodial leaves (25–450 mm long, 15–110 mm wide); roots with cross walls; fruits flattened and seed-like (to 2.5 mm wide), crowded into spherical clusters... *Sagittaria*
25. Plants lacking submersed, linear, phyllodial leaves; roots without cross walls; fruits globose, berry-like (4–40 mm wide) and borne singly...26
26. Leaves large (mostly >8 cm wide), veins branched and running toward margins; flowers bisexual, with >3 white, yellow, or pinkish petals; fruits large (4–40 mm wide)............ 28
26. Leaves smaller (<6 cm wide), veins unbranched and running toward tip; flowers unisexual with 3 whitish petals; fruits smaller (<1 cm wide).....................................27
27. Primary lateral veins of leaf blade forming a 75–90° angle with the midvein; spongy tissue confined to sides of midrib on undersurface of blade; stipules 2, distinct from the leaf stalk; petals broad (1.5 times or more or long as the sepals) ....*Hydrocharis*
27. Primary lateral veins of leaf blade forming a 30–80° angle with the midvein; conspicuous spongy tissue throughout undersurface of floating blade; stipules 1, its base fused to the leaf stalk; petals narrow (up to 1.5 times as long as the sepals) ....*Limnobium*
28. Leaf blade generally circular in shape, with a closed sinus and pointed lobes, usually purplish on underside; leaf stalk round in cross section; flowers white to pink, 5–19 cm wide with numerous petals; fruits maturing underwater on coiled stalks.........*Nymphaea*
28. Leaf blade circular-oblong, with an open sinus and rounded lobes, green on underside; leaf stalk round or flattened; flowers bright yellow, 1–4.5 cm wide, with 5–6, petal-like sepals; fruits maturing at water surface on straight stalks............................... *Nuphar*
29. Floating leaves pinnately compound with 3–9 round to oblong blades (leaflets); flowers with 4 white petals.. *Nasturtium*
29. Floating leaves simple, each with one blade; flowers otherwise.................................. 30
30. Floating leaves generally round or heart-shaped; flowers are emersed, often showy.... 31
30. Floating leaves elliptical, oblong, or egg-shaped; flowers are submersed or emersed, small (<5 mm wide) or showy...34
31. Leaf veins pinnately branching, blades tapering at base; submerged nodes sometimes bear erect, fleshy, white, spongy "air" roots which float; flowers yellow......................*Ludwigia*
31. Leaf veins parallel or centrally radiating, blades not tapering at base; nodes lack floating white spongy "air" roots; flowers yellow, white, or pale blue.......................................32

32. Floating blades with veins centrally radiating and branching, with or without a deep sinus at base; flowers with 5 white to yellow petals and 5 stamens.......................33

32. Floating leaves with parallel veins, blades shallowly lobed at base; flowers with 6 white to pale blue petals and 3 stamens...*Heteranthera*

33. Floating blades 3–15 cm long, margins unlobed to wavy, purple coloration may be present, especially on undersides; flowers showy, 5–25 mm wide, yellow or white; submersed clusters of slender fleshy roots may be present at leaf base......................... *Nymphoides*

33. Floating blades 1–7 cm long, margins lobed, lacking purple coloration; flowers whitish and small (5 mm); slender fleshy roots absent at leaf base; floating stems often with dense clusters of long thread-like roots at nodes... *Hydrocotyle*

34. Floating leaves tightly clustered into a rosette at the stem tip, blades small (5–30 mm long); submersed leaves arranged in opposite pairs and linear; flowers submersed, borne 1–3 in leaf axils...*Callitriche*

34. Floating leaves not clustered into a rosette, blades usually much larger (6–260 mm long); submersed leaves, if present, linear or broad, and alternate; flowers emersed or, if submersed, in spike-like clusters...35

35. Leaf veins parallel; floating and submersed leaves different in shape and texture; stipule usually present at base of each leaf; flowers greenish and inconspicuous.......*Potamogeton*

35. Leaf veins pinnately branching; floating and submersed leaves, if both present, no different; stipule present or absent at base of each leaf..36

36. Flowers bright yellow, borne singly in leaf axils; leaves hairless; stipule absent; submerged nodes sometimes bear erect, fleshy, white, spongy "air" roots which float... .... *Ludwigia*

36. Flowers pink, in crowded erect clusters at tip of stem; leaves sometimes hairy; a cylindrical stipule sheaths the stem at each node; nodes lacking erect, fleshy, white, spongy "air" roots ....*Persicaria*

KEY III: PLANTS WITH SOME LEAVES OR STEM PORTIONS EXTENDING ABOVE THE WATER SURFACE

1. Leaves or leaf-like branches held above water are linear, >10 times as long as wide............ 2

1. Leaves held above water with a more expanded blade, <10 times as long as wide............. 8

2. Plants with many submerged, flaccid, thread-like leaves or stems..............................3

2. Plants without submerged, flaccid, thread-like leaves or stems...................................5

3. Plants with 1 (or maybe 2) fully developed, emergent leaves attached to the main stem, leaf with internal cross walls; submerged thread-like leaves with internal cross walls; flower cluster multi-branched...*Juncus*

3. Emergent leaves lacking (no leaves attached to main stem); submerged thread-like leaves or stems lacking internal cross walls; flower cluster unbranched.......................................4

4. Erect, emergent stems round in cross section, narrower than flower cluster; flower cluster appears to come from side of stem (because a 2–20 mm long leaf-like bract is attached below flower cluster, appearing like a continuation of the stem); submerged leaves with a sheathing base...*Schoenoplectus*

4. Erect, emergent stems 3-sided in cross section, nearly as thick as the flower cluster; flower cluster attached to tip of stem; submerged leaf-like stems without a sheathing base.. *Eleocharis*

5. Leaves clustered in a basal rosette, each essentially round in cross-section and thickest at base, generally tapering to the tip; flowers, if present, with petals.............................. 6
5. Leaves not in a basal rosette, each generally flattened or thread-like; flowers are lacking petals..7
6. Base of plant swollen and bub-like, containing white spores; roots are not septate; leaves with four hollow lengthwise chambers, flexible or rigid; flowers, fruits or flowering stems never produced...*Isoëtes*
6. Base of plant not swollen and bulb-like; roots are septate; leaves rigid; flowers with three conspicuous white petals...*Sagittaria*
7. Leaves conspicuous (>0.5 m long, 2–10 mm wide); flowers are grouped into several spherical clusters, each with a leaf attached below; fruits are a spherical aggregate of hard, beaked drupes.. *Sparganium*
7. Plants delicate, grass-like, with short (5–8 cm tall) and slender (<0.5 mm wide) leaf-like stems; actual leaves scale-like and inconspicuous at stem base; flowers are grouped at the stem tip into a single cluster of overlapping scales; fruits are nut-like with bristles at the base .... *Eleocharis*
8. Leaves held above water are deeply divided or finely divided into narrow segments.........9
8. Leaves held above water are broad and flattened, not finely divided, but may have toothed margins..11
9. Emersed leaves greatly reduced and bract-like, <1 cm long...........................*Myriophyllum*
9. Emersed leaves well-developed, 1–3.5 cm long, essentially like submersed leaves..............10
10. Leaves whorled, each divided into 10–15 pairs of narrow segments.............*Myriophyllum*
10. Leaves alternate, each divided into 6–9 pairs of narrow segments.................*Proserpinaca*
11. Emersed leaf margins are toothed 12
11. Emersed leaf margins are without teeth..17
12. Submersed feather-like leaves present, attached to upright stems..........................13
12. Submersed feather-like leaves absent, leaves with round blades, attached to creeping stem..*Hydrocotyle*
13. Leaves held at or above water are attached alternately at top of a submersed stem, each with a triangular to diamond-shaped blade, and a long leaf stalk with an inflated portion; fruit with 4 horn-like spikes.. *Trapa*
13. Leaves held above water are alternate, opposite, or whorled on emersed portion of stems, each with a blade much not longer than wide, and a leaf stalk lacking an inflated portion; fruit with without 4 horn-like spikes... 14
14. Emersed leaves are opposite or whorled on a stem... 15
14. Emersed leaves are alternate on stem.. 16
15. Emersed leaves are opposite, 2 per node, and 2–4 cm long; flowers borne in a single, conspicuous, yellow, daisy-like cluster.. *Bidens*
15. Emersed leaves are whorled, 4–6 per node, and 0.4–1.8 cm long; flowers borne in axils of leaves forming a leafy spike... *Myriophyllum*
16. Flowers are unstalked, inconspicuous, purplish-greenish, without petals, borne in axils of emersed leaves; fruit is 3-sided, common; emersed leaves with sharp, forward-pointing teeth; submersed leaves sometimes absent...............................*Proserpinaca*
16. Flowers are stalked (stalks 5–15 mm long), conspicuous, with 4 white petals, borne in cluster above the emersed leaves; fruit a rounded pod, rare; emersed leaves with spreading teeth, some blades may be untoothed as well.............................. *Rorippa*
17. Emersed leaves pinnately compound with 3–9 leaflets, alternate on the stem...... *Nasturtium*
17. Emersed leaves simple with one blade, opposite or arising from a basal rosette..............18

18. Emersed leaves arising from a basal rosette, blade 3–30 cm long, on long stalks (>6 cm long) ……………… ……………………………………………………………………….. *Sagittaria*

18. Emersed leaves opposite on stem, blade 0.5–4 cm long, stalkless or short-stalked (<3 cm long)……………………………………………………………………………………………….19

19. Emersed leaves without stalks; stems green; flowers borne in a single, conspicuous, yellow, daisy-like cluster at stem tip; submersed leaves are finely divided into thread-like segments ………………………………………………………………………………………………… *Bidens*

19. Emersed leaves with stalks (5–25 mm long); stems reddish; flowers are inconspicuous, green-brown, borne singly in leaf axils; submersed leaves resembling emersed leaves……. ………………………………………………………………………………………… *Ludwigia*

Keys to Species & Descriptions

Aldrovanda — Droseraceae
Waterwheel plant

WATERWHEEL PLANT *Aldrovanda vesiculosa* L.

Waterwheel plant is a submersed, free-floating, rootless, perennial, with floating, branched stems (to 40 cm long). Leaves are 10–15 mm long, submersed, and whorled in clusters of 6–9. Each flattened leafstalk is tipped with 4–8, fine-toothed, bristles (6–8 mm long) surrounding an orbicular blade. The blade (2–3 mm long) consists of two semicircular halves, hinged along the midrib, which can rapidly close to trap invertebrates. Flowers (borne singly in leaf axils) are not produced in our area. Turions are produced at stem tips in late season.

HABITAT & DISTRIBUTION

Aldrovanda vesiculosa is a non-native, carnivorous species of shallow, stagnant lake waters. **Introduced** and uncommon in northern New Jersey. **Notes:** This unusual, globally rare, plant is native to Africa, Asia, and Australia but was introduced into US by carnivorous plant hobbyists in 1970s. Its peculiar, fast-acting, leaf traps have one of the quickest known plant movements (trap closure takes 10–20 milliseconds). Under optimal conditions, plants are known for rapid growth.

Azolla — Salviniaceae
Mosquito fern

EASTERN MOSQUITO FERN — *Azolla cristata* Mett.

Eastern Mosquito fern is a tiny, free-floating, aquatic fern with horizontal stems (0.5–1 cm long), slender roots, and overlapping, fuzzy leaves. Leaf blades are floating, very small (0.5–2 mm wide), dark green (or reddish), unequally two-lobed, covered in hairs, and positioned in two rows along a stem. Plants reproduce by spores.

HABITAT & DISTRIBUTION

Azolla cristata is a suspected native, moss-like, mat-forming fern species of stagnant lakes, ponds, or sluggish streams. It is ***rare*** in northern New Jersey, eligible for protection under the jurisdiction of the Highlands Preservation Area. This species has long gone by the name *A. caroliniana* Willd.

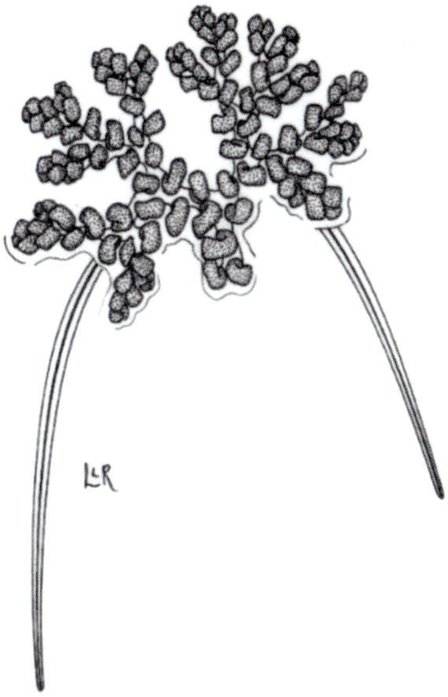

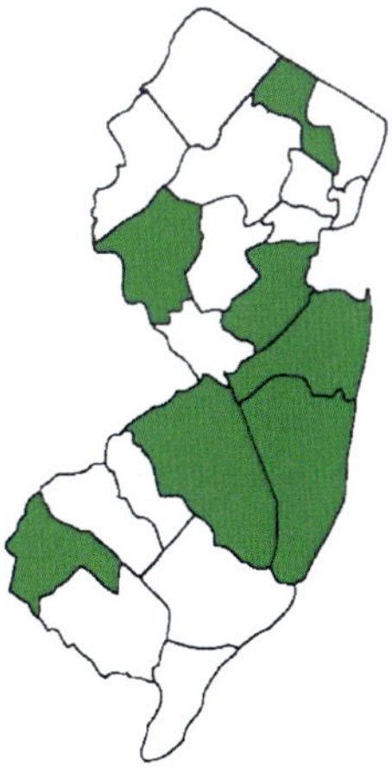

Bidens — Asteraceae
Beggar-ticks

BECK'S BEGGAR-TICKS *Bidens beckii* Torr. ex Spreng.

Beck's beggar-ticks, or Water marigold, is a submersed, rooted, perennial with rhizomes and elongated (to 200 cm), slender, flexible stems. Leaves are opposite, stalkless, 2–4 cm long, and dimorphic: submersed leaves, appearing whorled, are finely divided into thread-like segments; and emersed leaves are simple, lance-shaped, with toothed or untoothed margins. Flowers are borne, above water, in a single, conspicuous, yellow, daisy-like cluster (head) resembling a flower (2.5 cm diam.). Fruit is a yellowish to greenish brown, linear achene (10–15 mm) with 3–6 barbed extensions (13–15 mm long) at tip.

HABITAT & DISTRIBUTION

Bidens beckii is a native species in lakes, beaver ponds, and intermittent Coastal Plain ponds. It is critically imperiled in New Jersey and state-listed as ***endangered***.

Note: Fruits rarely mature in our region. It can occupy deep (to 7 m) waters where it will only produce submersed foliage. This species is listed as *Megalodonta beckii* in some references.

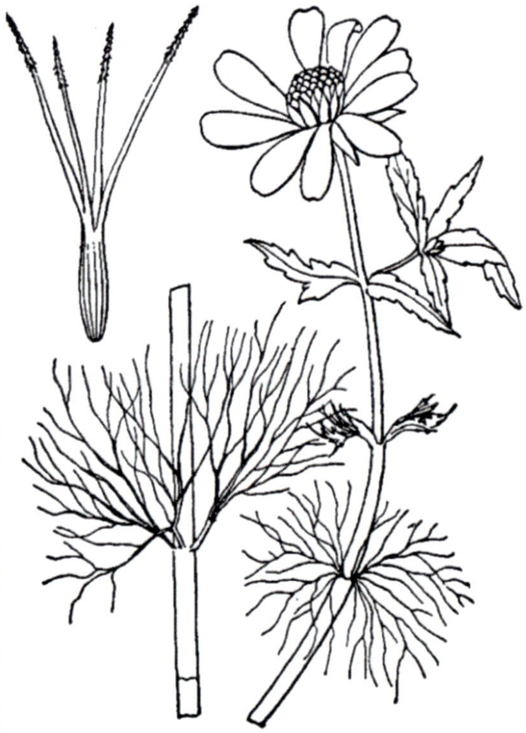

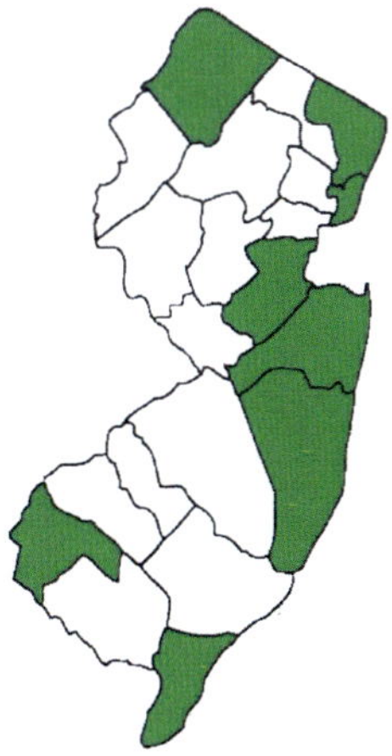

Brasenia — Cabombaceae
Watershield

WATERSHIELD *Brasenia schreberi* J.F. Gmel.

Watershield is a rooted, perennial, floating-leaved plant with creeping rhizomes and long, flexible, buoyant, branching stems. Leaves are alternate, floating, broadly oval (4–13 cm long), on long (to 60 cm) stalks centrally attached to the blades. Usually, all submerged portions are purplish and covered in a thick, translucent, jelly-like coating. Flowers (2 cm wide) are bisexual, mostly wind-pollinated, petals red purple (12–20 mm long), borne singly on elongated (to 15 cm) stalks that hold flowers about 2 cm above water. Fruit a small (6–10 mm long), leathery, few-seeded nutlet.

HABITAT & DISTRIBUTION

Brasenia schreberi is native and found in open, standing, or slow waters (1–3 m deep) of lakes, ponds, and streams. It is widespread and common in New Jersey. This species is highly tolerant and can reproduce asexually via rhizomes and winter buds which can result in dense, weedy colonies.

Notes: This is a very distinctive floating-leaved plant with its oval leaves and slippery, mucilaginous layer covering younger, underwater parts.

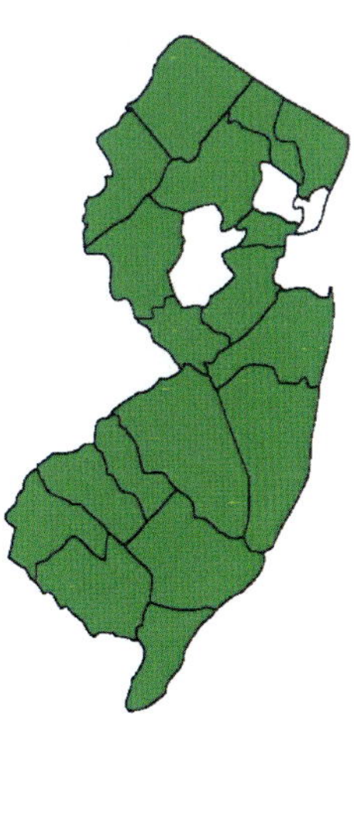

Cabomba — Cabombaceae
Fanwort

CAROLINA FANWORT *Cabomba caroliniana* Gray

Carolina fanwort is a rooted, submersed species with creeping rhizomes and long (up to 2 m), slender, branching, flexuous stems. Submersed leaves are opposite, rotund (1–3.5 cm long, 2.5–5 cm wide), palmately divided (3–7 divisions) into many narrow segments, and with distinct stalk (1–4 cm long). During periods of flowering only, a few inconspicuous, narrow (5–20 mm long, 1–4 mm wide), floating leaves are also produced at tips of stems. Flowers are bisexual, small (6–15 mm diam.), white, and borne singly above water on stalks (3–10 cm) from upper leaf axils. Fruit is a small (4–7 mm long), leathery, nutlet.

HABITAT & DISTRIBUTION

Cabomba caroliniana is a non-native plant, long naturalized in ponds and slow streams of the northeast. It is common in New Jersey. This plant can become abundant and problematic as it exhibits aggressive vegetative growth, prolific stem fragmentation, and broad ecological tolerances.

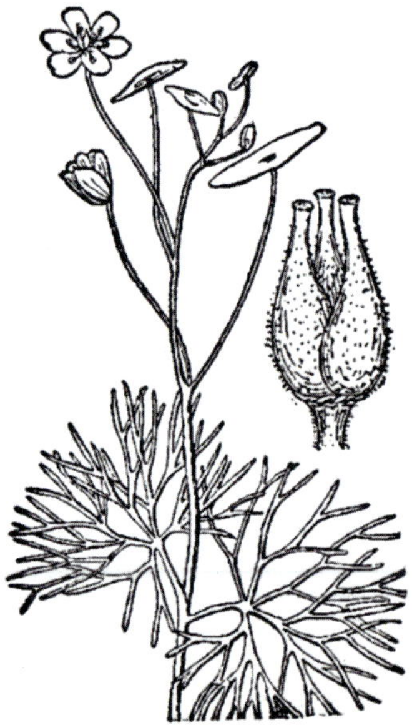

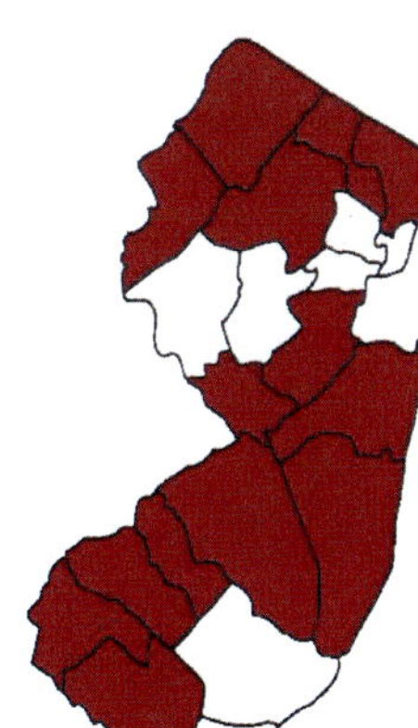

Callitriche — Plantaginaceae

Water starwort

The Water starworts are small, submerged, rooted, annuals with slender, branched stems. Leaves are opposite, toothless, often notched at tip, and dimorphic: submersed leaves are linear shaped and well-spaced along the stem, and floating, broader, spoon-shaped leaves are clustered into a rosette near the stem apex. The bases of adjacent leaves are slightly confluent, forming a narrow membranous wing across the sides of the stem (This feature is not always easily detected). Flowers and fruits have two translucent bracts (0.5–1.5 mm long) at base. Flowers are tiny, unisexual (on same plant), petal-less, and borne 1–3 per leaf axil. Female flowers have a flattened, 2-lobed ovary. Fruit splitting into four 1-seeded segments at maturity.

Three species occur in New Jersey, one non-native, which are very variable vegetatively. Mature fruits are essential for accurate identification.

Key to Species

1. Fruit 1.5–2 mm long, margins with a prominent wing extending along entire fruit length; floating leaf blades 5-8 mm wide with 5–7 veins.. *C. stagnalis*
1. Fruit 1–1.4 mm long, margins unwinged or with a wing absent at fruit base; floating leaf blades (when present) up to 5 mm wide, with 3 (–5) veins... 2
   2. Fruit longer than wide by 0.2 mm or more, top portion of each segment with a thin wing, pits of fruit surface aligned in vertical rows.. *C. palustris*
   2. Fruit as wide as long, lacking wings along margins, pits on fruit surface not aligned in rows .... *C. heterophylla*

C. heterophylla

C. palustris

C. stagnalis

GREATER WATER STARWORT *Callitriche heterophylla* Pursh

Greater Water starwort, or Two-headed Water starwort, is a submersed plant with loosely clustered stems (10–20 cm long). Floating leaf blades (when present) are egg-shaped (5–30 mm long, 2.5–5 mm wide), widest toward the apex, blunt tipped, usually with 3 veins. Submersed leaves are linear (5–25 mm long, 1.5 mm wide) and notched at tip. Fruits about as long as wide (1–1.4 mm long, 0.6–1.2 mm wide) with unwinged margins. Pits on fruit surface irregularly distributed.

HABITAT & DISTRIBUTION

Callitriche heterophylla is a native species of shallow lakes, ponds, bogs, vernal pools, and slow streams. It is widespread in New Jersey. Plants are generally found in circumneutral, shallow waters.

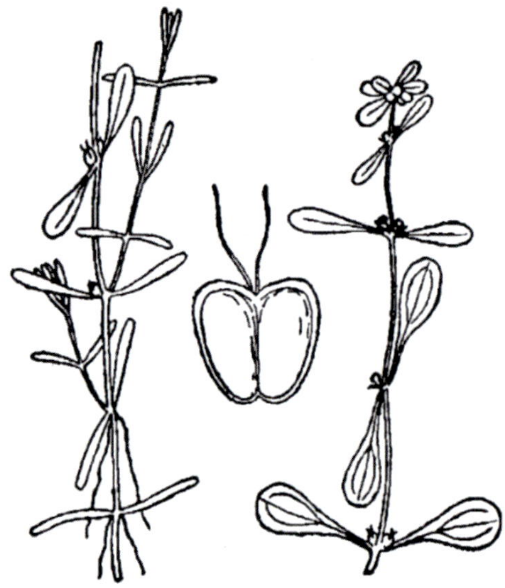

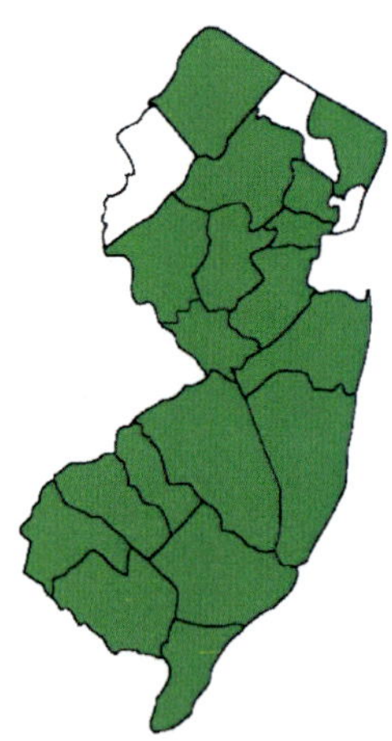

VERNAL WATER STARWORT — *Callitriche palustris* L.

Vernal Water starwort is a submersed plant with loosely clustered stems (10–20 cm long). Floating leaf blades (when present) are egg-shaped (5–30 mm long, 2.5–5 mm wide), widest toward the apex, blunt-tipped, usually with 3 veins. Submersed leaves are linear (5–15 mm long, 3 mm wide) and notched at tip. Fruits distinctly grooved, slightly longer than wide (1–1.4 mm long), widest above middle, with a thin wing along upper portions of each lobe. Pits on fruit surface aligned in vertical rows.

HABITAT & DISTRIBUTION

Callitriche palustris is a native species of springs, marshes, bogs, fens, pools, ponds, and slow rivers. It is **rare** and imperiled in New Jersey, eligible for protection under the jurisdiction of the Highlands Preservation Area.

Note: This species can grow as an emergent plant when exposed on wet shorelines or depressions.

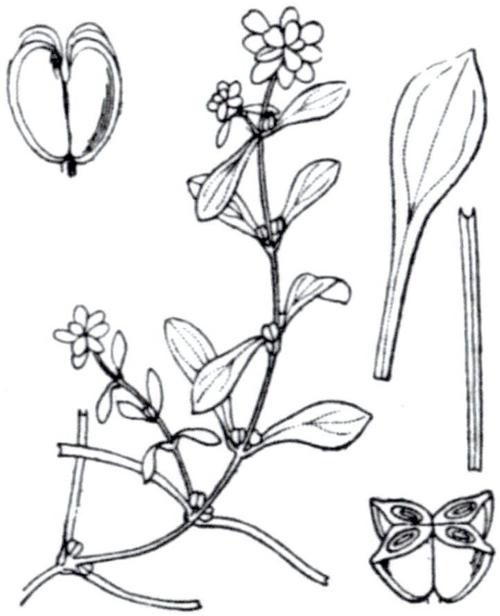

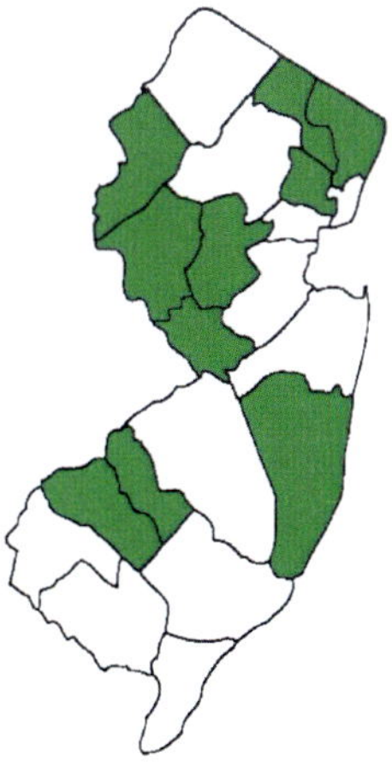

POND WATER STARWORT *Callitriche stagnalis* Scop.

Pond Water starwort is a submersed plant with loosely clustered stems (10–20 cm long). Floating leaf blades are egg-shaped (to 20 mm long, 5–8 mm wide), widest toward the apex, blunt-tipped, usually with 5–7 veins. Submersed leaves are usually linear (4–10 mm long), 1-veined, and notched at tip. Fruits distinctly grooved, nearly round (1.5–2 mm long), with a prominent wing extending evenly along whole length of margin.

HABITAT & DISTRIBUTION

Callitriche stagnalis is a non-native species of lakes and tidal rivers. It is throughout New Jersey where it is potentially **invasive**. Native to Europe, the plant can spread by seed or rooted stem fragments and form dense colonies. It does not grow in highly acidic waters.

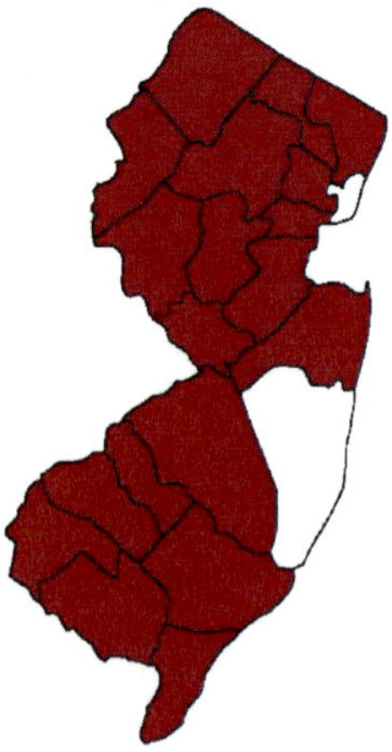

Ceratophyllum — Ceratophyllaceae
Hornwort

The Hornworts, or Coontails, are submerged, perennial, highly branched plants that float or are suspended in the water column. Plants are rootless but may become anchored to a substrate if segments become buried. Leaves are in whorls (of 3–11 leaves) along the stem, dichotomously divided, and forked into linear segments. Inconspicuous, submersed, unisexual flowers are borne in leaf axils. Fruits, if produced, are flattened, smooth-surfaced, dark green or reddish, achenes with spiny margins.

Two species occur in New Jersey, both native. *Ceratophyllum demersum* is one of the most common aquatic plants in the region.

Key to Species

1. Leaves usually forked 1–2 times and conspicuously serrated, ultimate segments somewhat flattened; fruits with 3 long spines.. *C. demersum*
1. Leaves usually forked 3–4 times, with few marginal teeth, ultimate segments threadlike; fruits with 4+ long and short spines... *C. echinatum*

C. demersum

COMMON HORNWORT *Ceratophyllum demersum* L.

Common hornwort is a highly branched, submersed plant with long (up to 3m) stems and whorled leaves. Leaves (10–30 mm long) are bright green, usually forked 1–2 times into somewhat flattened segments, curving upward, and more crowded at tips of branches. Leaf margins are conspicuously serrated with teeth, each arising from a raised green base. Flowers are small, at the leaf axils. Fruits are flattened and disk-like (3–6 mm long) with 3 long (0.5–12 mm) spines.

HABITAT & DISTRIBUTION

Ceratophyllum demersum is a native species of ditches, marshes, lakes, ponds, and slow streams. It is widespread and common in New Jersey where it can become abundant. It has a relatively stiff habit with coarsely textured leaves, maintaining its shape when out of water. This makes the stems somewhat brittle whereby they can detach, disperse, and form clonal populations.

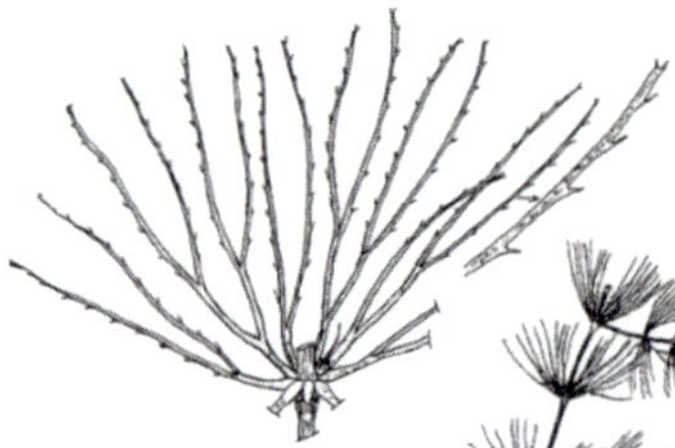

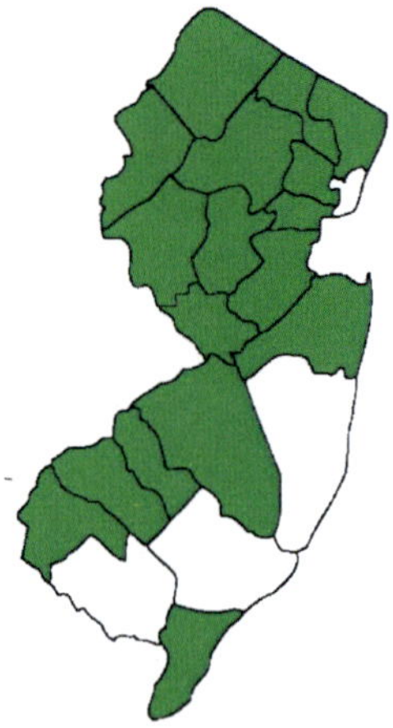

SPINELESS HORNWORT *Ceratophyllum echinatum* A. Gray

Spineless hornwort is a highly branched submersed plant with long stems (to 1 m) and leaves in whorls. Leaves are dark green, usually forked 3–4 times into threadlike segments, and not crowded at tips of branches. Leaf margins with few, weak, inconspicuous teeth. Flowers are small, at the leaf axils. Fruits are flattened, disk-like (4.5–6 mm long), and ornamented with 3 long (1–5 mm) spines and 2–13 shorter spines between the longer spines.

HABITAT & DISTRIBUTION

Ceratophyllum echinatum is a native species in lakes, ponds, bogs, and slow streams. It is rare and state-listed as ***endangered***. It prefers acidic, low nutrient, shaded, waters. This plant is somewhat stiff, yet not as stiff as *C. demersum*.

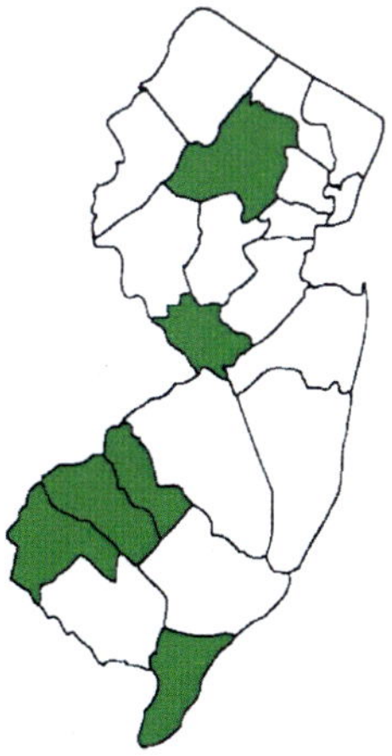

Echinodorus — Alismataceae
Burhead

DWARF BURHEAD — *Echinodorus tenellus* (Mart.) Buch.

Dwarf burhead is a diminutive (5 cm tall), inconspicuous, submersed, rooted annual. Leaves are basal, submersed, and lance-linear in shape (1–6 cm long, 2–3 mm wide). If stranded on shore, leaves have long (1–9.5 cm), ridged stalks and obvious blades. Flowers are bisexual, small (6–8 mm wide), white, stalked (5–30 mm), and borne in erect clusters.

HABITAT & DISTRIBUTION

Echinodorus tenellus is a native of wet, sandy, seasonal drawdown zones of pond shores. This globally **rare** species was known in New Jersey from Burlington Co. and is now considered *historical*.

Note: This species is cultivated as an ornamental aquarium plant (under Pigmy chain sword). It has been called *Helanthium tenellum* (Mart.) Britt.

Egeria — Hydrocharitaceae
South American waterweed

BRAZILIAN WATERWEED *Egeria densa* Planch.

Brazilian waterweed, or Brazilian elodea, is a submersed, rooted perennial with elongated (to 3 m), flexuous, branched stems. Leaves are in crowded, overlapping whorls of 4–6, lance-shaped (1.5–4 cm long, 3–6 mm wide), bright to dark green, recurved, with finely tooted margins (under magnification). Flowers are unisexual (on separate plants), white, 20 mm in diam., and borne singly from upper leaf axils on slender stalks reaching water surface. Only male plants are known in the US.

HABITAT & DISTRIBUTION

Egeria densa is a non-native species of lakes, ponds, and sluggish rivers. It is uncommon in New Jersey, where it is **invasive**. The species is native to southeastern Brazil and introduced through the aquarium trade. In the US it reproduces strictly asexually via fragments, grows rapidly, and can outcompete native plants. Similar to Waterweeds (*Elodea*) and Hydrilla (*Hydrilla*).

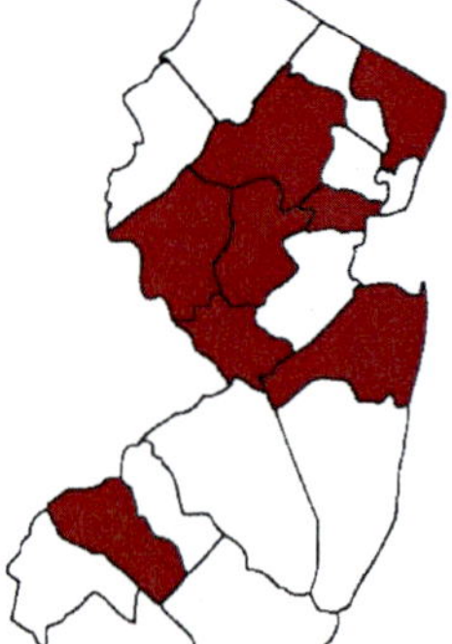

Eichhornia — Pontederiaceae
Water hyacinth

COMMON WATER HYACINTH *Eichhornia crassipes* (Mart.) Solms.

Common Water hyacinth is a free-floating perennial with a buoyant cluster of spongy leaves above the water surface and long, feathery, black roots hanging in water column. Leaves are in a basal rosette, green, glossy, and usually with greatly inflated stalks (3–33 cm long). Leaf blades are oval to round (2.5–11 cm long, 4–12 cm wide). Flowers are large (5–7 cm wide) and showy, blue or purplish-blue with a yellow spot, clustered in 4–15-flowered spikes, borne on erect stems (5–12.5 cm long) above the leaves.

HABITAT & DISTRIBUTION

Eichhornia crassipes is a non-native species and popular water garden plant. It is uncommon in New Jersey, found where plants escaped cultivation or were introduced during the same season. The species cannot tolerate winter in our area.

Notes: Native to the tropical Americas, it is one of the most aggressive aquatic weeds known in warmer climates where it forms dense floating rafts. Its flowers open for one day only—within two hours after sunrise and then wilt by night.

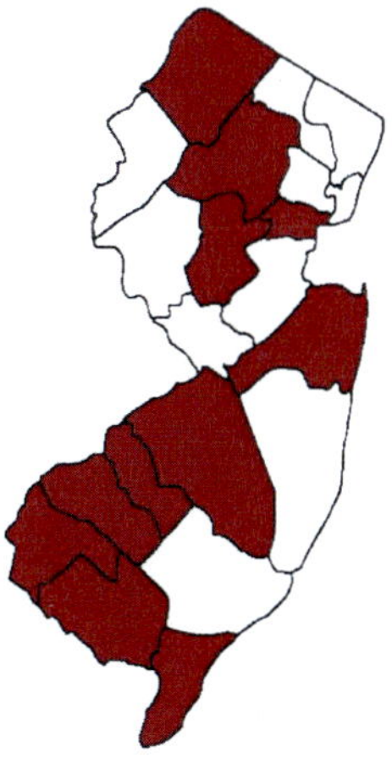

Elatine — Elatinaceae
Waterwort

The Waterworts are diminutive, mat-forming, submersed plants which can easily be overlooked. Individuals are sometimes emersed in mud when stranded by receding waters. Plants have simple, paired leaves along the stems and roots at the lower nodes. Single, white or pinkish, bisexual flowers are borne in upper leaf axils which mature into capsules.

Three species are known in New Jersey, including one non-native. All species are annuals and lack asexual reproduction, so population recruitment is strictly from seeds. *Elatine* taxonomy is confusing and species identification is difficult. Species documentation in New Jersey is generally sparse so the distribution maps provided here should be regarded as tentative. Waterworts are popular aquarium plants.

Key to Species

1. Leaves oblong and rounded, 1–5 mm long; flowers with 2 petals and stamens; seed surface with rounded pits; plants holding their shape when removed from water............. *E. minima*
1. Leaves much longer than wide, 3–8 (–15) mm long; flowers with 3 petals and stamens; seed surface with longer 6-sided, angular-ended pits, plants limp and collapsing when out of water...2
    2. Leaf blades obovate or broadly spatulate, the larger blades 1.5–5 mm wide, tips rounded .... *E. americana*
    2. Leaf blades linear to egg-shaped, 0.5–3 mm wide, tips acute or sometimes notched......... .... *E. triandra*

American Waterwort *Elatine americana* (Pursh) Arnott

American waterwort is an erect or prostrate herb with short (1.5–5 cm long), branched stems. Leaves are egg-shaped or broadly spoon-shaped, 3–8 mm long, larger blades 1.5–5 mm wide, with rounded tips. Minute flowers are borne singly in the leaf axils and develop into rounded capsules (1.5 mm wide). Seeds are cylindrical and marked on the surface with 6-sided, angular-ended pits.

Habitat & Distribution

Elatine americana is a native species in shallow (<1 m) waters and muddy shores of tidal rivers and their tributaries and less frequently ponds. It is **rare** and imperiled in New Jersey, eligible for protection under the jurisdiction of the Highlands Preservation Area.

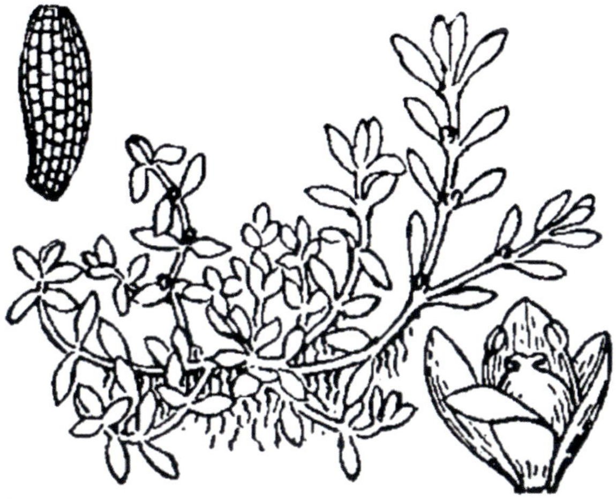

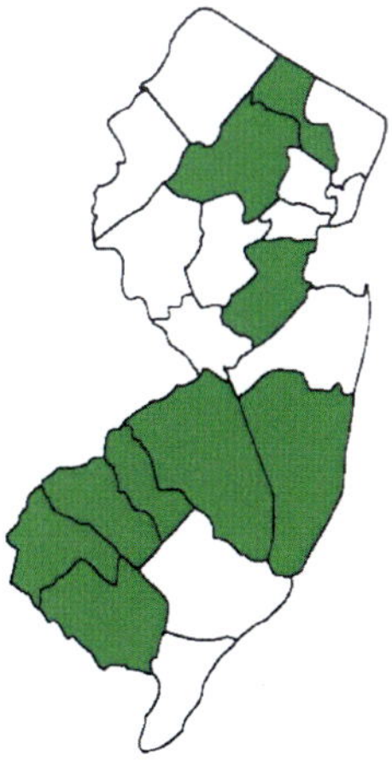

SMALL WATERWORT *Elatine minima* (Nutt.) Fisch. & CA Mey.

Small waterwort is a small, erect, herb with short (to 3 cm long), sometimes few-branched, stems. Leaves are rounded and small (1–5 mm long). Minute flowers are borne singly in the leaf axils and develop into papery capsules containing 4–9 seeds. Seeds are cylindrical and marked on the surface with 8–9 rows of rounded pits.

HABITAT & DISTRIBUTION

Elatine minima grows in shallow (1–2 m) waters of lakes, ponds, tidal or nontidal streams, and exposed mudflats. It is native and **rare** in New Jersey, eligible for protection under the jurisdiction of the Highlands Preservation Area. Flowers are self-pollinating, and seeds are dispersed by water. Colonies can become very dense (up to 2500 plants per m^2) reaching highest densities in shallow water.

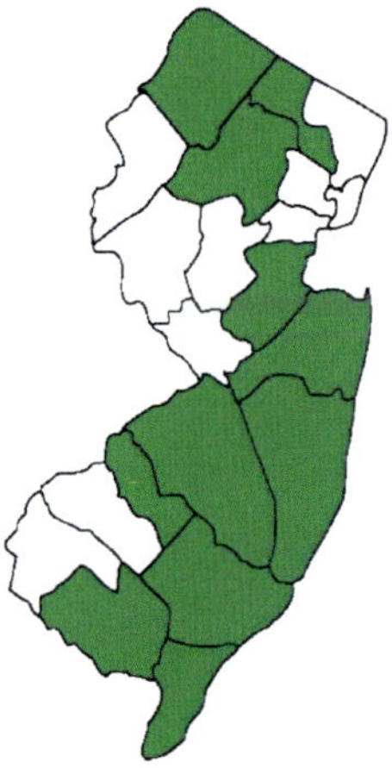

LONG-STEM WATERWORT *Elatine triandra* Schkuhr

Long-stem waterwort is a prostrate herb with short (2–10 cm), highly branched, bright yellow-green stems. Leaves are linear to egg-shaped, 3–8 (–15) mm long, 0.5–3 mm wide, with acute or sometimes notched tips. Minute flowers are borne singly in the leaf axils and develop into papery capsules. Seeds are oblong and marked on the surface with 6-sided, angular-ended pits.

HABITAT & DISTRIBUTION

Elatine triandra is a non-native species (at least to the northeast) in shallow waters (to 1 m) of lakes, ponds, tidal or nontidal streams, and mudflats. It is infrequent, or at least poorly documented, in New Jersey. Introduced from Eurasia, where it is a weed in rice fields, this species is now widespread throughout North America. It can form dense carpets on lake bottoms and its seedbanks can be persistent.

Notes: It is very similar to Asian Waterwort (*E. ambigua* Wight), a non-native species, which has become introduced—most likely through aquarium disposal—into nearby southern New England. Distinguishing between these two species is nearly impossible when plants are found submersed. When emersed, *E. ambigua* produces longer (0.5–2.5 mm), recurved fruit stalks (fruit stalks in *E. triandra* are ≤ 0.5 mm and erect).

Eleocharis — Cyperaceae
Spikesedge

The Spikesedges, or Spikerushes, are rooted, grass-like plants, with green upright stems (or "culms") and very reduced, inconspicuous leaves (represented by a closed, thin sheath at base of stems). Flowers are tiny, borne above water, in a single cluster (spikelet) of overlapping scales at the tip of a stem. Fruits are small and nut-like with bristles at the base, and a distinctive tubercle at top.

Many species of Spikesedge occupy shallow, marshy wetlands and wet mud in New Jersey [e.g., *E. obstusa* (Willd.) Schultes, *E. palustris* (L.) Roem. & Schultes, *E. tuberculosa* (Michx.) Roem. & Schultes, and others]. These species are more wholly emergent (and not detailed here). Three species, all native, can be found more submerged at times in New Jersey.

Key to Species

1. Stem much narrower than the spikelet, stems generally round in cross-section, flexible, slender (<0.5 mm), typically short (5–8 cm tall), and often forming a dense turf................2
1. Stem nearly as thick as the spikelet, flowering stems triangular in cross-section, stiff, 16–70 cm tall.. *E. robbinsii*
   2. Plants of freshwater ponds and lakes (rarely brackish), without root-tubers at ends of rhizomes; nutlet with longitudinal rows of fine horizontal ridges .... *E. acicularis*
   2. Plants of brackish or saline coastal tidal marshes, with curved root-tubers at ends of rhizomes; nutlet without longitudinal rows of fine horizontal ridges .... *E. parvula*

NEEDLE SPIKERUSH *Eleocharis acicularis* (L.) Roem. & Schult.

Needle spikerush is a delicate, rooted, perennial with white, threadlike rhizomes. Upright stems are clustered, flexible, short (5–8 cm tall), slender (<0.5 mm wide), and more slender than the spikelet. Spikelet is small (2–8 mm long) with dark brown scales with green mid-rib. Nutlet is 3-angled, with 2–4 bristles, and a tubercle separated from body by narrow constriction.

HABITAT & DISTRIBUTION

Eleocharis acicularis is a native species of shallow marshes and lake or river shores. It is common and widespread in New Jersey. Plants can grow in dense clusters and form a turf. In deep water, plants may not produce flowers/fruits and can grow much taller (30+ cm).

Note: It closely resembles Little-headed spikesedge (*E. parvula*) of coastal saline or brackish tidal waters which are stouter and have curved, root-tubers on ends of the rhizome.

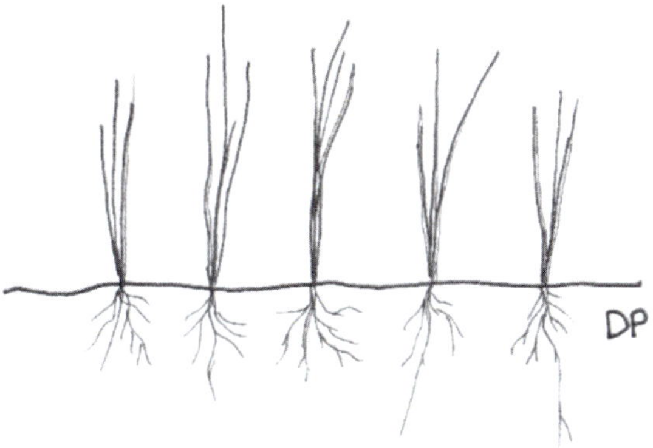

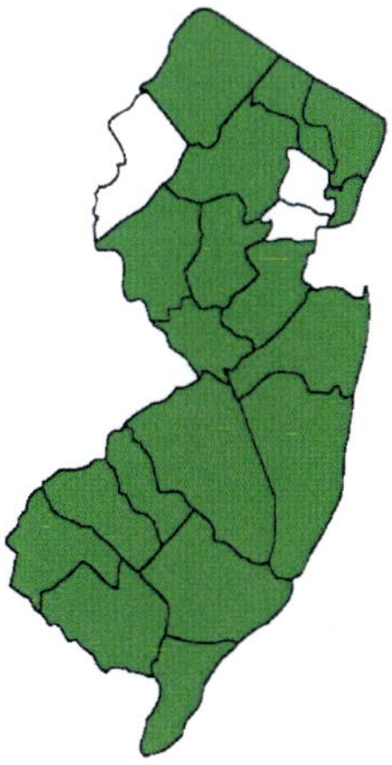

LITTLE-HEADED SPIKESEDGE *Eleocharis parvula* (Roem. & Schult.) Link

Little-headed spikesedge is a delicate, rooted, perennial with slender rhizomes terminated by pale, oblong, usually markedly curved, tubers (2–5 mm long). Upright stems are clustered, flexible, short (5–8 cm tall), and narrower than the spikelet. Spikelet is small (2–4 mm long) with light brown scales. Nutlet is 3-angled, lacking longitudinal rows of fine horizontal ridges, with 5–7 bristles, and a tubercle continuous with the fruit body.

HABITAT & DISTRIBUTION

Eleocharis parvula is a native species of coastal brackish or saline tidal waters in New Jersey. In deep water, plants may not produce flowers/fruits.

Note: It closely resembles Needle spikesedge (*E. acicularis*) of more freshwater habitats, which lacks root-tubers at ends of rhizomes.

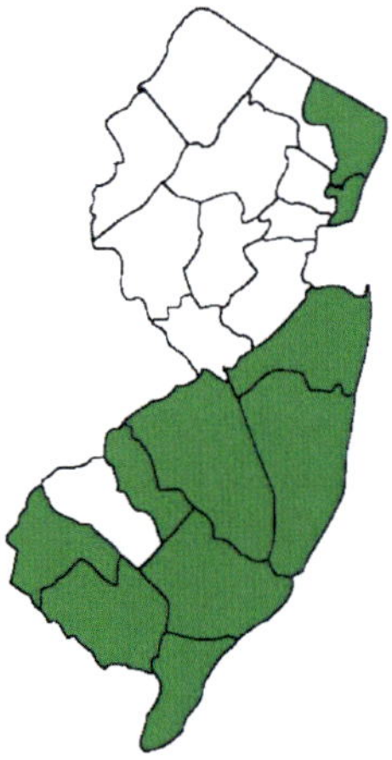

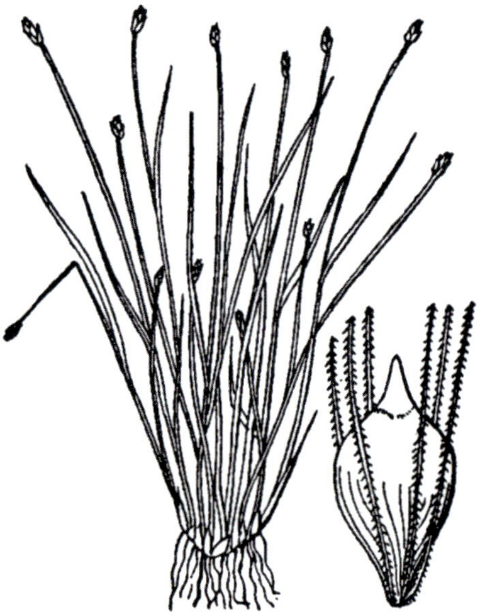

ROBBINS' SPIKERUSH *Eleocharis robbinsii* Oakes

Robbins' spikerush is a rooted, perennial with buried, reddish, rhizomes (1–2 mm thick). Flowering stems are stiff, erect (16–70 cm tall, 1–2 mm wide), 3-sided, and nearly as thick as the spikelet. Numerous submersed, thread-like, flexible stems (resembling leaves) lacking spikelets are frequently present attached to base of plant. Spikelet is 9–33 mm long. Nutlet is 2-sided, with 6–7 bristles, and a distinct tubercle.

HABITAT & DISTRIBUTION

Eleocharis robbinsii is a native species of swamps, lakes, and ponds where it forms clumps. It is scattered in New Jersey.

Note: Similar to Water bulrush (*Schoenoplectus subterminalis*). Water bulrush is distinguished by alternate leaves and flowering stems with only their top portions held above water which have a single bract (2–20 mm long) attached below the flower cluster appearing like a continuation of the stem.

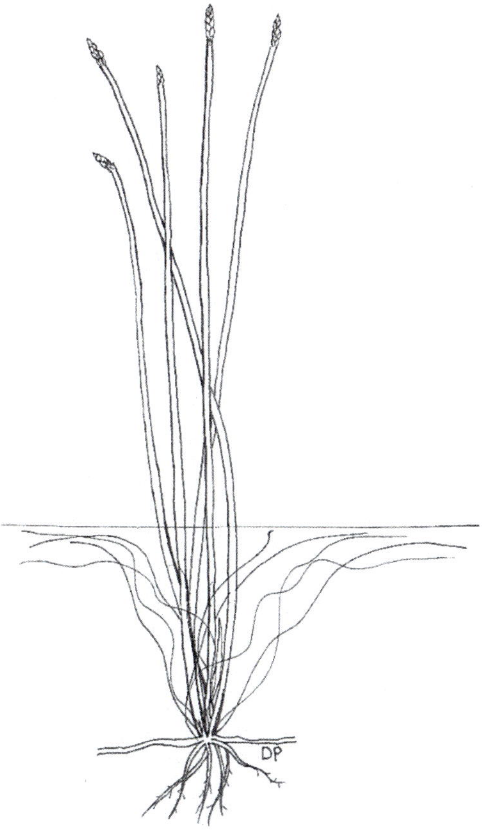

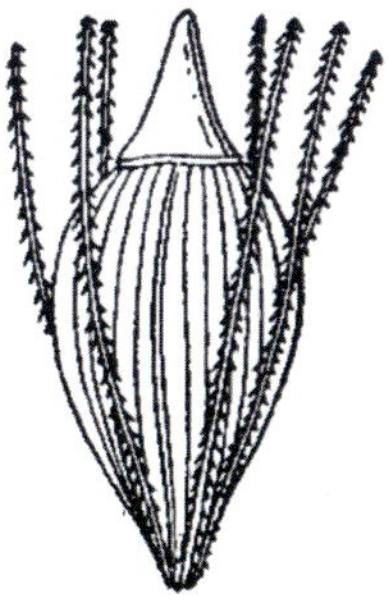

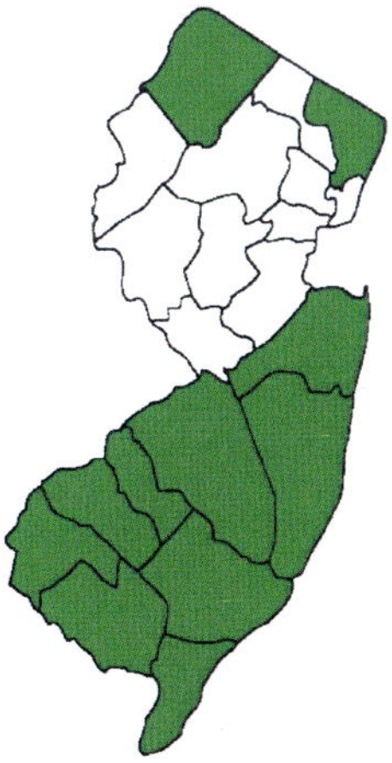

Elodea — Hydrocharitaceae
Waterweed

The Waterweeds are rooted, submersed aquatics with elongated, slender, branching stems which are somewhat brittle. Plants are leafy with small (<15 mm long, <5 mm wide), stalkless, bright green, recurved leaves borne in whorls of 2–3 per node. Flowers are unisexual (on different plants), white, and borne at the water surface.

Two species, both native and extremely similar vegetatively, are known from New Jersey. Waterweeds are commonly sold as aquarium "oxygenating" plants.

Key to Species

1. Leaves oblong, mostly 2 mm wide (ranging 1–5 mm wide), firm, blunt-tipped, densely crowded and overlapping towards stem tips.. *E. canadensis*
1. Leaves narrowly lance-shaped, mostly 1.3 mm wide (ranging 0.9–1.7 mm wide), weak, pointed, more or less equally spaced along stem.. *E. nuttallii*

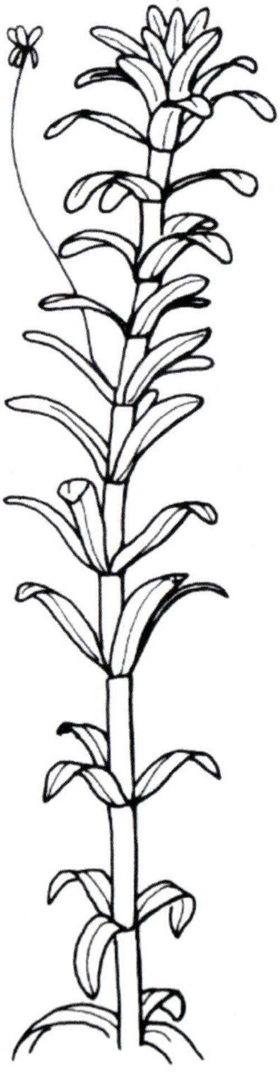

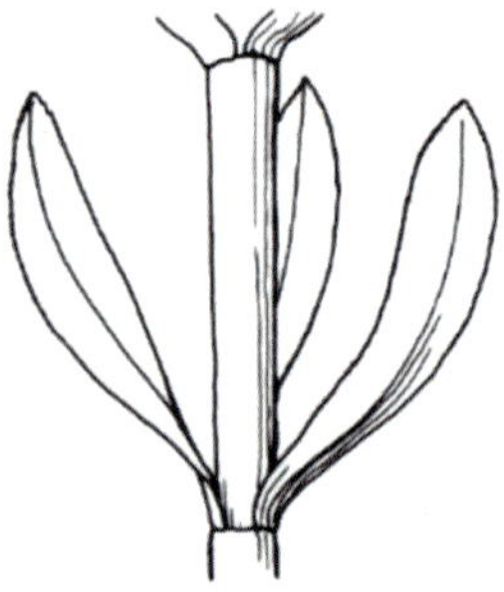

Common waterweed *Elodea canadensis* Michx.

Common waterweed is a submersed, perennial with elongated (≥1 m), flexuous stems rooting from nodes. Leaves are mostly in whorls of 3, oblong, blunt tipped, mostly 2 mm wide (6–10 mm long, 1–5 mm wide), firm, and flat. Leaves in upper whorls can grow closely together and overlap. Flowers are unisexual (on separate plants), small (petals 2–5 mm long), borne singly, and white. Female flowers attached to long thread-like stalks at leaf axils, with sepals 2–3.5 mm long. Male plants are uncommon, but have flowers also elevated on long (2–30 cm) stalks.

Habitat & Distribution

Elodea canadensis is a native species of lakes, ponds, and slow rivers. It is widespread in New Jersey but most common in neutral to calcareous waters. Plants grow rapidly in favorable conditions and form dense masses. It spreads by the detachment of resilient, densely leaved stem fragments (turions).

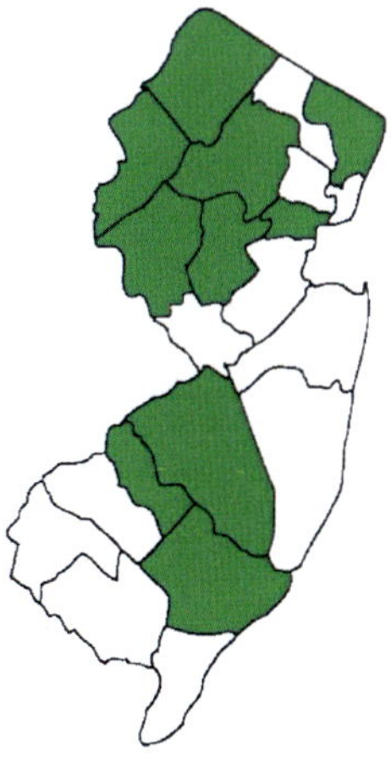

FREE-FLOWERED WATERWEED *Elodea nuttallii* (Planch.) St. John

Free-flowered waterweed is a submersed, perennial, with elongated, flexuous stems rooting from nodes. Leaves are mostly in whorls of 3, narrowly lance-shaped, pointed, mostly 1.3 mm wide (4–15 mm long, 0.9–1.7 mm wide), weak, and edges slightly folded along midvein. Leaves more or less equally spaced along stem. Flowers are unisexual (on separate plants), small (petals 2.5 mm long), borne singly at leaf axils, and white. Female flowers attached to long thread-like stalks, with sepals 1–1.8 mm long. Male flowers are stalkless and released from plant to float on water surface.

HABITAT & DISTRIBUTION

Elodea nuttallii is a native species of lakes, ponds, slow rivers, and sometimes brackish tidal waters. It is widespread in New Jersey. Plants are found in acidic to moderately alkaline waters.

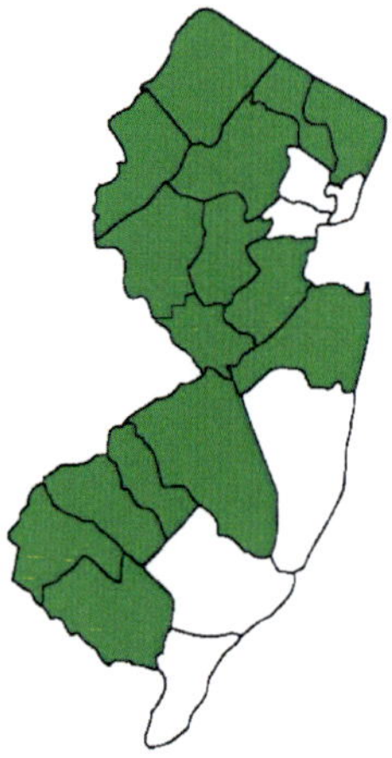

Eriocaulon — Eriocaulaceae

Pipewort

The Pipeworts, or Hatpins, are diminutive, submerged, tufted, erect perennials with conspicuously white roots bearing distinctive cross-walls. Leaves are green, in dense, basal rosettes, narrow, tapered to a point from a flattened, pale, spongy base. Leaves are smooth, veiny, and somewhat translucent. Soft, flowering heads of minute, whitish flowers are borne at tips of erect, slender, longitudinally ridged stalks, and held above water surface.

Four species occur in New Jersey, three being aquatic. All are native and very similar in appearance. Pipeworts superficially resemble the related Hairy pipewort, or Bogbuttons [*Lachnocaulon anceps* (Walt.) Morong]. This emergent wetland species of pine barrens, bogs, and ponds (not detailed herein) is distinguished by its hairy leaves and flower stalks and dark roots lacking cross-walls.

Key to Species

1. Flower head 10–20 mm wide, stalk with 10–12 ridges; plants coarse, 20–70 cm tall………………………………………………………………………………………………*E. compressum*
1. Flower head 4–6 mm wide, stalk with 4–7 ridges; plants low, to 20 cm tall……………………2
   2. Flower cluster 4–6+ mm wide, white to gray-white, globose in shape, atop a 5–7 ridged stalk; usually a single flowering stalk per plant……………………………………*E. aquaticum*
   2. Flower cluster 3–4 mm wide, dull gray or rarely yellow-brown, hemispherical in shape, atop a 4–5 ridged stalk; 1–4 flowering stalks per plant……………………………………*E. parkeri*

E. aquaticum

SEVEN-ANGLED PIPEWORT *Eriocaulon aquaticum* (Hill) Druce

Seven-angled pipewort is a tufted, submersed plant with basal, green, tapered leaves, 1–10 cm long (to 40 cm), 2–5 mm wide. Flowering stalks (1 mm wide), usually one per leaf rosette, with 5–7 vertical ridges. Flower cluster 4–10 mm wide, white to gray-white, and globose in shape.

HABITAT & DISTRIBUTION

Eriocaulon aquaticum is a native plant of freshwater lakes, ponds, and slow-moving rivers and streams. It is widespread and common in New Jersey. Plants are usually abundant on sandy substrates of shallow, low nutrient, acid waters.

Note: Flowering stalks can be notably long (2 m) when in deeper waters

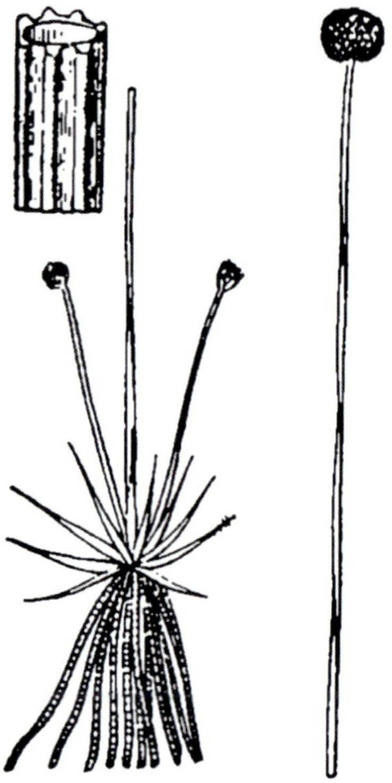

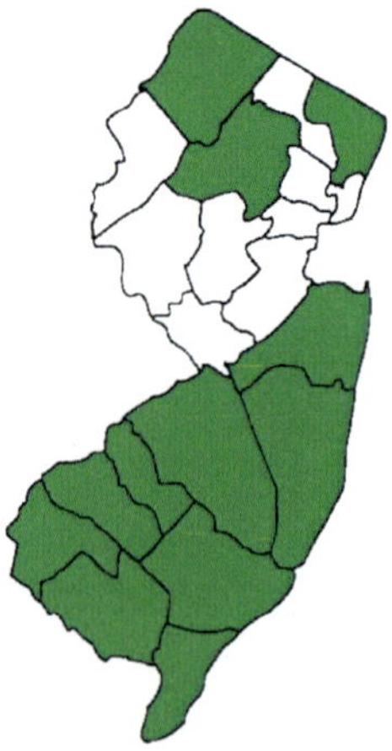

FLATTENED PIPEWORT *Eriocaulon compressum* Lam.

Flattened pipewort is a tufted, submersed plant with basal, green, tapered leaves, 5–30 cm long. Flowering stalks 30–100 cm tall, 1–3 mm wide, 1–3 per leaf rosette, with 10–12 vertical ridges. Flower cluster 10–20 mm wide, chalk white, and globose in shape.

HABITAT & DISTRIBUTION

Eriocaulon compressum is a native plant of freshwater lake shores, pine barren ponds, and pools. This southeastern Coastal Plain species is at the northern limit of its range in southern New Jersey. Plants occur on sandy substrates of shallow, low nutrient, acid waters.

Note: Similar to Ten-angled pipewort (*E. decangulare* L.) of moist, sandy areas (seldom in aquatic or permanently wet situations). Its flower heads are notably hard (rather than soft, like in the other three species) and leaf tips blunt.

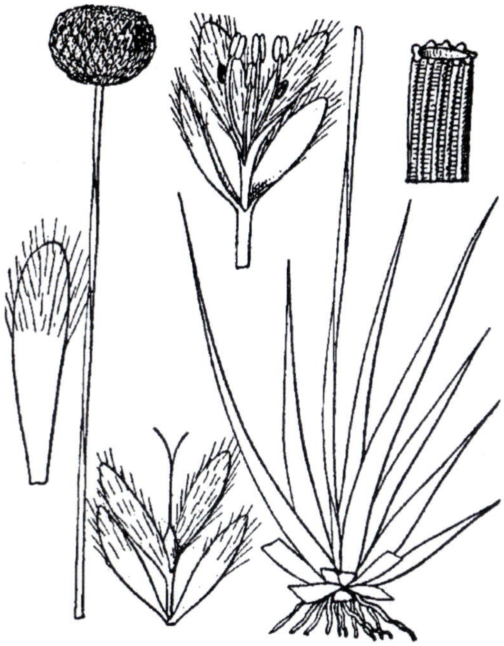

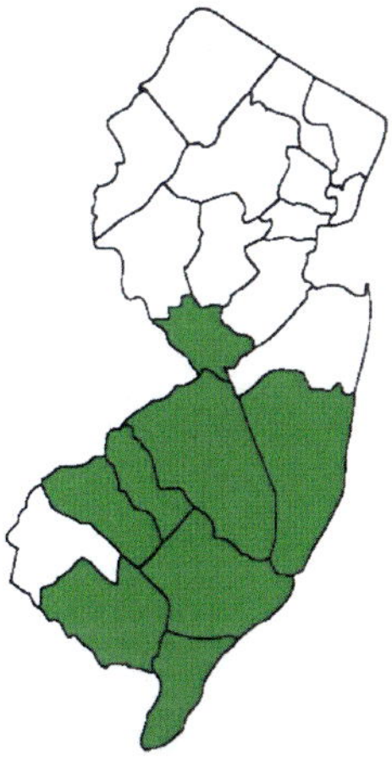

Estuary Pipewort — *Eriocaulon parkeri* B.L. Robins.

Estuary pipewort, or Parker's pipewort, is a tufted submersed plant with basal, green, tapered leaves, 2–6 cm long, 1–2 mm wide. Flowering stalks, 1–4 per leaf rosette, are 2.5–10 cm long, with 4–5 vertical ridges. Flower cluster 3–4 mm wide, dull gray or rarely yellow-brown, and hemispherical in shape.

Habitat & Distribution

Eriocaulon parkeri is a native species of fresh to brackish tidal shores and open mudflats of estuaries. Restricted to coastal regions and tidally influenced tributaries of the Delaware River in New Jersey. It is **rare** and imperiled in New Jersey, eligible for protection under the jurisdiction of the Highlands Preservation Area.

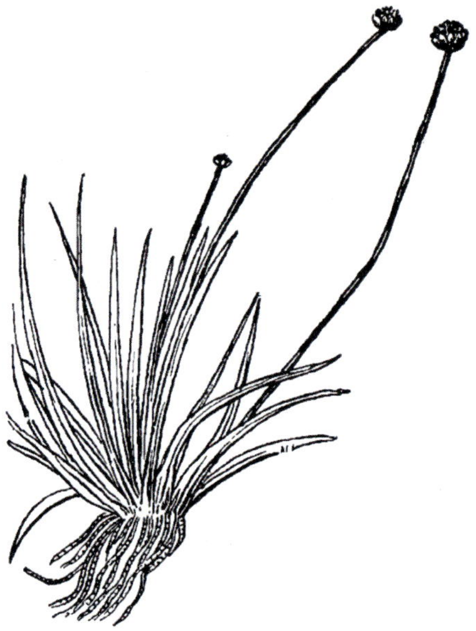

This species was first described in 1903 from specimens collected in the Delaware River, near Camden.

Notes: Plants are usually exposed at low tide, found at intertidal reaches to shores above high tide, and tolerant of oligohaline (salinity 0.5–5.0 ppt) waters.

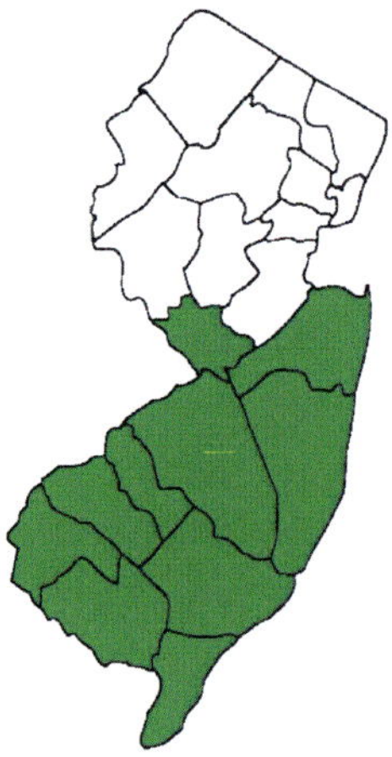

Glossostigma — Phrymaceae
Mud-mat

MUD-MAT *Glossostigma cleistanthum* W.R. Barker

Mud-mat is a diminutive (1–2 cm tall), mat-forming, submersed, perennial herb with creeping, slender rhizomes, rooting at the nodes (nodes to 18 mm apart). Leaves are opposite in pairs, erect, small (9–25 mm long, 1–3 mm wide), strap-shaped but widening toward tip. Flowers are small, with 2 stamens, borne singly on short (0–2 mm) stalks between the leaf pairs. When submersed, flowers are closed and self-pollinating. Fruit a capsule (<2 mm).

HABITAT & DISTRIBUTION

Glossostigma cleistanthum grows in shallow to deep (4 m) waters, or on exposed muddy or sandy shorelines of lakes, ponds, and streams. This Australia native was recently introduced and established in the northeast—presumably via improper aquarium disposal—where it is known in central New Jersey. It thrives in acidic, nutrient-poor waters with full sun. This fast-spreading **invasive** weed can form dense, carpet-like colonies (>25,000 plants/m^2), potentially threatening native hydrophytes. It can be confused with Atlantic Mudwort (*Limosella australis*).

Notes: Two ecotypes (submersed or emersed) exist: if growing emersed on open shores, plants exhibit shorter leaves (5–11 mm long), shorter internodes (1–10 mm), longer flower stalks (>4 mm), and behave as annuals with open, insect-pollinated flowers.

1 2 3 4
CENTIMETERS

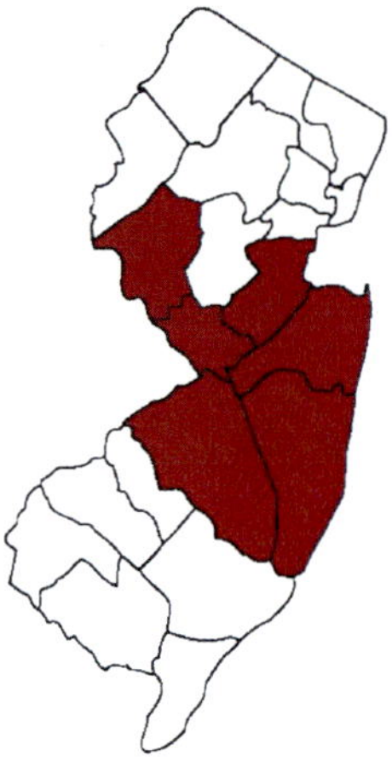

Glyceria — Poaceae
Manna grass

NORTHERN MANNA GRASS *Glyceria borealis* (Nash) Batch.

Northern manna grass, or Small Floating manna grass, is a rooted, perennial grass (60–100 cm tall) with creeping rhizomes and narrow (1.5–5 mm), ascending, hairless stems. Leaves are typically floating on surface, especially early in season (becoming weakly erect with age). Leaf blades are linear (15–45 cm long, 2–7 mm wide), flat, abruptly tapered to a point, hairless, dark bluish-green, with a prominent midvein. Leaf blades are tubular at base and sheath the stem (sheaths, deep red when submerged, have fused margins for most of their length). Flower clusters are emergent, weakly erect (18–40 cm tall), several-branched, and borne from the uppermost leaf sheath. Flowers are enclosed in small (10–20 mm), linear, spikelets.

HABITAT & DISTRIBUTION

Glyceria borealis is a native grass of shallow lake and stream margins. It is state-listed as ***endangered*** in New Jersey, considered *historic*. Mid-stem leaf blades have a dense covering of minute, pimply projections on their upper surface making them strongly hydrophobic.

Note: It can be confused with other widespread species, like Eastern manna grass (*G. septentrionalis* A.S. Hitchc.). Those plants (not detailed here) differ mostly by finer details of flowers.

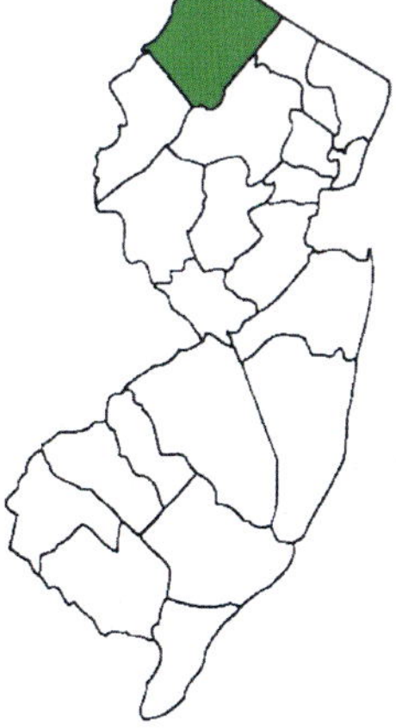

Gratiola — Plantaginaceae
Hedge-hyssop

GOLDEN HEDGE-HYSSOP *Gratiola aurea* Pursh.

Golden hedge-hyssop, or Golden pert, is a rooted, submersed, perennial with slender rhizomes. Plants are diminutive (1–5 cm tall), somewhat fleshy/stout, with smooth, somewhat four-angled, upright stems. Leaves are opposite, stalkless, small (≤5 mm long), narrow, awl-like and pointed, with toothless margins. Plants of this submersed life-form are sterile (vegetative only).

HABITAT & DISTRIBUTION

Gratiola aurea is a native species of low nutrient, mostly acidic, lake waters with full sun exposure. It is most common in southern New Jersey. Plants can be locally abundant, forming dense, turf-like, beds in either shallow or deep (4 m) waters.

Notes: The dwarfed, truly aquatic life-form (f. *pusilla* Fassett) is described here. At many occurrences, the species instead exists as a larger, fertile, emergent life-form on wet sandy shores of marshes, lakes, and rivers. The emergent form has taller stems (10–30 cm) with gland-tipped hairs, larger leaves (1–3 cm long) with conspicuous glandular dots, and bright yellow flowers (12–16 mm long) borne singly in leaf axils.

The submersed form is similar in appearance to Waterwort (*Elatine*) which has rounded leaves and evident flowers/fruits.

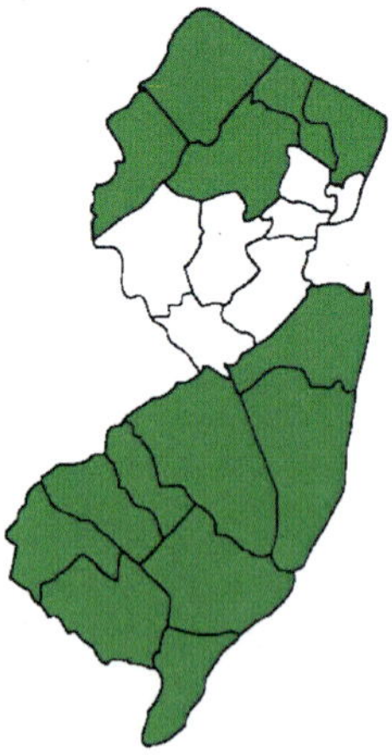

Heteranthera — Pontederiaceae
Mud-plantain

The Mud-plantains are submerged or creeping perennials or annuals with elongated stems rooted in mud. Leaves are linear and submerged or with broad blades and floating, with sheathing bases. Flowers are conspicuous, yellow, white, or purplish, with 6 petal-like segments, 3 stamens, and borne above water. Fruits are elongated capsules.

Three species occur in New Jersey, all native. Individual flowers are short-lived and only bloom for one day.

KEY TO SPECIES

1. Leaves linear, ribbon-like, and mostly submersed; flowers pale yellow and borne singly.. *H. dubia*
1. Leaves with stalked, kidney-shaped or elliptical blades and floating (or emersed); flowers white to pale blue, borne in elongated clusters of 2–16 flowers.................................... 2
   2. Flowers white, 2–8 per cluster, stamens with white hairs; mature leaf blades wider than long.. *H. reniformis*
   2. Flowers purplish to white, usually 7–16 per cluster, stamens with dark purple hairs; mature leaf blades as long as wide.. *H. multiflora*

GRASS-LEAVED MUD-PLANTAIN *Heteranthera dubia* (Jacq.) MacM.

Grass-leaved mud-plantain, or Water star-grass, is a submersed (or emersed on exposed mud), rooted, perennial with ribbon-like leaves, buried horizontal stems, and elongated, flexible, branching stems growing to water surface. Leaves are alternate, submersed, linear (3–10 cm long, 1–5 mm wide), sheathing at base, thin, lacking a distinct mid-rib, and blunt-tipped. Flowers are yellow, with six linear (4–11 mm long) petal-like lobes, three yellow stamens, and borne singly at water surface.

HABITAT & DISTRIBUTION

Heteranthera dubia is found in ponds, streams, and tidal rivers. It is native to New Jersey and frequent in the north. Plants exhibit the most extensive growth in alkaline waters and can become weedy.

Notes: Flowers open within 2 hours after dawn and wilt by dusk. When not flowering, this species resembles narrow-leaved Pondweed (*Potamogeton*) species but lacks the conspicuous midvein of the latter. Older references may list this plant as *Zosterella dubia*.

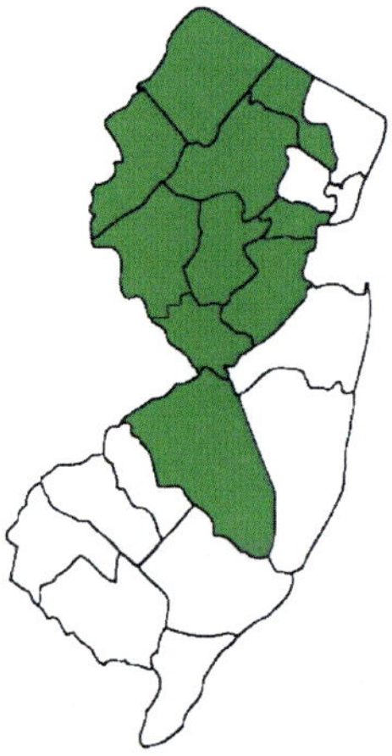

BOUQUET MUD-PLANTAIN *Heteranthera multiflora* (Griseb.) Horn

Bouquet mud-plantain is a submersed or creeping, annual or short-lived perennial, with elongated, flexible, branching stems growing upright in water. Leaves are alternate, mostly floating (or emersed) with broad, kidney-shaped blades (2–5 cm long, 2–5 cm wide), long (5–15 cm) stalks, and stipules (3–5 cm long), and submersed, thin, linear (4–7 cm long, 4–6 mm wide) leaves in basal rosettes. Flowers are pale purple or white (with 2 yellow spots in a purple blotch), with six petal-like lobes (3–6 mm long), borne in clusters of usually 7–16 above water surface.

HABITAT & DISTRIBUTION

Heteranthera multiflora is found in shallow pond margins. It is native to New Jersey where it reaches its northern limits on the Coastal Plain.

Note: Similar to Kidney-leaved mud-plantain, but Bouquet mud-plantain has a dark purple blotch on the upper petal, purple haired stamens, and more flowers per cluster.

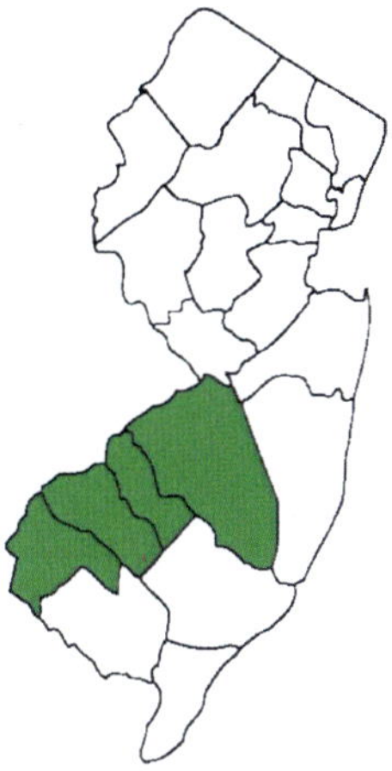

KIDNEY-LEAVED MUD-PLANTAIN *Heteranthera reniformis* Ruiz & Pavón

Kidney-leaved mud-plantain is a submersed or creeping, annual or short-lived perennial, with elongated, flexible, branching stems growing upright in water. Leaves are alternate, mostly floating (or emersed) with broad, kidney-shaped blades (1–4 cm long, 1–5 cm wide), long (2.5–4 cm) stalks, and stipules (1–5 cm long), and submersed, thin, linear (2.5–4 cm long, 3–8 mm wide) leaves in basal rosettes. Flowers are white (with 2 yellow or green spots), with six petal-like lobes (3–6.5 mm long), borne in clusters of 2–8 above water surface.

HABITAT & DISTRIBUTION

Heteranthera reniformis is found in tidal river mudflats and ponds characterized by fluctuating water depths. It is native and frequent in New Jersey.

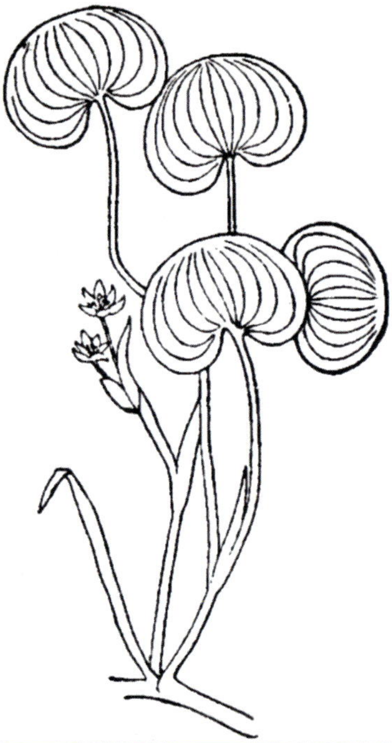

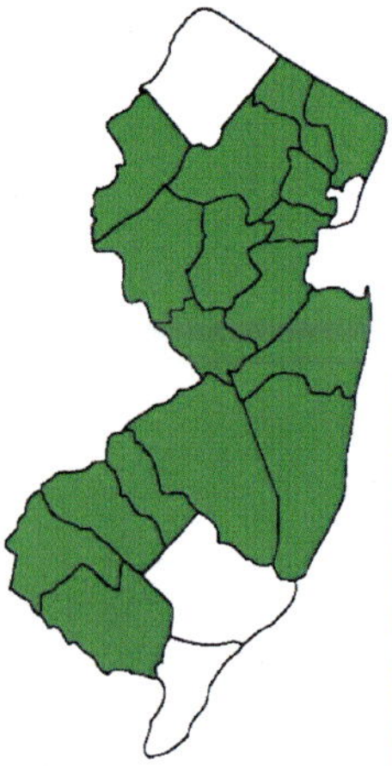

Hottonia — Primulaceae
Featherfoil

AMERICAN FEATHERFOIL *Hottonia inflata* Ell.

American featherfoil is a submersed, short-lived annual with long (30–50 cm), flaccid, hollow stems, rooted at base. Leaves are alternate (or whorled/clustered near top), submersed (or floating at surface), oblong (2–8 cm long), feathery, and finely divided into linear segments. Flower clusters are floating on water surface, with swollen, air-filled, spongy stalks (to 30 cm long) bearing whorls of (3–10) inconspicuous white flowers. Fruit is a globose (1.5–3 mm) capsule.

HABITAT & DISTRIBUTION

Hottonia inflata is a native Coastal Plain species found in still, acidic waters of ponds, swamps, and ditches. It is rare in New Jersey and state-listed as ***endangered***.

Note: This odd-looking plant is unmistakable in spring with its buoyant, swollen, flower clusters. These clusters can detach and become free-floating. As a "winter annual" species, after fruiting plants typically wither and die by mid-July. Abundance at a site can vary greatly from year to year as a function of precipitation.

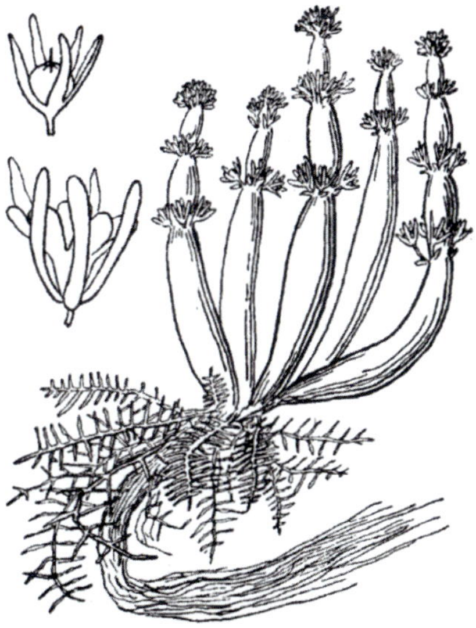

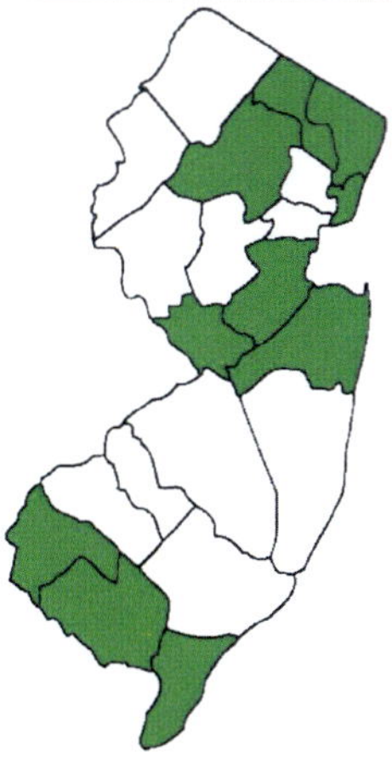

Hydrilla — Hydrocharitaceae
Hydrilla

HYDRILLA *Hydrilla verticillata* (L.f.) Royle

Hydrilla, or Water-thyme, is a submersed, perennial with rhizomes and elongated, flexuous, branched stems. Leaves are in whorls of 4–8, linear (8–15 mm long, 1–4 mm wide), sharply pointed, with saw-toothed margins, and bottom surface with minute prickles or bumps along midvein. Flowers are unisexual (on same or separate plants), small, white, and borne singly from upper leaf axils. Female flowers with elongated (10–50 mm) floral tubes reaching water surface. Fruit a small (4–6 mm long) capsule.

HABITAT & DISTRIBUTION

Hydrilla verticillata is a non-native species of lakes, ponds, and rivers. It is known from much of New Jersey where it is **invasive**.

Native to Asia, it was introduced into the US as an aquarium plant. It produces two types of overwintering turions: underground, pale brown, tuber-like ones and dark green, stiff-scaled ones on upright stems.

Notes: A problematic weed that is fast-growing, easily and rapidly dispersed, and with remarkably broad ecological tolerances (of water depth, pH, salinity, and nutrient levels). Anywhere it is found it poses a serious threat to the waterbody. It may be confused with Waterweeds (*Elodea*).

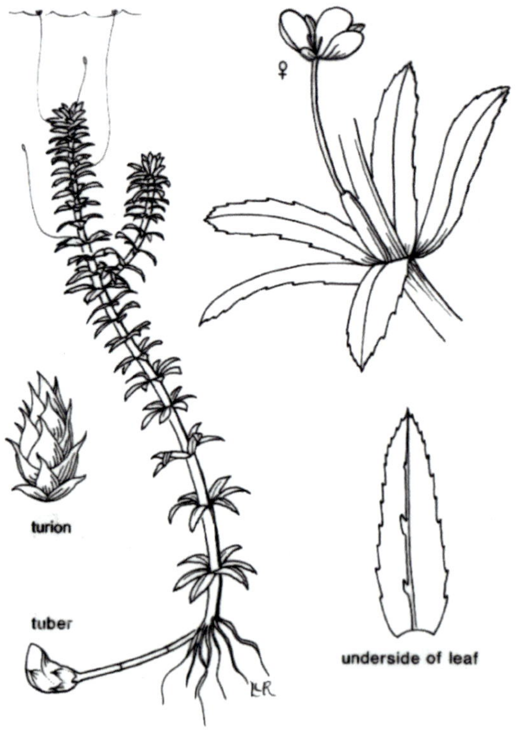

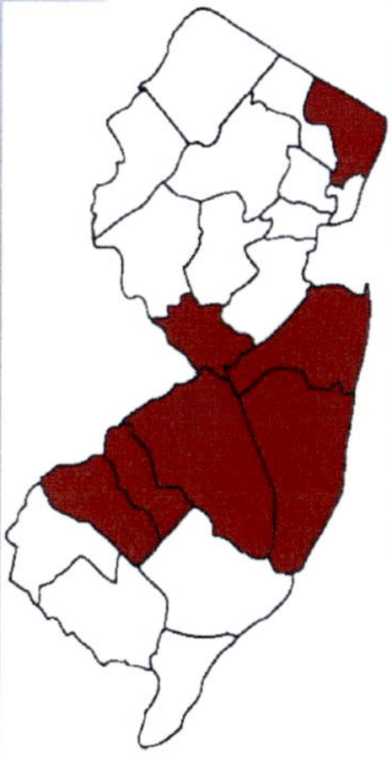

Hydrocharis — Hydrocharitaceae

Frog-bit

EUROPEAN FROG-BIT *Hydrocharis morsus-ranae* L.

European frog-bit is a perennial, free-floating or rooted floating-leaved plant, with horizontal stoloniferous stems and branched roots. Leaves are in basal rosettes and floating with long stalks (4–6 cm long) and a slight spongy central region on lower blade surface. Leaf blades are leathery, broad (1.5–6.5 cm long, 1–6 cm wide), heart shaped to near circular (with 5–7 broadly arching veins), with rounded tips. Each leaf with two stipules at base of leaf stalk. Flowers are unisexual (on different plants) with three whitish petals (yellowish at base) and held above water. Fruits, if produced, round (4–12 mm wide), berry-like, on recurved stalks. Turions develop at ends of stolons in late summer.

HABITAT & DISTRIBUTION

Hydrocharis morsus-ranae is a non-native species of quiet, shallow lakes, sheltered pools, and slow river margins. It is known from a few locations in New Jersey where it is **invasive**. Native to Eurasia, this species was introduced into North America as a water garden escape.

Notes: A problematic weed that can develop dense, floating mats easily dispersed by fragmentation. Individual plants are known to form up to 100–150 turions, which can remain dormant for 2+ years.

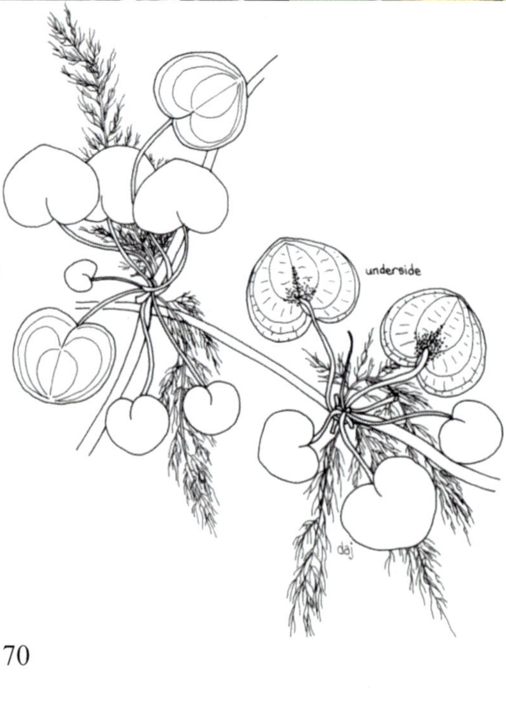

Hydrocotyle — Araliaceae
Water pennywort

The Water pennyworts are submerged, floating, or creeping perennials with branching, fleshy stolons, rooting at the nodes. Leaves are submerged, floating, or emersed, one per node, with thick, green, nearly-round blades (1–7 cm wide) and long (4–30 cm), erect, leafstalks. Flowers clusters, one per node, are borne at tip of long stalks. Flowers are minute and whitish. Fruits are round, ribbed, and dry.

Two aquatic species occur in New Jersey, both native. Other species (e.g., *H. americana*, *H. prolifera*, *H. verticillata*) occur in moist woods or marshes of New Jersey. These less aquatic species, excluded here, are more emergent in habit.

Key to Species

1. Leaf blades deeply notched, a sinus extending to point of stalk attachment, with 3–7 lobes; flower clusters not overtopping leaves ....*H. ranunculoides*

1. Leaf blades with stalk centrally attached to underside of blade, lacking a sinus extending to leafstalk, merely round-toothed on margins; flower clusters overtopping leaves............ ....*H. umbellata*

FLOATING MARSH PENNYWORT *Hydrocotyle ranunculoides* L.f.

Floating marsh pennywort, or Swamp marsh pennywort, is a small, floating-leaved plant with floating or creeping stems, freely rooting at nodes. Leaves are floating (emersed if stranded), with dark green, nearly-round (1–7 cm wide), 3–7 lobed (with distinct, central lobe) blades. Leaves have long (to 30 cm), stout stalks attached to blades at base of a deep sinus. Flowers clusters, one per node, are borne at tip of stalks (1–6 cm long) that are shorter than the leaves. Flowers (4–10 per cluster), connected at same point on stalk, are minute and whitish. Fruits are round (2–3 mm wide), ribbed, brownish, and dry.

HABITAT & DISTRIBUTION

Hydrocotyle ranunculoides occurs in pools, pond shores, bogs, and streams. It is a rare native species in New Jersey where it is state-listed as ***endangered***.

Notes: This species can occupy swiftly flowing waters. The roots on floating stems can be notably numerous and long.

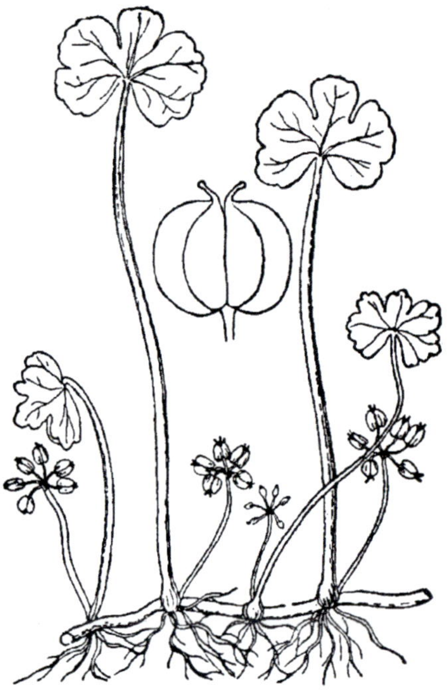

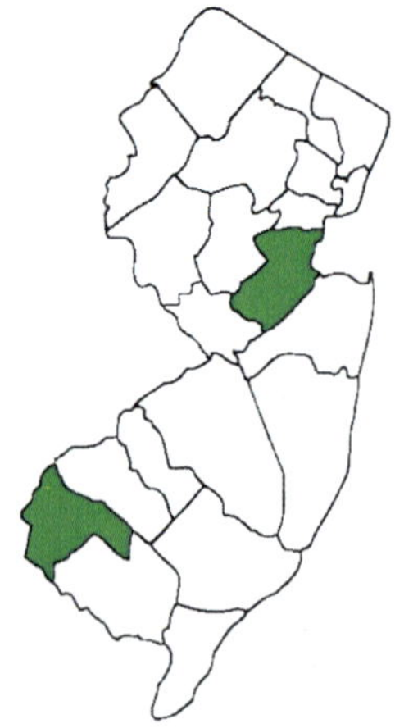

Many-flowered marsh pennywort is a small, floating-leaved plant with slender, floating or creeping stems, rooting at the nodes. Leaves are floating (emersed if stranded), one per node, with thick, green, nearly-round blades (1–4 cm wide) and round-toothed margins. Leaves have long stalks (to 20 cm) centrally attached to underside of blade (peltate). Flowers clusters (1–3 cm wide), one per node, are borne at tip of stalks that are equaling or longer than the leaves. Flowers (10–100 per cluster), connected at same point on stalk, are minute and whitish. Fruits are round (2–3 mm wide), ribbed, and dry.

HABITAT & DISTRIBUTION

Hydrocotyle umbellata occurs in shallow (<1 m) pond shores, marshes, bogs, and ditches. It is native and frequent in the Coastal Plain of New Jersey. This species reproduces vegetatively by stem elongation and detached stem fragments and has broad ecological tolerances.

Notes: Similar to the rare, state-listed Whorled marsh pennywort (*H. verticillata* Thunb.) of coastal New Jersey. The rare species produces flowers in spike-like clusters, each with multiple (2–12) whorls of flowers, and wider fruits (3–4 mm).

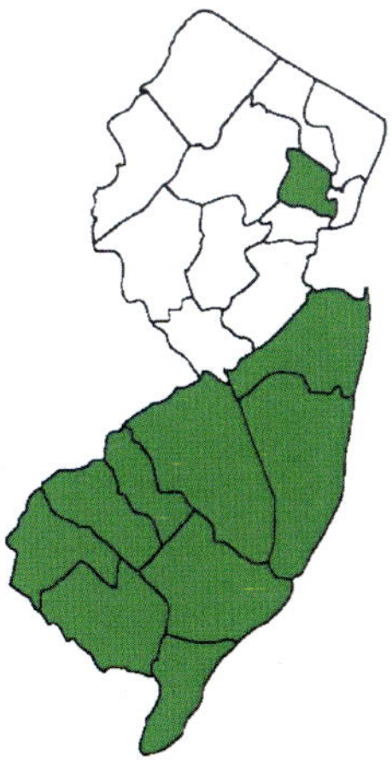

Hypericum — Hypericaceae
St. John's-wort

NORTHERN ST. JOHN'S-WORT ***Hypericum boreale*** (Britt.) E. Bickn.

Northern St. John's-wort is a delicate, submersed, rooted, perennial, with slender rhizomes and flaccid, elongated, mostly unbranched stems (1–2 mm wide). Leaves are opposite, small (6 mm long), rounded, toothless, 3-veined, and without stalks (round bases of blade clasping stems). Plants usually lack flowers.

HABITAT & DISTRIBUTION

Hypericum boreale is a native species that occurs in shallow ponds, streams, and marshes. It is widespread in New Jersey.

Notes: The flexuous, sterile, submersed life-form (f. *callitrichoides* Fassett) is described here. In many cases, the species also occurs nearby as the typical, fertile, emergent life-form on wet shores or marshes. Emergent plants have erect stems (10–40 cm tall), larger, more oblong, leaf blades (1–3 cm long) with scattered translucent dots on surface and 3–5 veins, and small, yellow flowers borne near tips of spreading upper branches. The submersed life-form is similar to Water starworts (*Callitriche*).

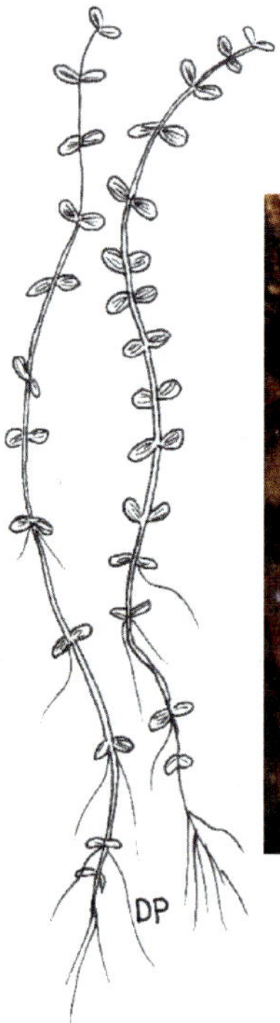

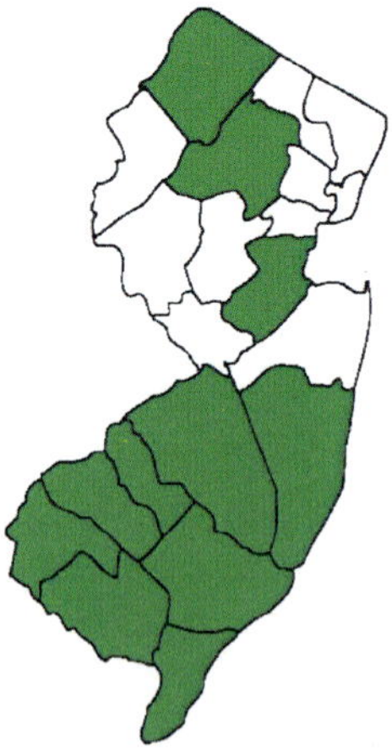

Isoëtes — Isoëtaceae
Quillwort

The Quillworts are tufted, submersed, perennial, spore-producing (i.e., non-flowering) plants with grass-like leaves arranged in rosettes, and rooted below a bi-lobed stem. Leaves are linear, green, with four hollow lengthwise chambers, scattered cross-walls, and swollen, whitish bases where the spore-producing structures (sporangia) are enclosed.

Vegetatively, most species are very similar in appearance. Species identification is challenging and requires microscopic examination of sculptural details of mature macrospores. These diagnostic, larger, spherical spores (bone-white when dry), usually borne in bases of outer leaves, are typically available from our plants only after July.

Five aquatic species occur in New Jersey, all native. Many species are known to hybridize frequently. Black spored quillwort (*I. melanopoda* Engem.) is a more terrestrial species of transient waters known historically from Cape May Co. The more northern Acadian Quillwort (*I. acadiensis* Kott) has also been reported for New Jersey in some references. Both of these species are omitted here.

Key to Species

1. Megaspores densely covered with thin, sharp, spine-like projections; leaves deciduous……. ………………………………… *I. echinospora*

1. Megaspores covered with ridges; leaves evergreen, lasting 1+ years…………………2

2. Megaspore diameter averaging <0.5 mm, patterned with an unbroken network of ridges.. ………………………………… *I. engelmannii*

2. Megaspore diameter averaging >0.5 mm, patterned with crest-like, wrinkled or network of broken, unconnected ridges…………………3

3. Leaves light green with abundant stomates; plants occasionally emergent; megaspores girdle (area just below equatorial ridge) obscure………………… *I. riparia*

3. Leaves dark green to red-brown with few or no stomates; plants always submerged; megaspore girdle evident…………………4

4. Megaspore diameter averaging >0.6 mm; leaves coarse and firm, abruptly tapering to the tip; plants typically in deep (1–3+ m) water………………… *I. lacustris*

4. Megaspore diameter averaging <0.6 mm; leaves soft and flaccid, gradually tapering to the tip; plants typically in shallower (0.5–1 m) water………………… *I. tuckermanii*

I. lacustris

I. echinospora

Leaves are bright green to reddish green, mostly 5–25 cm (to 40 cm) long, 0.5–1.5 mm wide, with slender tips. Leaves usually stiff in ponds and soft in flowing water.

A widespread species in New Jersey, where it reaches the southern end of its range. occupying clear, low nutrient, slightly acidic lakes, ponds, rivers, and streams.

Note: This species may be listed as *I. tenella* Léman in some references.

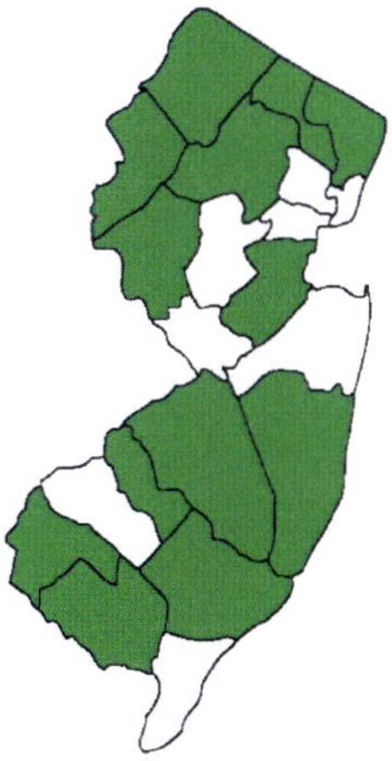

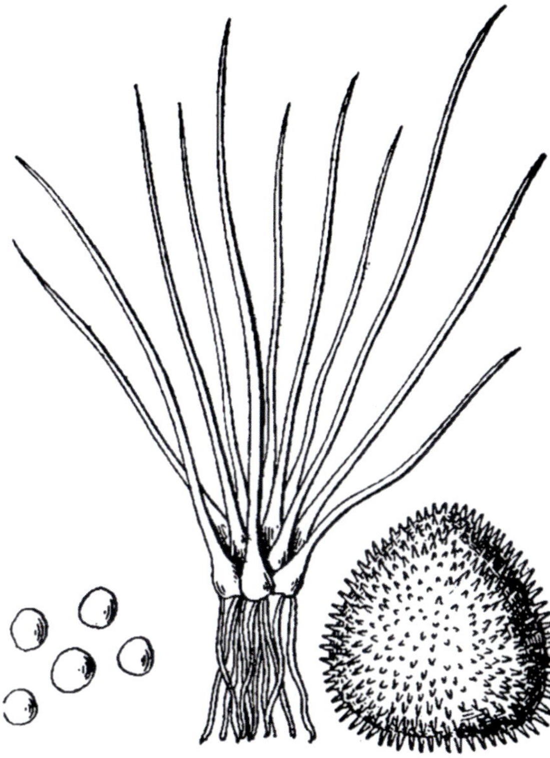

ENGELMANN'S QUILLWORT *Isoëtes engelmannii* A. Braun

Leaves are 6–50 cm long, 0.5–2 mm wide. Usually in shallow ponds and slow streams with fluctuating waters. Plants can be emersed later in season. The most common Quillwort in New Jersey.

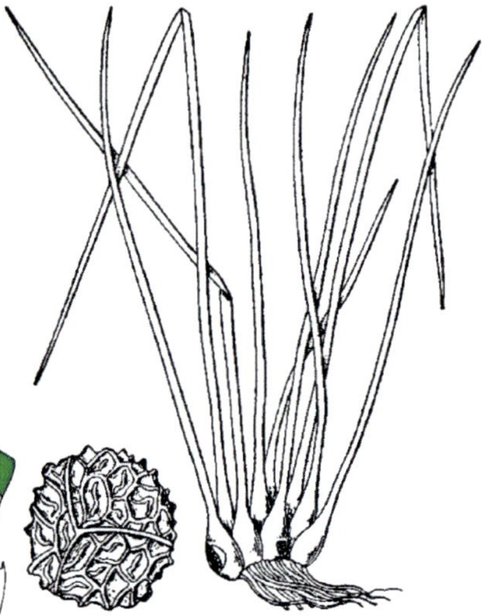

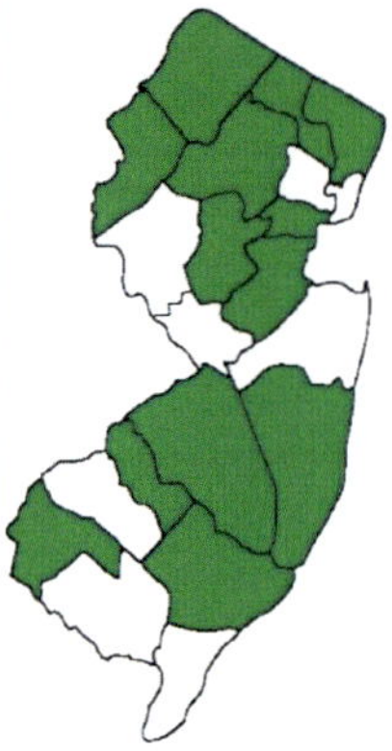

LAKE QUILLWORT *Isoëtes lacustris* L.

Leaves are dark green, coarse and firm, short (5–10 cm long, 1–2 mm wide), abruptly tapering to the tip, with few or no stomates. Plants are submerged in deep (1–3+ m), cold, clear lakes, ponds and streams. Critically imperiled in New Jersey where it is state-listed as ***endangered***.

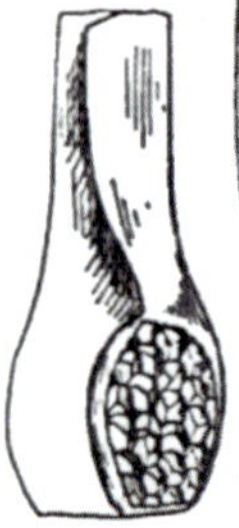

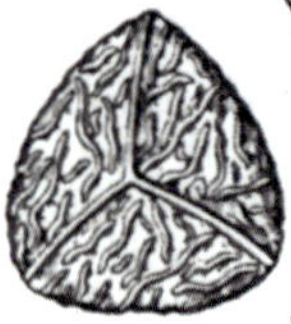

RIVERBANK QUILLWORT *Isoëtes riparia* Engelm. ex A. Braun

Leaves are bright green to yellow-green (whitish-green at base), 10–20 cm long, 0.5–1.5 mm wide, often twisted, with abundant stomates. Plants usually submersed, occasionally emergent, in shallow waters (<0.5m deep) of streams and lakes with a sterile sand, gravel, boulder substrate. Also along mudflats of brackish tidal riverbanks and estuaries.

It is ***rare*** and imperiled in New Jersey, eligible for protection under the jurisdiction of the Highlands Preservation Area. Historically common along the Delaware River and tributaries.

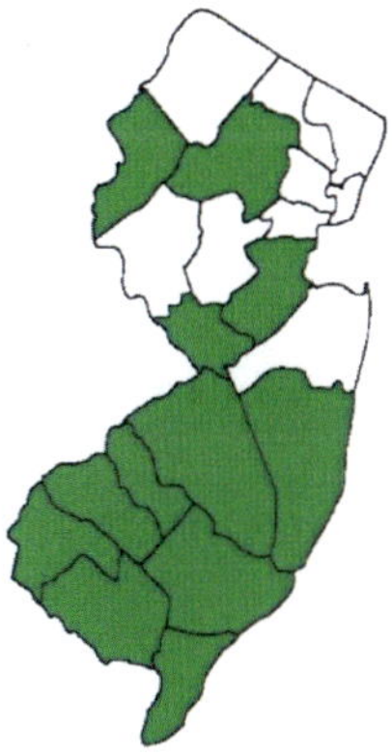

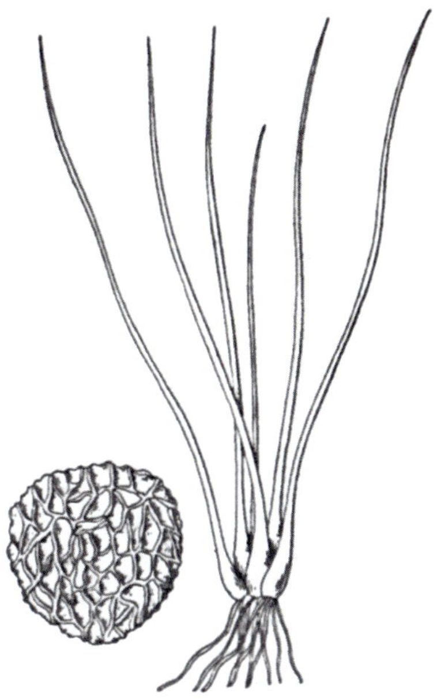

TUCKERMAN'S QUILLWORT *Isoëtes tuckermanii* A. Braun ex Engelm.

Leaves are olive green to reddish, thin, soft and flaccid, mostly 5–20+ cm long, 0.25–1.5 mm wide, gradually tapering to the tip. Plants are always submerged, in slightly acidic ponds and lakes 1–3 m deep. At the southern limits of its range in New Jersey, it is ***endangered*** and considered *historic*.

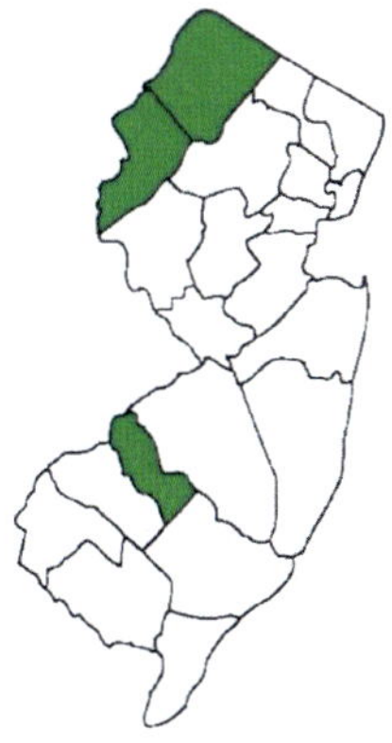

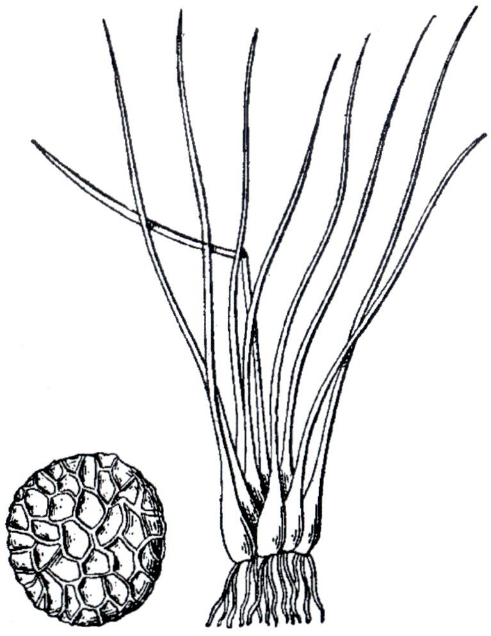

Juncus — Juncaceae
Rush

The Rushes are rooted, grass-like perennials, with submersed rhizomes and upright stems (culms) round in cross-section. Leaves can be of two types: one to several, emersed, stiff, hollow leaves attached to the erect stem and, in some cases, many, submerged, flaccid, thread-like leaves attached to rhizomes. The emersed leaves are round or oval in cross-section and have hardened internal cross-walls at regular intervals. Flowers are minute, straw-colored, and borne in a multi-branched cluster on top of stem.

Rushes can be difficult to identify, and flowers/fruits are often required for correct species determination. Sometimes mistaken for grasses or sedges, Rushes differ by flowers with 3 stiff petals & sepals, capsule fruit, and at times leaves with internal partitions. The firm leaf partitions can be felt by pressing and pulling the leaf between your fingers.

Numerous species of Rushes can occupy the shallow marshy wetlands, pond shores, and wet mud or sand of New Jersey. Most of these species, however, are more wholly emergent (and not detailed here). Two truly aquatic species, both native, can be found more submerged at times in New Jersey.

Key to Species

1. Stems stout (5–12 mm wide, 30–150 cm tall) with leaves usually overtopping flower structures; numerous, long, thread-like, submersed leaves with floating tips often present, attached to rhizomes; flowers crowded into hemispherical heads (6–8 mm wide) of 5–13 flowers each; flowers never replaced with bulbs.. *J. militaris*

1. Stems slender (1–2 mm wide, 5–30 cm tall) with leaves not overtopping flower structures; long thread-like submersed leaves absent; flowers borne singly or paired, not clustered in heads; flowers often replaced with small bulbs of reduced leaves .... *J. pelocarpus*

J. militaris

Bayonet rush has stout (5–12 mm wide), tall (to 150 cm), erect stems, round or oval in cross-section. Leaves are of two types: many, submerged (or tips floating), flaccid, thread-like leaves attached to rhizomes, and usually a single, emersed, stiff leaf attached to the erect stem. The emersed leaf is stout (50–100 cm long, 2–4 mm wide), round or oval in cross-section, with hardened internal cross-walls, pointed, attached near middle of stem, and overtopping the flower cluster. Flowers are minute, straw-colored or brown, borne in a multi-branched cluster (4–15 cm tall) at stem tip. Fruit is a small (2–3 mm long), straw-colored capsule.

HABITAT & DISTRIBUTION

Juncus militaris is a native species of shallow ponds, lakes, and streams. It is near its southern limits in New Jersey.

Notes: The submersed hair-like leaves are found particularly in deeper waters, where plants may remain sterile. Plants can form dense colonies. Similar to Robbins' spikerush (*Eleocharis robbinsii*) and Water bulrush (*Schoenoplectus subterminalis*), but neither possess emersed leaves or internal cross-walls.

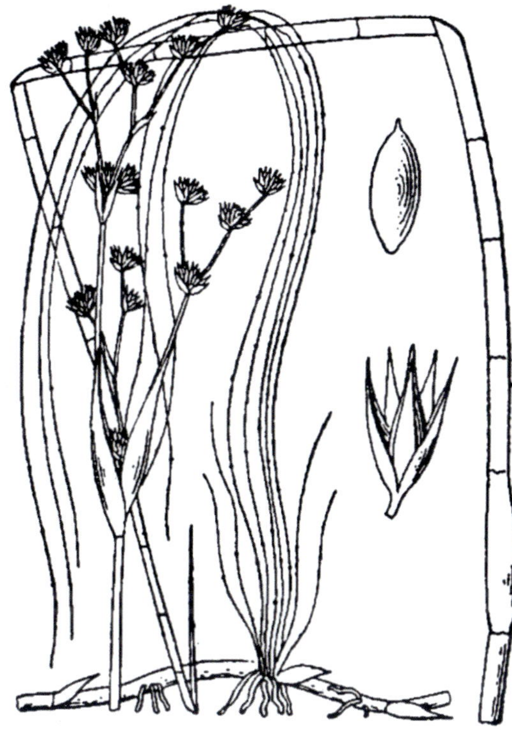

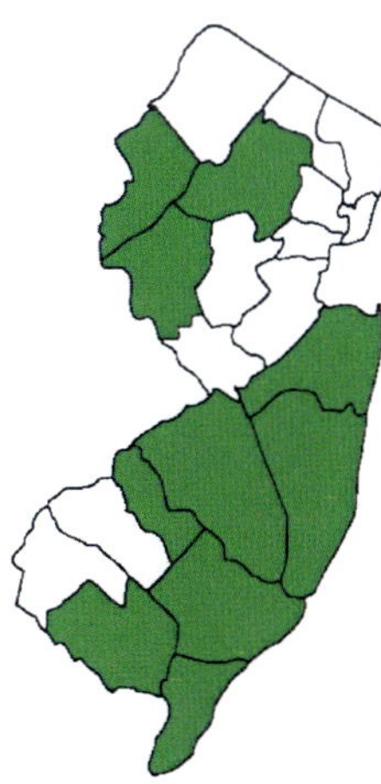

Brownfruit Rush *Juncus pelocarpus* Mey.

Brownfruit rush has slender (1–2 mm wide, 5–30 cm tall), erect stems, round or oval in cross-section. Leaves are usually emersed (1.5–11 cm long, 1 mm wide), round or oval in cross-section, with hardened internal cross-walls, not overtopping the flower cluster. Flowers are minute, straw-colored or brown, borne singly or paired along branches of a broad multi-branched cluster (more than a fourth as tall as plant) positioned at stem tip. Flowers are often replaced with small bulbs of reduced leaves. Fruit is a small (1.5–3.5 mm long) chestnut brown capsule.

Habitat & Distribution

Juncus pelocarpus is a native species of pond shores, swamps, and bogs. It is scattered throughout New Jersey.

Note: This plant can be found in a completely submersed growth form (forma *submersus* Fassett) in lakes with the typical emersed form often growing on nearby shores. This sterile aquatic form consists of leaves tufted along rhizomes and lacking upright stems. The internal cross-walls in these leaves can be more scattered.

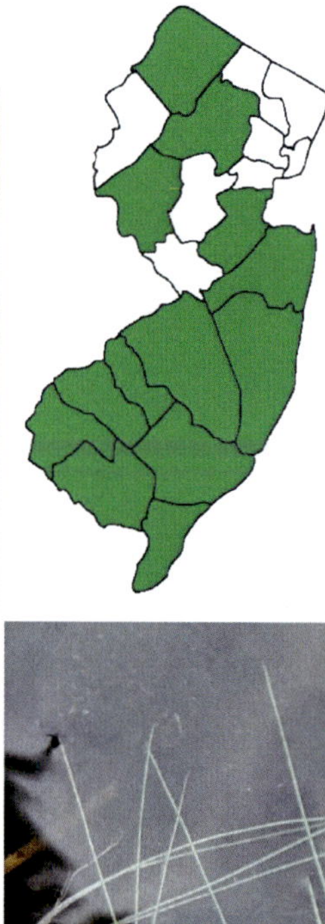

Lemna — Araceae
Duckweed

The Duckweeds are small (<15 mm long), green, perennials, mostly floating on surface of quiet waters. Plant body (sometimes called a thallus or frond) is greatly reduced (not differentiated into stem and leaf), flattened, oblong to narrowly egg-shaped, very obscurely 1–5 veined above, and one root below extending into water. There is a reproductive pouch on both sides of the body where new plants are produced. Usually 1–several plants are connected. Flowers and fruits are tiny, rarely seen.

Five species occur in New Jersey. Identification is best when plants are fresh. Individuals consistently reproduce vegetatively and are usually abundant, often intermixed with other duckweeds (*Spirodela* and *Wolffia*).

Key to Species

1. Plant bodies 6–15 mm long, oblong to broadly lance-shaped in outline, tapering to a conspicuous narrow stalk by which mature plant bodies remain attached laterally to parents, floating just below water surface in tangled masses; root often absent.... *L. trisulca*
1. Plant bodies 1–6 mm long, round, egg-shaped, or narrowly oblong in outline, without stalks, usually floating on surface of water; root present... 2
   2. Plant bodies with 1 vein.. *L. valdiviana*
   2. Plant bodies with 3–7 veins.. 3
3. Root sheath winged at base; root tip usually sharp pointed; roots up to 3 cm long; plant body green with a pointed tip, and 1 very distinct raised, pimple-like, projection (papilla) near apex on upper surface... *L. perpusilla*
3. Root sheath not winged; root tip mostly rounded; roots often longer than 3 cm; plant body green or red, rounded at tip, with or without raised, pimple-like, projections near apex on upper surface... 4
   4. Plant bodies not reddish on lower surface, upper surface flat, lacking a row of raised projections (papillae)..*L. minor*
   4. Plant bodies often reddish on lower surface beginning at point of root attachment, upper surface flat or convex, with a row of distinct raised projections near apex............*L. obscura*

L. minor

COMMON DUCKWEED *Lemna minor* L.

Common duckweed is a diminutive, perennial, floating on water surface. Its body, or thallus is small (1–6 mm long, 1–3 mm wide), flattened, egg-shaped, with 3–5 obscure veins on top surface, without a row of raised projections along midvein. Root is mostly over 3 cm long (to 15 cm), with a rounded tip, extending into water. Turions not produced.

HABITAT & DISTRIBUTION

Lemna minor is a native species of ponds, lakes, marshes and streams. It is common and widespread in New Jersey.

Notes: Similar to the rare Minute duckweed (*L. perpusilla*) which has a much shorter (<3 cm long), pointed roots, a body with a prominent, raised projection at tip, and a winged root sheath.

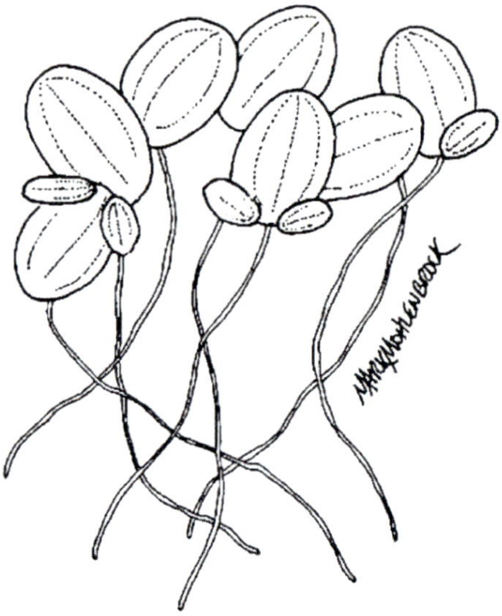

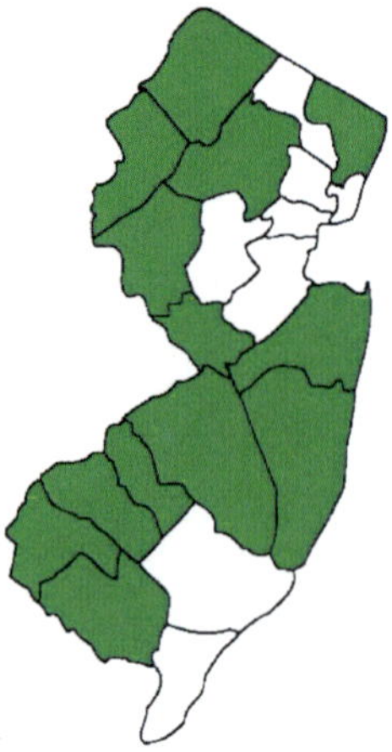

LITTLE DUCKWEED *Lemna obscura* (Austin) Daubs

Little duckweed is a diminutive, perennial, floating on water surface. Its body, or thallus is small (1–3 mm long), flattened or convex, egg-shaped, with 3 obscure veins on top surface, with a row of distinct, raised, pimple-like projections near apex. Lower surface often reddish, beginning at point of root attachment. Root is mostly over 3 cm long (to 15 cm), with a rounded tip, extending into water. Turions not produced.

HABITAT & DISTRIBUTION

Lemna obscura is a native species of ponds, lakes, and streams. It is nearing the northeastern limit of its range in New Jersey. Probably more frequent than indicated.

Notes: This plant, once recognized as a southeastern variety of Common duckweed (i.e., *L. minor* var. *obscura* Austin), was described based on plants collected in 1862 from New Durham Meadows, NJ. As such, it is very similar to Common duckweed.

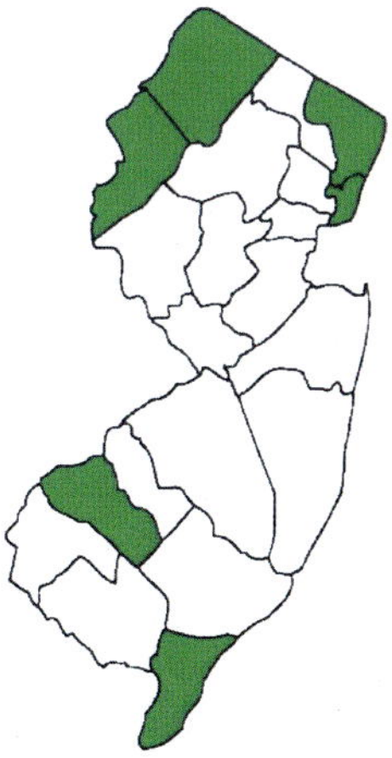

MINUTE DUCKWEED *Lemna perpusilla* Torr.

Minute duckweed is a diminutive, perennial, floating on water surface. Its body, or thallus is small (1–4 mm long, 1–3 mm wide), flattened, egg-shaped, with a pointed tip, 3 veins, and one very distinct, pimple-like projection near apex on top surface. Root is up to 3.5 cm long, with a sharp tip, extending into water. Root sheath is laterally winged at base. Turions not produced.

HABITAT & DISTRIBUTION

Lemna perpusilla is a native species of ponds, lakes, springs, and streams. It is critically endangered in New Jersey where it is state-listed as ***endangered***.

Note: This is one of the few duckweeds to regularly flower and fruit.

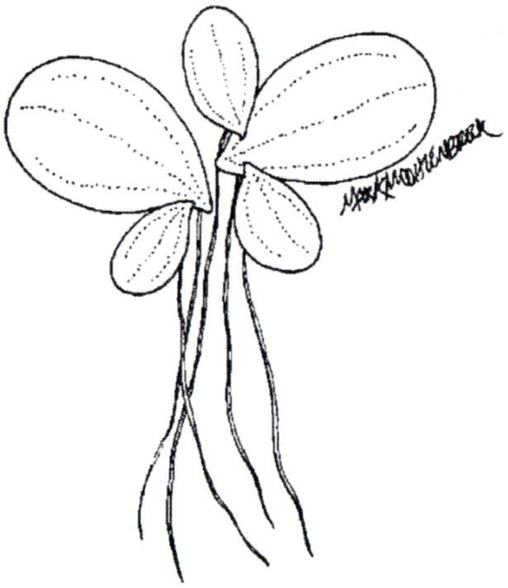

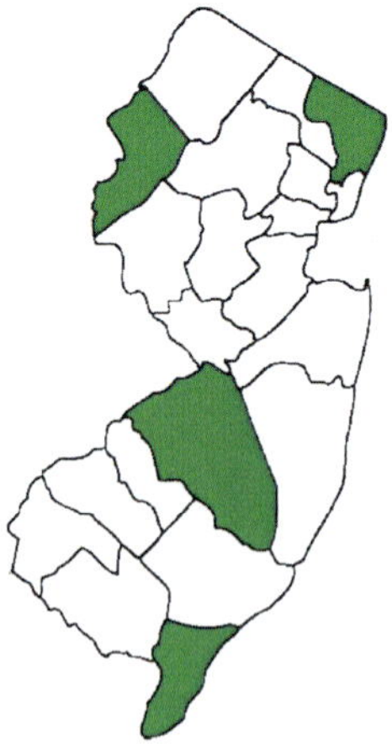

IVY-LEAVED DUCKWEED *Lemna trisulca* L.

Ivy-leaved duckweed is a diminutive perennial, suspended just below the water surface. Its body, or thallus, is 6–15 mm long without stalk (1.4–4 mm wide), flattened, oblong to broadly lanceolate in outline, with a somewhat toothed margin towards tip, tapering at base to a conspicuous, narrow stalk (2–20 mm long). Root deciduous and sometimes absent. Mature plant bodies remain attached to parents via stalks, forming branched chains.

HABITAT & DISTRIBUTION

Lemna trisulca is a native species of ponds and lakes, most common in alkaline waters. In New Jersey it reaches its southern limits in the northeast where it is **rare** and imperiled.

Notes: One of the more distinctive duckweeds with its long stalks. This species often forms extensive, tangled colonies where 3–50 clones can be interconnected. Bodies become shorter and thicker when flowering.

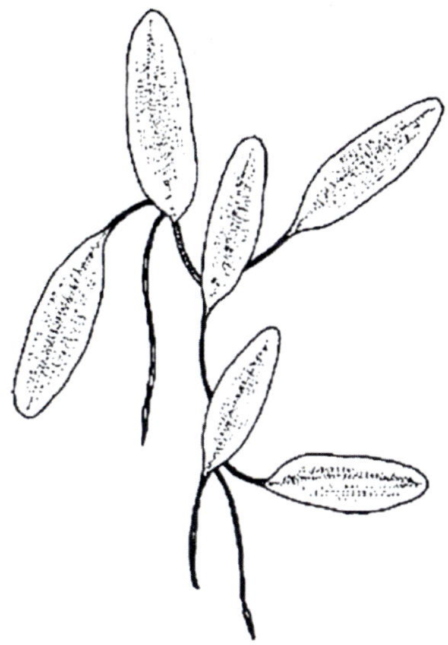

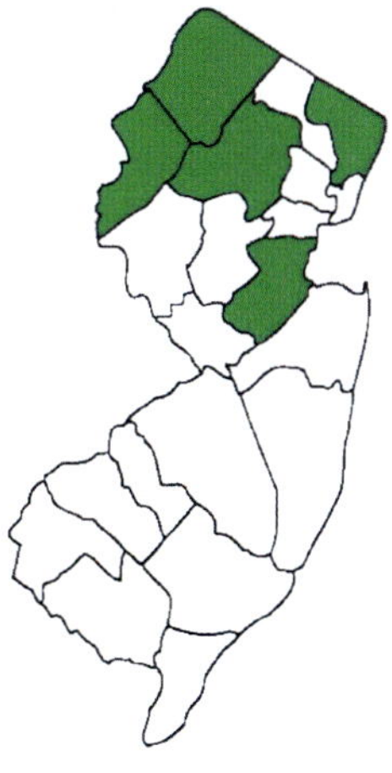

Pale duckweed is a diminutive, perennial, floating on water surface. Its body, or thallus is small (1–5 mm long, 0.6–3 mm wide), oblong, sides somewhat parallel, with 1 pronounced vein on top surface, with or without a row of raised projections along midvein. Root to 1.5 cm long, with a rounded to pointed tip, extending into water. Turions not produced.

HABITAT & DISTRIBUTION

Lemna valdiviana is a native species of ponds, lakes, and marshes. It is critically endangered in New Jersey where it is state-listed as ***endangered***.

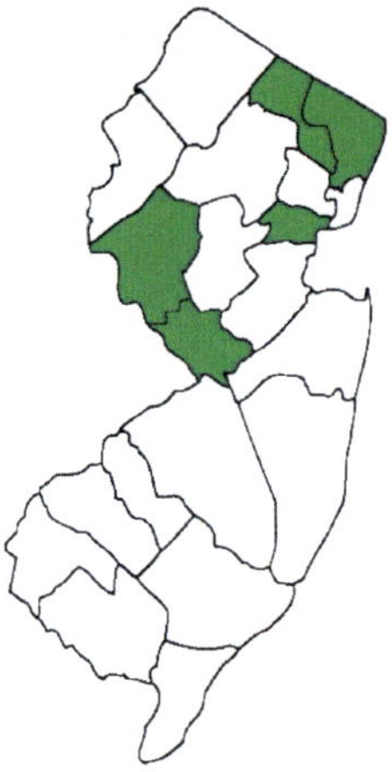

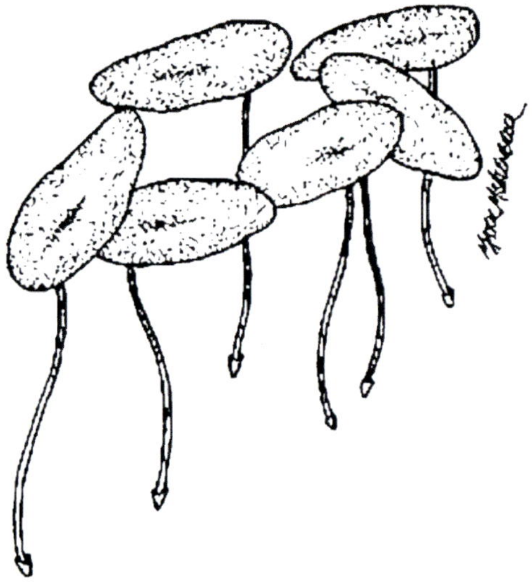

Lilaeopsis — Apiaceae
Grasswort

EASTERN GRASSWORT *Lilaeopsis chinensis* (L.) Kuntze

Eastern grasswort is a low, submersed or emergent, perennial with creeping, horizontal rhizomes which root at nodes. Leaves are 1–few, arising from the rhizome, linear or spatulate in shape, without an expanded blade, 1–5 cm long, hollow, rounded to flattened, transversely divided with 4–6 septa. Flowers inconspicuous, bisexual, and borne 4–10 in clusters from base of leaves. Flower cluster stalks are about as long as or longer than the leaves. Fruits are small (<3mm), rounded nutlets with 5 corky ribs.

HABITAT & DISTRIBUTION

Lilaeopsis chinensis is a native species in shallow waters and exposed mudflats of freshwater to brackish marshes, tidal streams, canals, and ditches, or saltmarshes. Restricted mostly to seaside areas in New Jersey.

Notes: This is a coastal species typically occupying intertidal areas which become inundated at high tide. It can form dense colonies in sunny areas. Submersed plants may remain sterile.

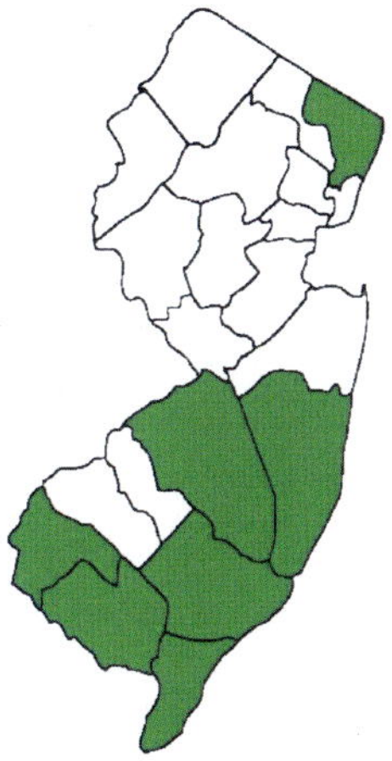

Limnobium — Hydrocharitaceae
Spongeplant

AMERICAN SPONGEPLANT *Limnobium spongia* (Bosc) Steud.

American spongeplant, or American frogbit, is a perennial, free-floating or rooted floating-leaved (or emergent) plant, with horizontal stoloniferous stems and branched roots. Leaves are in basal rosettes and of two forms: floating with short stalks and a thick, broad, spongy pad on lower blade surface and/or emergent with flat, leathery blades on long spongy stalks. Leaf blades are broad (2–8 cm long, 2–5 cm wide), heart shaped to round, (faintly 5–7 veined), usually with pointed tips. Each leaf with a stipule fused to base of leaf stalk. Flowers are unisexual (on same plant), whitish or yellowish, and held above water. Fruits round (4–12 mm wide), berry-like, on recurved stalks.

HABITAT & DISTRIBUTION

Limnobium spongia is a native Coastal Plain species of shallow margins of usually hard water, nutrient-rich, ponds. It is critically imperiled in New Jersey where it is state-listed as ***endangered***. It is more common in southeastern US.

Notes: The conspicuous broad, spongy pad on the undersides of leaf blades is most prominent on young floating leaves (and becomes less prominent with age).

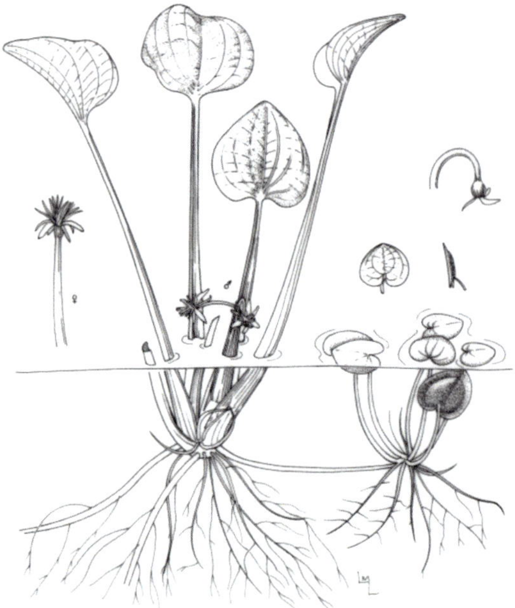

Limosella — Scrophulariaceae
Mudwort

ATLANTIC MUDWORT — *Limosella australis* R. Br.

Atlantic mudwort, or Awl-leaf mudwort, is a diminutive, rooted, submersed, herb with horizontal stoloniferous stems rooting at nodes. Leaves are fleshy, linear (2–5 cm long, 1–2 mm wide), round in cross-section, and tufted, 5–10 leaves clustered at bottom of plant. Flowers are small (3 mm wide), with 5 white petals (3.5–4 mm long) and 4 stamens, borne singly on erect stalks (about half of leaf length) that arise from nodes, several per plant. Fruit is a round capsule.

HABITAT & DISTRIBUTION

Limosella australis is a native species of shallow, tidally exposed, sand or mud of estuaries, rivers, and coastal pools. It is critically imperiled in New Jersey, where it is state-listed as ***endangered***.

Notes: This succulent, sometimes mat-forming, plant is tolerant of brackish water (to 18 ppt salinity) and exposure at low tides. It is most common and abundant in shallower waters. Technically a perennial species that acts as an annual due to difficulty in surviving winter conditions.

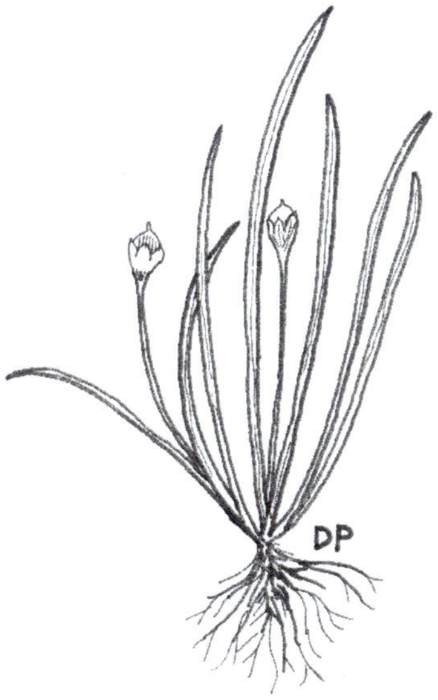

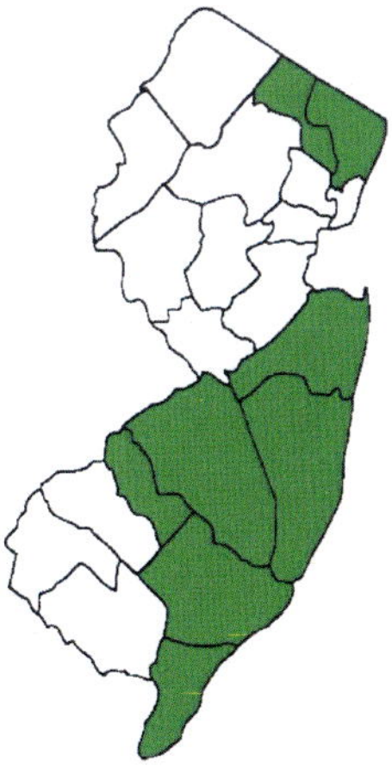

Lobelia — Campanulaceae
Lobelia

WATER LOBELIA *Lobelia dortmanna* L.

Water lobelia is a short, rooted, submersed, perennial plant. Leaves are clustered in basal rosettes, 2–5 cm long, linear, tubular (two hollow tubes in cross section), blunt-tipped, and arching outward. Flowers (1–2 cm long) have white to bluish, united petals, borne loosely towards the end of an emergent stalk. Flower stalks protrude from water surface about 30 cm (but can be 2–3 m long overall). Fruit a green, barrel-shaped, nodding, capsule.

HABITAT & DISTRIBUTION

Lobelia dortmanna is a native northern species of still, shallow waters of lake and pond shores. It is ***endangered*** in New Jersey, considered *historical*. This slow-growing plant prefers soft, clear, nutrient-poor waters with a sandy substrate. It is intolerant of high-nutrient conditions.

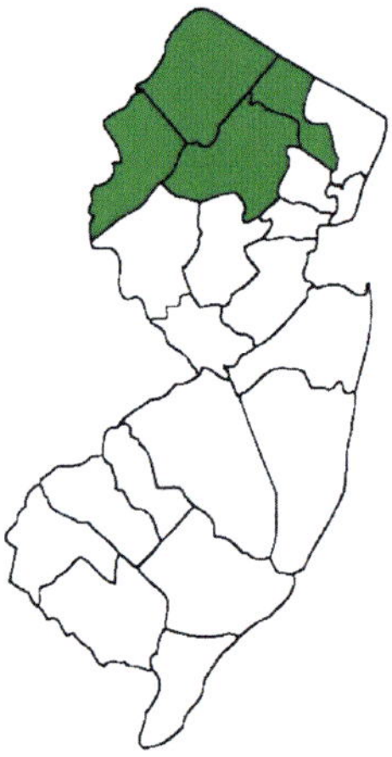

Ludwigia — Onagraceae
Water-primrose

The Water-primroses are perennial herbs with reddish stems either submersed, floating or creeping and ascending to erect near surface of quiet waters. Leaves are toothless often with roots at nodes. Flowers and capsules are produced in leaf axils.

Several *Ludwigia* species occur in wetlands of New Jersey, but only two species are truly aquatic.

KEY TO SPECIES

1. Leaves opposite, blades 0.5–3 cm long, leafstalks 0.1–2.5 cm long; flowers inconspicuous, without petals, and nearly stalkless (stalks 0–0.5 mm); fruit 2–5 mm long.............. *L. palustris*
1. Leaves alternate, blades 4–10 cm long, leafstalks 0.7–6 cm long; flowers conspicuous, with five yellow petals (1-1.5 cm long), with long stalks (stalks 7–60+ mm); fruit 10–40 mm long .... *L. peploides*

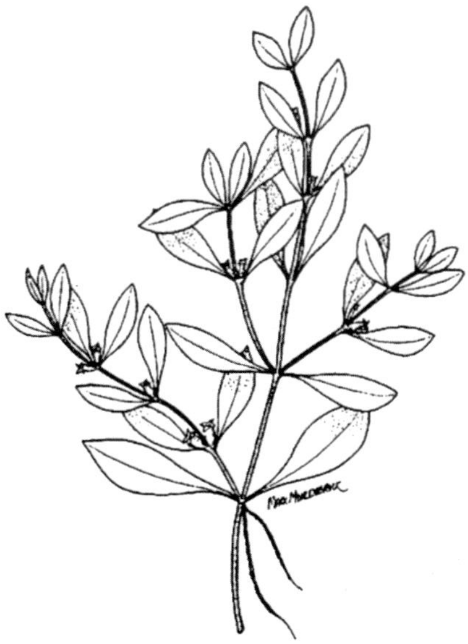

COMMON WATER-PRIMROSE *Ludwigia palustris* (L.) Ell.

Common water-primrose, or Water purslane, is mostly submersed (or emergent on mud), with reddish, many-branched stems (3–50 cm long) laying on sides or partly floating and rooting at lower nodes. Leaves are opposite, green to reddish-bronze, abruptly stalked (stalks 5–25 mm long) with egg-shaped to oval, toothless, blades (5–30 mm long, to 20 mm wide). Flowers are inconspicuous, bisexual, borne singly in leaf axils, green-brown, bell-shaped, and topped with 4 triangular sepals. Fruits are oblong (2–5 mm long, 2–3 mm wide), 4-sided capsules with four longitudinal green bands.

HABITAT & DISTRIBUTION

Ludwigia palustris is a native species occupying waters of marshes, swamps, rivers, and ponds. It is common and widespread in New Jersey. Plants can form dense mats in shallow waters.

Note: Similar to the rare Toothcup [*Rotala ramosior* (L.) Koehne] of sandy coastal pond shores. Toothcup, a more emergent species, however, has somewhat 4-sided stems, more lance-shaped leaves, and small white petals.

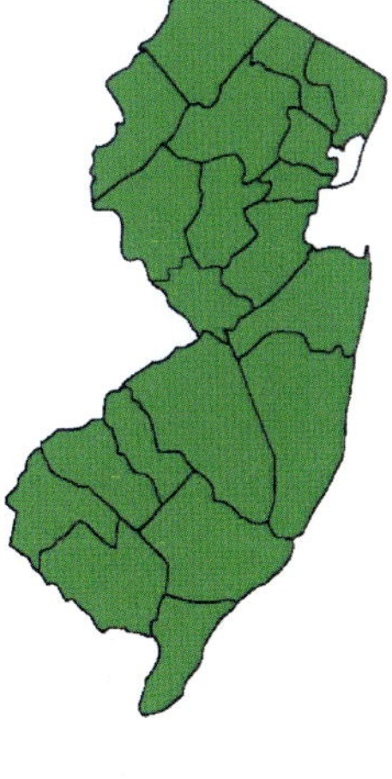

FLOATING PRIMROSE-WILLOW *Ludwigia peploides* (Kunth) Raven

Floating primrose-willow, or Creeping water-primrose, is sprawling plant mostly floating (or emergent on mud) with long (to 3 m long), often reddish, branched or unbranched stems rooting at nodes. Submerged nodes sometimes bear erect, fleshy, white, spongy "air" roots which float. Leaves are floating (or emersed at ascending stem tips), alternate, and stalked (0.7–6 cm long) with egg-shaped to nearly round, shiny, blades (4–10 cm long, to 4 cm wide). Flowers are conspicuous, borne singly in leaf axils at water surface, with 5 large (7–24 mm long), yellow petals. Fruits are cylindrical (25–40 mm long, 3–4 mm wide), long stalked (35–90 mm long), with 4 persistent sepals at apex.

HABITAT & DISTRIBUTION

Ludwigia peploides is native to our south but **introduced** into New Jersey, occupying slow-moving rivers, creeks, and ponds. Plants can become aggressive and form dense shoreline mats that drift several meters into the waterbody. Our plants are subspecies *glabrescens* (Kuntze) P.H. Raven

Note: This plant is very similar to the invasive Water primrose [*L. hexapetala* (Hook. & Arn.) Zardini, Gu, & Raven] which also has floating stems, alternate leaves, air roots, and yellow flowers but has soft-hairy upright flowering stems. This species has been introduced into nearby waters of Pennsylvania.

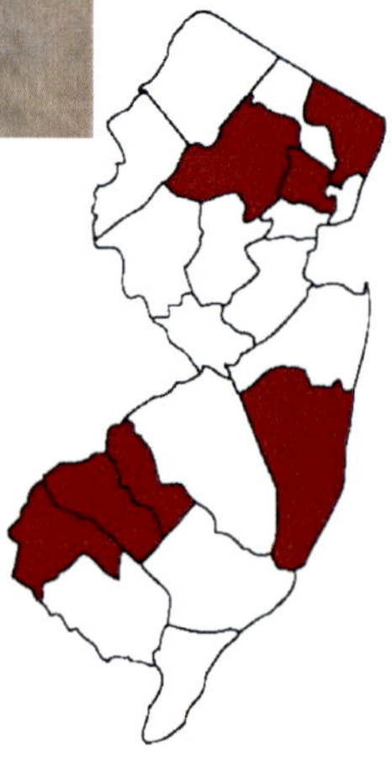

Marsilea — Marsileaceae
Water-clover

EUROPEAN WATER-CLOVER *Marsilea quadrifolia* L.

European water-clover, or Water-shamrock, is a perennial, aquatic fern that grows from long, creeping rhizomes, rooting mostly at nodes. Leaves are usually floating, with blades centrally divided into four triangular segments (each 7–21 mm long, 6–19 mm wide). Leaf stalks are narrow, flexible, and long (6–16 cm). Reproduces by spores, borne in hairy, pea-shaped (5 mm) structures (sporocarps) produced near base of leaf stalks.

HABITAT & DISTRIBUTION

Marsilea quadrifolia is a **non-native** plant established in shallow ponds or slow rivers. It is uncommon in New Jersey. The species was first introduced from Europe into Connecticut in the mid-1800s. As a popular water garden ornamental, it is now naturalized throughout the northeastern US.

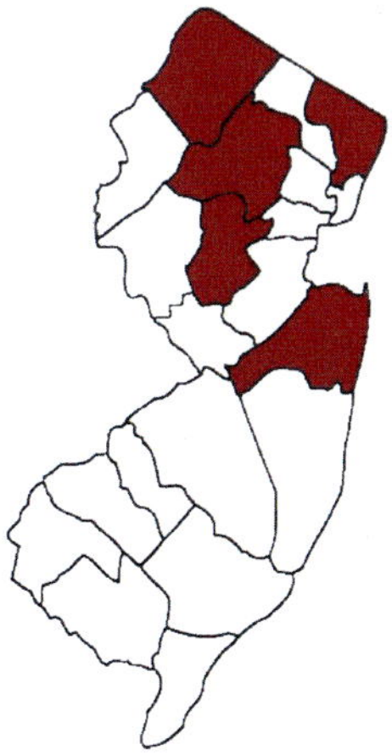

Myriophyllum — Haloragaceae
Water-milfoil

The Water-milfoils are slender, submersed, rooted, perennials with upright stems growing from rhizomes. Leaves are opposite, alternate, or whorled, and mostly feather-like, delicate and finely divided into thread-like segments. The emersed, bract-like, leaves associated with flowers, if present, usually differ in form and are reduced in size. Flowers are unisexual (on same plant), minute, and inconspicuous, borne singly either in leaf axils of submersed leaves or clustered on upright spikes above water. Flowering spikes have male flowers in uppermost positions and female flowers lowermost. Fruits are tiny (to 2.5 mm long), nut-like clusters of four 1-seeded segments.

Eight species occur in New Jersey, including five rare species and two non-natives. A few species are aggressive and highly invasive. Most species are highly variable so reproductive structures and existence of winterbuds (turions) are often essential for proper identification. Winterbuds are formed in late summer and autumn as highly condensed clusters of green, apical leaves.

Key to Species

1. Leaves (if present) simple, reduced to minute scales (<1 mm long) or bumps, on stiffly upright stems (2–20 cm); floral bracts toothless...*M. tenellum*
1. Leaves well-developed, pinnately divided into narrow segments, on elongated flexuous stems; floral bracts toothless, toothed, or deeply divided...2
    2. Leaves alternate, or alternate and whorled on same stem; male flowers with four stamens, 0.5–1 mm long; flowers in axils of submersed leaves or on spikes emersed above water 3
    2. All leaves whorled; male flowers commonly with 8 stamens (4 in *M. heterophyllum*), 1–2 mm long, flowers in emersed spikes... 4
3. Flowers and fruits borne in axils of reduced, pinnately divided, bract-like leaves on emersed spikes; leaves both alternate and whorled on same stem .... *M. pinnatum*
3. Flowers and fruits borne in axils of submersed leaves, not emersed above water in a spike; leaves alternate.. *M. humile*
    4. Emersed spikes with bracts (mostly 25–35 mm long, divisions 4–8 mm long) similar to submersed leaves, but rigid; submersed leaves with stalks 5–7 mm long........ *M. aquaticum*
    4. Emersed spikes with conspicuously reduced bracts (<20 mm long, teeth or divisions <4 mm long); submersed leaves with stalks 0–2 mm long..5
5. Floral bracts inconspicuous, bracts under lower flowers <2 times as long as the flowers or fruits; bracts under upper flowers with toothless to small-toothed edges........................ 6
5. Floral bracts conspicuous, bracts under lower flowers ≥2 times as long as the flowers or fruits; bracts under upper flowers with deeply divided to sharp-toothed edges........................ 7
    6. Middle leaves with 5–12 segments on each side; uppermost leaves rounded at tip; cylindrical turions formed in autumn; stems sparingly branched and vertical, stem diameter uniform throughout; non-flowering stem tips usually green and knob-shaped.... ....*M. sibiricum*

6. Middle leaves with 13–20 segments on each side; many uppermost leaves flat-topped at end (as if cut off); turions never formed; stems much-branched, often laying on water surface, and thickened (1.5–2 times as thick as lower stem) just below flowering spikes; non-flowering stem tips usually red and tassel-like………………………………*M. spicatum*

7. Bracts under female (i.e., lower) flowers sharply toothed; fruits 1–1.5 mm long; turions not widened at tip, formed at base of stems or rhizomes in fall; stems often reddish…………………………………………………………………………………………………… *M. heterophyllum*

7. Bracts under female flowers pinnately lobed or deeply divided; fruits 2–2.5 mm long; turions club-shaped and widened at tip, formed on stems in fall; stems olive green…………………………………………………………………………………………………….*M. verticillatum*

PARROT'S-FEATHER WATER-MILFOIL *Myriophyllum aquaticum* (Vell.) Verde.

Parrot's-feather water-milfoil is a submersed, densely leaved plant with elongated, flexuous, stems often with considerable leafy portions at tips emersed above water. Submersed leaves are whorled (3–6 per whorl), 8–45 mm long, pinnately divided into 10–15 pairs of narrow segments (4–8 mm long), appearing markedly feather-like, often reddish, with 5–7 mm long stalks. Emersed foliage is crowded, rigid, and grayish-green. Flowers, rarely produced, are borne in axils of emersed, mostly 25–35 mm long, leafy bracts—similar in appearance to submersed leaves. Fruits never produced in our region.

HABITAT & DISTRIBUTION

Myriophyllum aquaticum is an **invasive** species of exposed, shallow, ponds and lakes. It is uncommon in New Jersey. Native to South America, this species was introduced through aquarium and water garden trade. It prefers alkaline nutrient-rich waters and can form thick floating mats.

Notes: The emersed leaves and stems are highly hydrophobic and repel water. Submersed leaves are often shed or brown and deteriorating. Only female plants occur in North America.

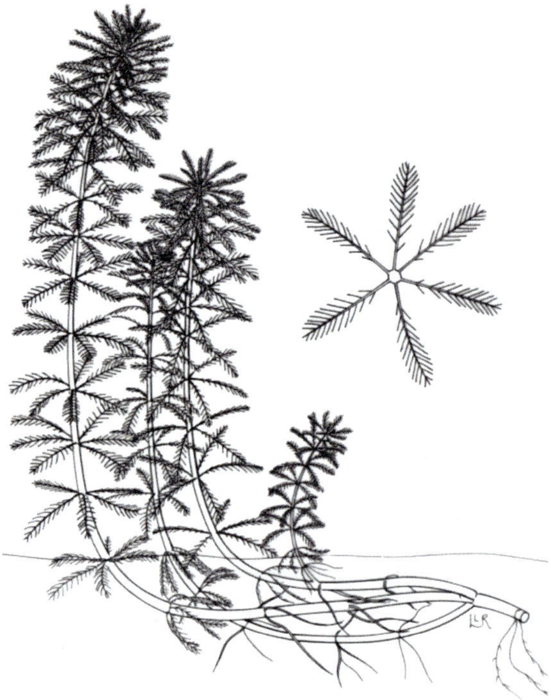

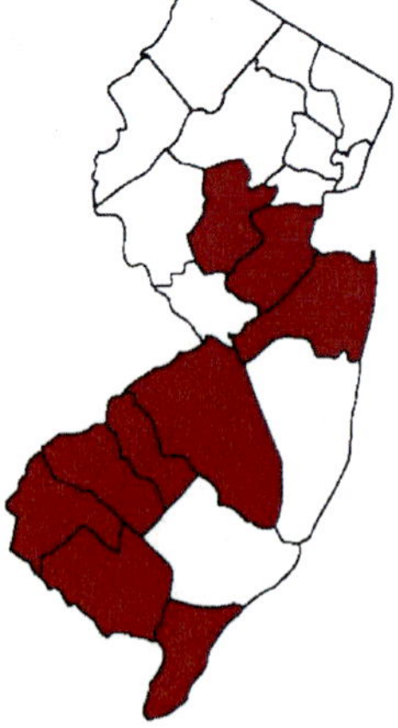

VARIABLE-LEAVED WATER-MILFOIL *Myriophyllum heterophyllum* Michx.

Variable-leaved water-milfoil is a submersed, densely leaved plant with relatively stout, reddish, elongated, much-branched stems, swollen just below the flowering spikes. Submersed leaves (2–4 cm long, 1–3 cm wide) are whorled (4–6 per whorl), closely spaced (whorls <10 mm apart), and pinnately divided into 6–14 pairs of thread-like segments. Flowers are borne in long (15–30 cm tall), leafy, upright, spikes, emersed above water. Floral bracts are whorled, conspicuous, leaf-like, oval (4–18 mm long, much-longer than flowers or fruits), with sharp-toothed edges (bracts near waterline may be somewhat lobed). Male flowers commonly have 4 stamens. Fruits (1–1.5 mm long) are rounded. Turions are produced in fall, at base of stems or rhizomes.

HABITAT & DISTRIBUTION

Myriophyllum heterophyllum is a native species of lakes, ponds, and streams. More common in southeastern U.S., it is **rare** in New Jersey eligible for protection under the jurisdiction of the Highlands Preservation Area.

Notes: Plants have potential to grow rapidly, aggressively spread by stem fragmentation, and develop dense beds which hinder waterbody uses. It is non-native to the north in New England where it is invasive and prohibited.

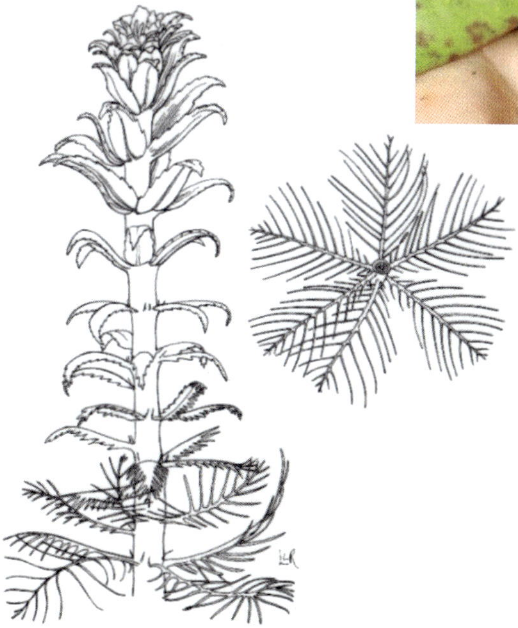

Low water water-milfoil is a delicate, normally submersed, densely leaved plant with elongated, flexuous stems. Leaves are alternate (sometimes some near-opposite), 10–25 mm long, and pinnately divided into 5–12 pairs of narrow segments. Leaves and stems may be brownish red. Flowers and fruits submersed, borne in axils of submersed leaves. Male flowers commonly have 4 stamens (0.5–1 mm long). Fruit (0.7–1.3 mm long) is smooth-sided. No turions produced.

HABITAT & DISTRIBUTION

Myriophyllum humile is a native species in shallow, nutrient poor, mostly acidic, waters of ponds, lakes, and streams. It is most common on the Coastal Plain and Piedmont in New Jersey.

Notes: This northern species is highly variable in form with stem length and leaf number increasing with water depth. When stranded on receding pond shores, a rigid, simple-leaved "terrestrial" growth form can occur. It is our only water-milfoil with submersed flowers and fruits.

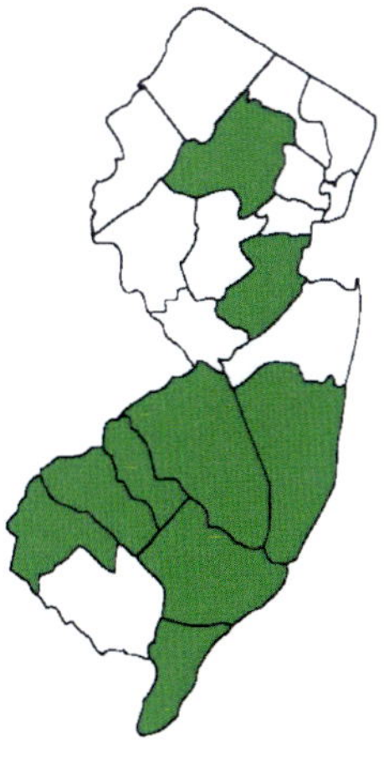

CUT-LEAVED WATER-MILFOIL *Myriophyllum pinnatum* (Walt.) BSP

Cut-leaved water-milfoil is a submersed, densely leaved plant with elongated, slender stems. Leaves (10–30 mm long) are submersed, both alternate and whorled on same stem, and pinnately divided into 8–10 pairs of narrow segments. Flowers are borne on elongated (10–20 cm tall), upright, leafy spikes, emersed above water. Leafy floral bracts are conspicuous (usually more than twice the flower length), alternate, and pinnately divided into flat segments. Male flowers commonly have 4 stamens (0.5–1 mm long). Fruits (1.3–1.8 mm long) have vertical, bumpy ridges on outer surface. Turions never produced.

HABITAT & DISTRIBUTION

Myriophyllum pinnatum is a native, Coastal Plain species occurring in shallow, freshwater or brackish ponds. It is critically imperiled in New Jersey where it is state-listed as ***endangered***.

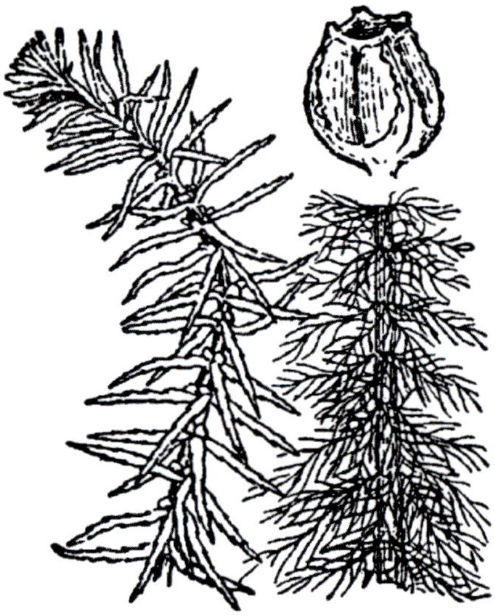

NORTHERN WATER-MILFOIL *Myriophyllum sibiricum* Komarov

Northern water-milfoil is a submersed, densely leaved plant with slender, few-branched, mostly vertical stems. Tips of non-flowering stems are usually green (except during turion formation) and knob-like. Submersed leaves (1.5–3 cm long) are whorled (3–4 per whorl, whorls ≤10 mm apart), and with well-developed middle leaves, pinnately divided into 5–12 pairs of thread-like segments. Many uppermost leaves rounded at tips. Flowers are borne in upright (4–10 cm tall) spikes, emersed above water. Floral bracts are whorled and inconspicuous. Upper bracts are shorter than flowers with toothless to small-toothed edges and lower bracts <2 times as long as the flowers or fruits. Male flowers have 8 stamens. Dark green, cylindrical (≥2 cm long) turions are produced at stem tips in autumn.

HABITAT & DISTRIBUTION

Myriophyllum sibiricum is a native species of primarily clear, alkaline waters. It approaches the southern end of its range in New Jersey, where it is critically imperiled and state-listed as ***endangered***.

Note: Similar to Eurasian water-milfoil (*M. spicatum*) but stems essentially unbranched and vertical, fewer segments per leaf, and formation of turions in late season.

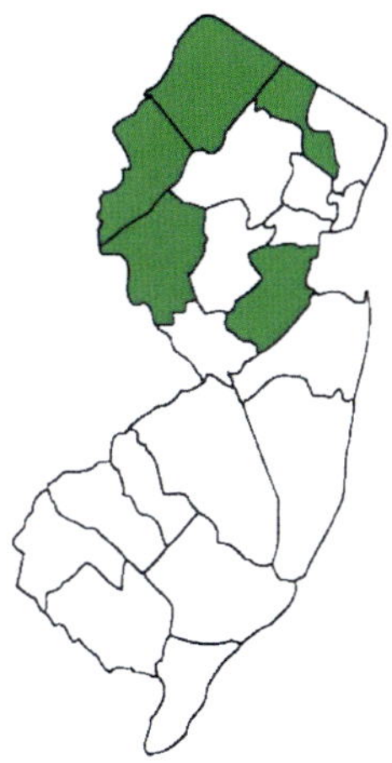

EURASIAN WATER-MILFOIL *Myriophyllum spicatum* L.

Eurasian water-milfoil is a submersed, rhizome-less, densely leaved plant with long (1 m+), slender, much-branched stems, swollen (nearly twice as thick) just below the flowering spikes, and curved to lie parallel to water surface. Tips of non-flowering branches are usually reddish and tassel-like. Submersed leaves (3–3.5 cm long, 1–2.5 cm wide) are whorled (3–4 per whorl), widely spaced (whorls 10–30 mm apart), distinctly stalked, and with well-developed middle leaves, pinnately divided into 13–20 (mostly 14–17) pairs of thread-like segments, and flat (segments all in one plane). Many uppermost leaves flat-topped across at end (as if cut off with scissors). Flowers are borne in upright (6–10 cm tall) spikes, emersed above water. Floral bracts are whorled and inconspicuous. Upper bracts are shorter than flowers with toothless to small-toothed edges and lower bracts <2 times as long as the flowers or fruits. Male flowers have 8 stamens. Turions are never produced.

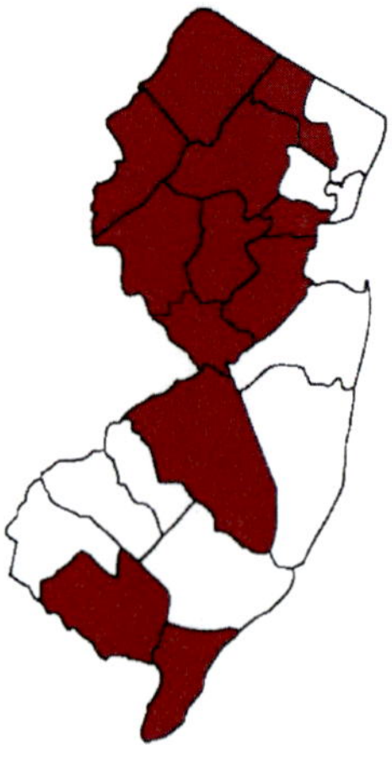

HABITAT & DISTRIBUTION

Myriophyllum spicatum is a non-native species established in lakes and ponds. It is **invasive** in New Jersey. Occurrences are scattered, primarily in more alkaline waters.

Notes: This species, a renown aggressive weed, exhibits broad environmental tolerances (e.g., depth, pH, temperature, salinity, exposure, nutrient load, turbidity), rapid growth, and easy dispersal via stem fragmentation. It is similar to non-flowering Northern water-milfoil (*M. sibiricum*) plants but has more leaf segments, reddish, tassel-like stem tips, and lacks turions.

SLENDER WATER-MILFOIL *Myriophyllum tenellum* Bigel.

Slender water-milfoil is a slender submersed plant with short (2–20 cm tall), stiff, upright, unbranched stems arising singly from buried rhizomes. Leaves are alternate, inconspicuous, stubby, reduced to minute scales (<1 mm long), and few, or absent. Flowers are borne in the upper leaf axils of wiry, emergent stems. Floral bracts are alternate, toothless, and about the length of the flowers. Fruits are about 1 mm long. Turions never produced.

HABITAT & DISTRIBUTION

Myriophyllum tenellum is a native species of shallow, mostly acidic, ponds and lakes. It is rare in New Jersey, where it is critically imperiled and state-listed as ***endangered***.

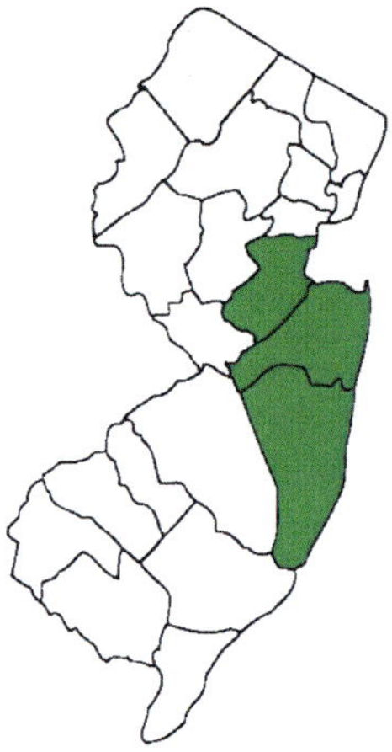

Notes: This inconspicuous northern species is unlike other water-milfoils in New Jersey as plants are essentially leafless. Sterile plants are usually abundant, and populations can be dense, propagating largely by vegetative means. Flowering is infrequent and occurs only in very shallow (e.g., 5 cm deep) water where upright stems may reach 30 cm. It can be easily overlooked.

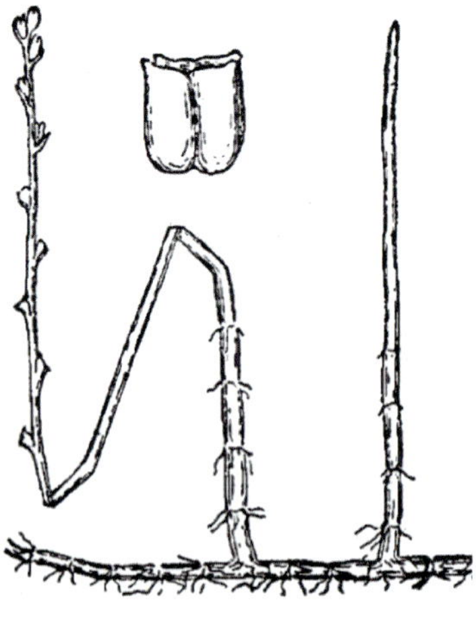

WHORLED WATER-MILFOIL *Myriophyllum verticillatum* L.

Whorled water-milfoil is a submersed, densely leaved plant with elongated, olive green, sparingly-branched stems. Submersed leaves (2–4.5 cm long, 1.5–2.5 cm wide) are whorled (4–5 per whorl) and pinnately divided into 9-17 pairs of thread-like segments. Flowers are borne in long (7–20 cm tall), leafy, upright, spikes, emersed above water. Floral bracts are whorled, conspicuous (to 20 mm long), lower bracts ≥2 times as long as the flowers or fruits, with mostly deeply divided or pinnately lobed edges. Male flowers commonly have 8 stamens. Fruits (2–2.5 mm long) are rounded. Dark, yellow green, distinctively club-shaped (wider at tip than at base) turions (1–3 cm long) are formed on stem tips in fall.

HABITAT & DISTRIBUTION

Myriophyllum verticillatum is a native species of lakes and streams, with an affinity for alkaline waters. More common in northern areas, it reaches its southern limits in New Jersey, where it is state-listed as ***endangered***, considered *historic*.

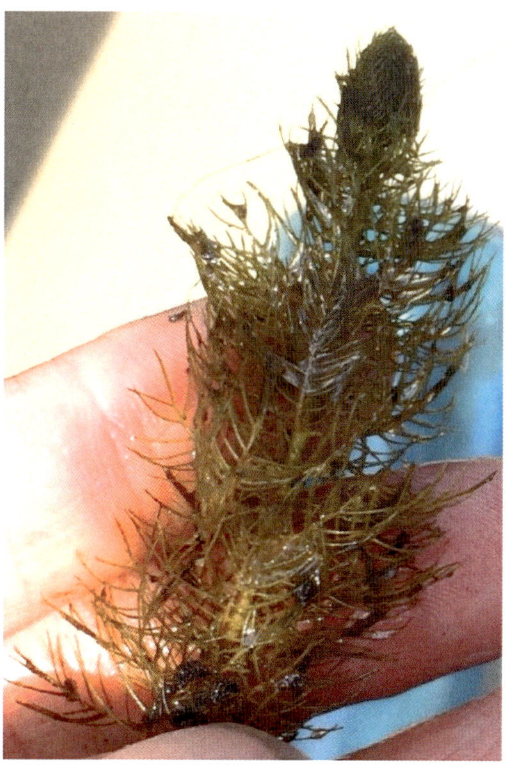

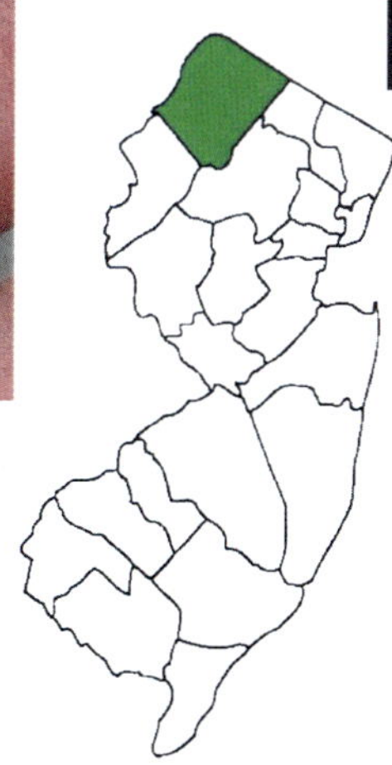

Najas — Hydrocharitaceae
Waternymphs

The Waternymphs, or Naiads, are slender, rooted, much-branched, submersed annuals. Their leaves are opposite (or appearing whorled when extra leaves present), toothed along margins, with linear (<2 mm wide) blades that widen to a stem-sheathing base. Flowers are unisexual (on same plant), submersed, and borne 1–3 per leaf axil. Fruits are small (2–4 mm long), with a thin, membranous covering, one-seeded, and tapered at tip.

Five species occur in New Jersey, one being non-native. Fruits and foliage serve as important waterfowl food.

Key to Species

1. Leaf margins with 20–100 minute teeth per side (visible with hand lens); top of basal leaf sheath tapered or sloping.......... 2

1. Leaf margins with 7–17 teeth per side; top of basal leaf sheath distinctly lobed or abruptly widened.......... 4

   2. Leaves tapered from about the middle, to long, slender, pointed tips; seeds smooth and glossy, widest above the middle, deep brown to yellow.......... 3

   2. Leaves abruptly pointed, tapered only from last 2–3 mm, or rounded at tip; seeds minutely pitted and dull, widest at middle, yellowish white with purple tinge, greenish, or reddish brown.......... *N. guadalupensis*

3. Seeds broad (seed length:width ratios <3).......... *N. flexilis*

3. Seeds thin and elongate (seed length:width ratios 3–4).......... *N. canadensis*

   4. Leaves generally stiff and recurved in age, with 7–15 course teeth per side (visible without magnification), top of leaf sheath lobed and finely toothed; seeds slightly curved.......... *N. minor*

   4. Leaves spreading and lax in age, with 13–17 fine teeth per side (visible with magnification), top of leaf sheath abruptly widened, but not lobed, and coarsely jagged; seeds straight.......... *N. gracillima*

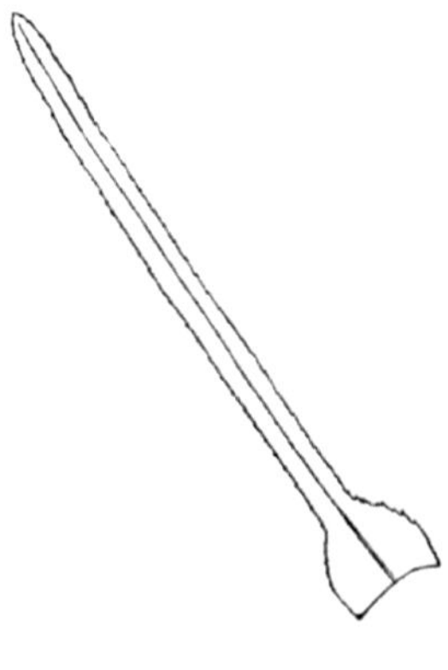

N. flexilis

N. minor

CANADIAN WATERNYMPH *Najas candensis* Michx.

Canadian waternymph is completely submersed and possesses the same vegetative morphology as its sister species *N. flexilis* (see below). Seeds smooth and shining, length to width ratios 3–4.

HABITAT & DISTRIBUTION

Najas canadensis is a native species of lakes and rivers. Its range overlaps that of its sister species Northern waternymph (*N. flexilis*), where it can occupy the same bodies of water.

Note: Work by Les et al. (2015) confirmed this cryptic tetraploid species, which is remarkably similar to, yet genetically distinct from, *N. flexilis*. It can be separated by its subtly different "thinner" elongate seeds (i.e., seed length to width ratios >3). This plant used to be called *N. muenscheri* R.T Clausen.

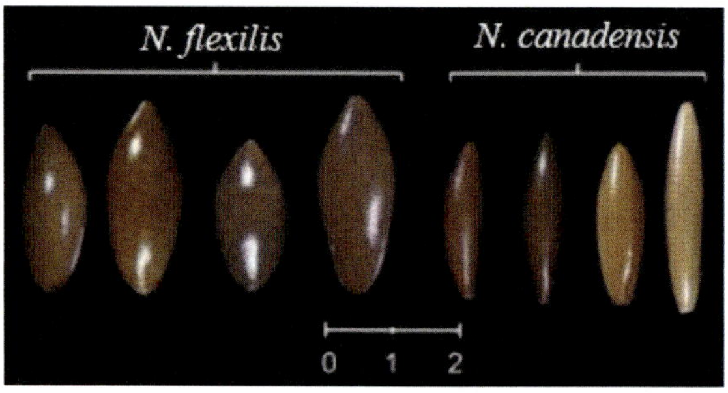

Modified from Les et al. 2015. Mol. Phylogen. Evol. 82: 15–30.

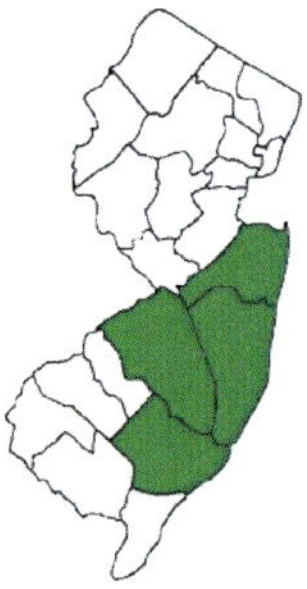

NORTHERN WATERNYMPH *Najas flexilis* (Willd.) Rostk. & Schnidt

Northern waternymph is completely submersed, 25–50 cm tall, with much-branched stems. Leaves are 1.5–4 cm long, 0.5–1 mm wide (above widened base), tapered to a slender tip, with 35–80 fine teeth per side (visible with hand lens). Top of basal leaf sheath is gradually tapered. Usually 1 fruit per leaf axil. Seeds smooth and shining, deep brown to yellow, and widest above the middle, length to width ratios <3.

HABITAT & DISTRIBUTION

Najas flexilis is a native species of lakes, ponds, and streams. It is common and widespread throughout New Jersey.

Notes: Les et al. (2015) revealed this species is nearly indistinguishable from the cryptic *N. canadensis*. In general, both species have smooth shiny seeds, but the diploid *N. flexilis* has longer and broader seeds (i.e., "thicker" seeds = seed length to width ratios <3) compared to the thinner seeds of *N. canadensis* (tetraploid). Without seeds, it is difficult to distinguish from Southern waternymph too.

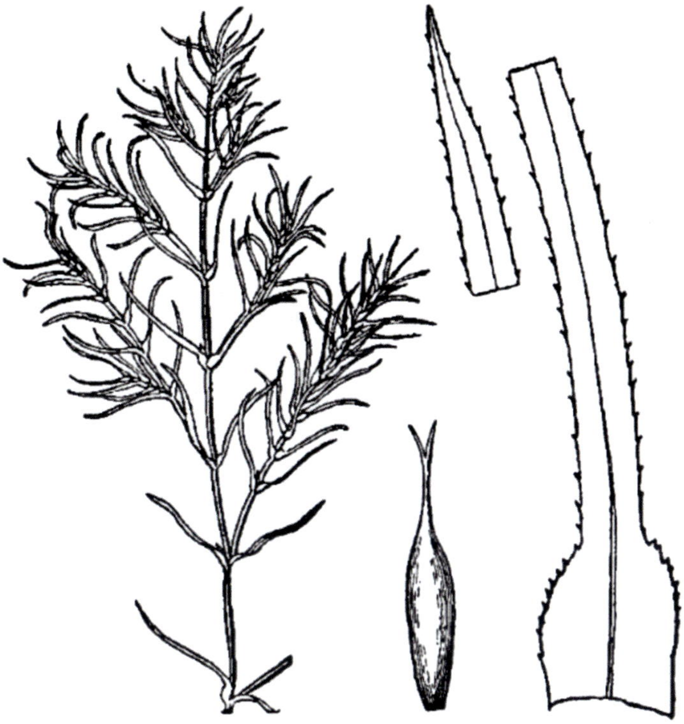

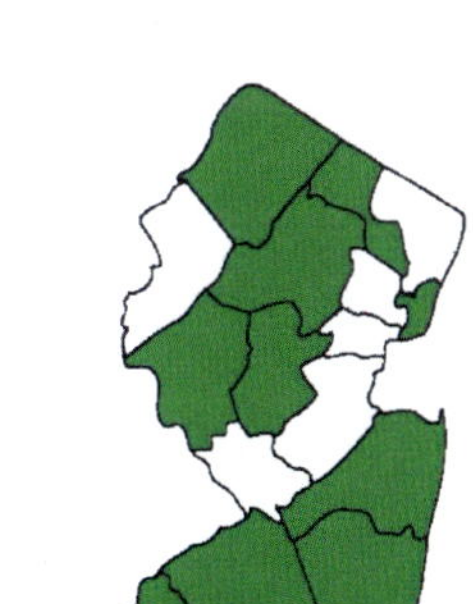

SLENDER WATERNYMPH *Najas gracillima* (A. Braun) Magnus

Slender waternymph is completely submersed, 4–48 cm tall, with slightly branched, slender (to 0.7 mm wide) stems. Leaves are 0.6–2.8 cm long, 0.1–0.5 mm wide (above widened base), pointed at tip, with 13–17 fine teeth per side (visible only with magnification). Top of basal leaf sheath is abruptly widened, but not lobed, and coarsely jagged. Fruits with style positioned off to one side of apex. Seeds straight, dull, light brown.

HABITAT & DISTRIBUTION

Najas gracillima is a native species of lakes and streams, most abundant in acidic waters. It is imperiled and **rare** in New Jersey, eligible for protection under the jurisdiction of the Highlands Preservation Area. Most similar vegetatively to Northern waternymph (*N. flexilis*) however its leaves have fewer teeth and lack a tapered leaf sheath.

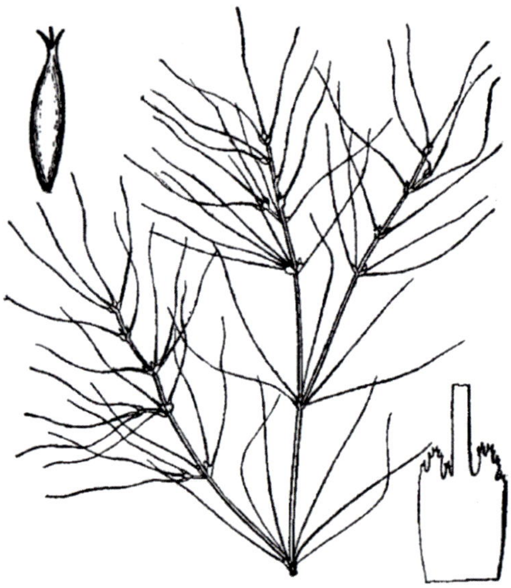

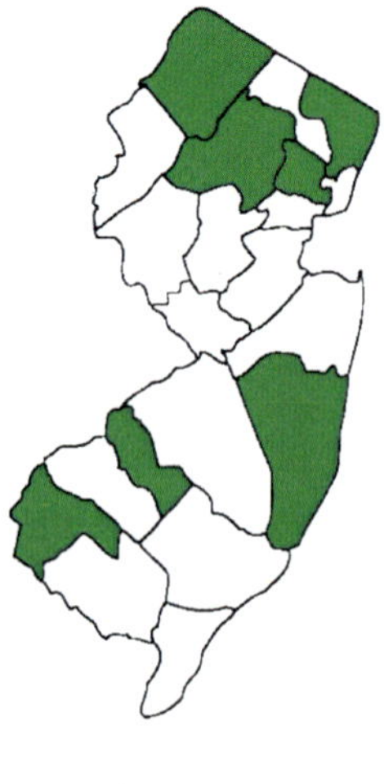

SOUTHERN WATERNYMPH *Najas guadalupensis* (Spreng.) Magnus

Southern waternymph, or Guppy grass, is completely submersed, 10–90 cm tall, with much-branched stems. Leaves are 0.5–3 cm long, 0.2–2.1 mm wide (above widened base), abruptly pointed or rounded at tip, with 20–100 fine teeth per side (visible only with magnification). Top of basal leaf sheath is gradually tapered. Seeds minutely pitted and dull, yellowish white with purple tinge, greenish, or reddish brown, and widest at middle.

HABITAT & DISTRIBUTION

Najas guadalupensis is a native species of alkaline, fresh, or brackish lakes, reservoirs, ponds, and rivers. It is imperiled and **rare** in New Jersey, eligible for protection under the jurisdiction of the Highlands Preservation Area.

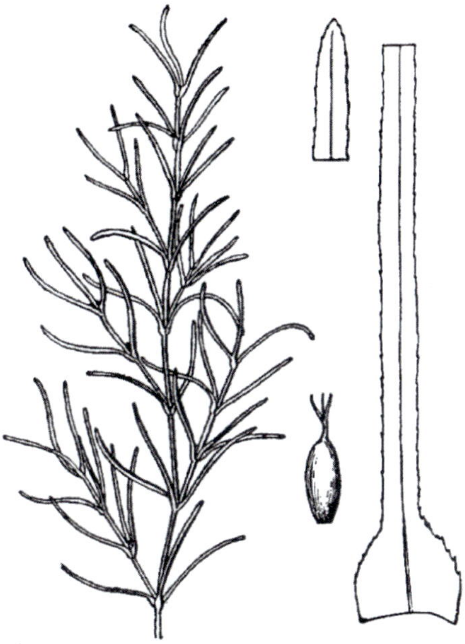

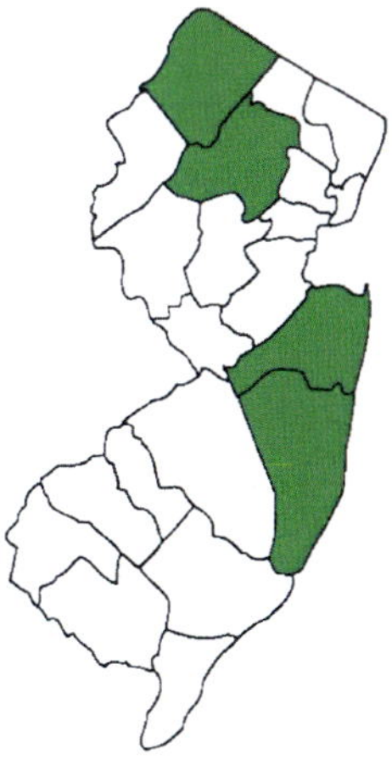

BRITTLE WATERNYMPH — *Najas minor* All.

Brittle waternymph, or Brittle naiad, is completely submersed, 11–120 cm tall, compact, with heavily branched stems. Leaves are stiff and recurved in age, 0.5–3.4 cm long, 0.1–1.2 mm wide (above widened base), pointed at tip, with 7–15 course teeth per side (visible without magnification). Top of basal leaf sheath is lobed and finely toothed. Seeds are slightly curved, dull, and purplish brown.

HABITAT & DISTRIBUTION

Najas minor is a non-native species naturalized in lakes and rivers. It is **invasive** in New Jersey. Native to Eurasia, the species can be a problematic weed. Plants are easily spread by stem fragmentation and highly tolerant of turbidity and nutrient-rich waters.

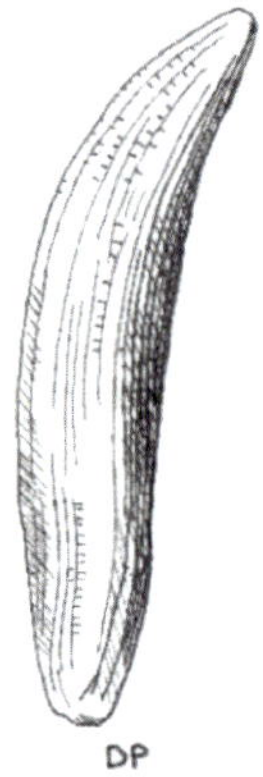

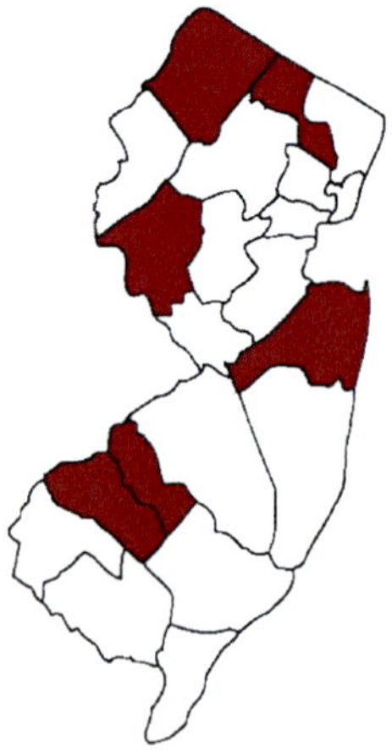

Nasturtium — Brassicaceae
Water Cress

WATER CRESS *Nasturtium officinale* Ait. f.

Water cress is a mat-forming perennial, submersed, floating, or emersed, with unbranched, prostrate stems rooting at nodes. Leaves are alternate and pinnately compound (2–15 cm long) with 3–9 round to oblong blades (leaflets) or may be simple (i.e, one blade) if plants deeply submersed. The terminal leaflet is usually larger than those on sides. Flowers are bisexual, each with four, white or pink petals (3–6 mm long) and borne on elongated clusters above water. Fruits are linear pods (2–3 mm long, 1–2 mm wide), compressed in cross section, with seeds in two rows.

HABITAT & DISTRIBUTION

Nasturtium officinale is a non-native species of cold springs, ditches, slow streams, lake margins and marshes. It is widespread in New Jersey.

Note: This Eurasian species became naturalized throughout North America long ago. Plants are rapidly growing and often floating on water surface or sprawling on mud.

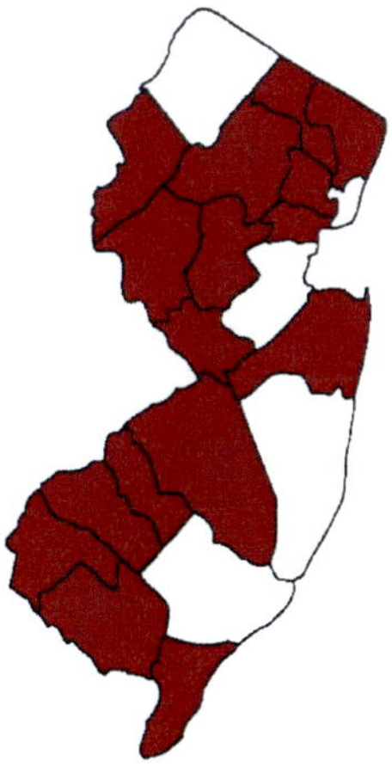

Nelumbo — Nelumbonaceae
Lotus

The Lotuses are robust, rooted, perennials with spongy, buried rhizomes. Their circular, bluish green leaves, either floating or emersed, are usually massive, with stout, centrally attached stalks. The satiny leaf blade surfaces possess an extreme ability to repel water. Flowers are likewise massive (>10 cm wide), showy, held above leaves, and capable of generating (and regulating) heat to attract pollinators. Hard, 1-seeded fruits are embedded in leathery, flat-topped structures.

Two species occur in the region, one non-native. The species are exceedingly like each other, yet very distinguishable from all other aquatic plants. Both are cultivated as ornamental water garden plants with numerous cultivars produced between and within species. Interestingly, *Nelumbo* seeds can remain viable for extraordinary periods of time (>150 years).

KEY TO SPECIES

1. Flowers pale yellow, outermost 1–5 petals usually persistent after others are shed...*N. lutea*
1. Flowers pink, all petals easily detached and shed at an early stage... .... *N. nucifera*

AMERICAN LOTUS *Nelumbo lutea* Willd.

American lotus, or Water lotus, is a rooted, perennial with long, slender, horizontal rhizomes and massive, round leaves and flowers. Leaves are circular, without a sinus, large (to 60 cm), floating (flat) or emergent (concave), blue green, with centrally radiating veins, and long (to 2 m), centrally attached stalks. Flowers are very large (10–20 cm wide), bisexual, pale yellow, borne singly, above water, on long stalks (to 2 m). Flowers have a central, green, cone-shaped, flat-topped, receptacle. Fruits are nut-like, roundish (10–16 mm long), and embedded in a leathery receptacle (abruptly tapered at base).

HABITAT & DISTRIBUTION

Nelumbo lutea is a native species occurring in still, usually shallow (<1 m), waters of lakes, ponds, or tidal marshes, in full sun. It is critically imperiled in New Jersey, where it is state-listed as ***endangered***.

Notes: This distinctive plant is cultivated as an ornamental plant in water gardens. It is fast-growing and can become aggressive. It possesses water-repellant (hydrophobic) leaves and its flowers generate heat to attract pollinators.

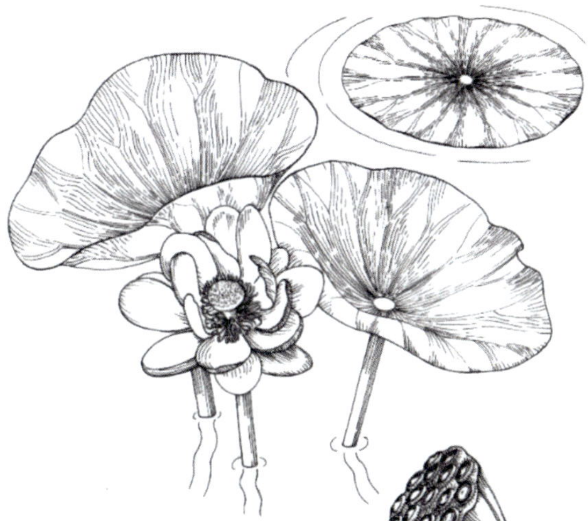

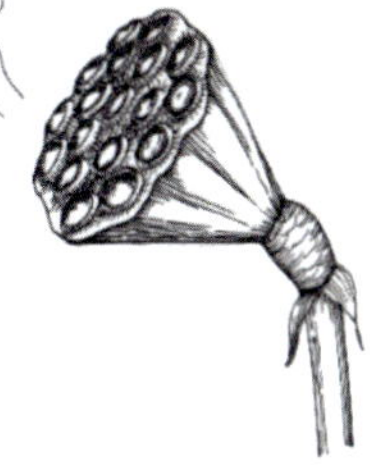

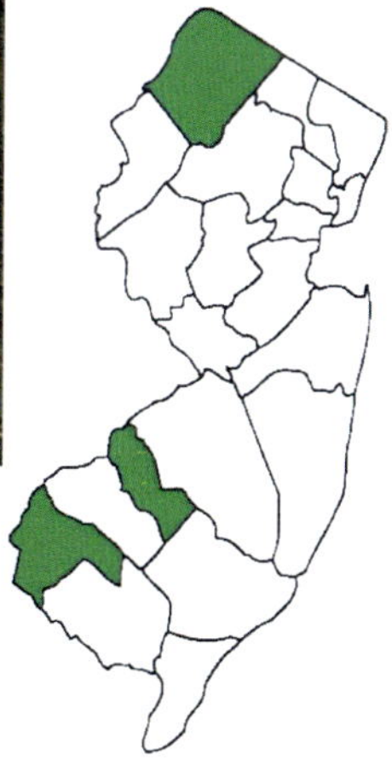

SACRED LOTUS *Nelumbo nucifera* Gaertn.

Sacred lotus, or Indian lotus, is a rooted, perennial with long, slender, horizontal rhizomes. Leaves are circular, without a sinus, large (to 60+ cm wide), floating (flat) or emergent (concave), blue green, with centrally radiating veins, and long (to 2 m), centrally attached stalks. Flowers are very large (10–20 cm wide), bisexual, pink to pinkish-white, fragrant, borne singly, above water, on long stalks (to 2 m). Flowers have a central, green, cone-shaped, flat-topped, receptacle. Fruits are nut-like, oval (10–20 mm long) and embedded in a leathery receptacle (gradually tapering to rounded at its base).

HABITAT & DISTRIBUTION

Nelumbo nucifera is native to eastern Asia and sporadically **introduced** as a water garden escape. It occurs in still, mostly acidic, waters of lakes or ponds, with full sun exposure. It is uncommon in New Jersey.

Note: For thousands of years, this plant has been grown as an ornamental specimen and utilized in traditional Asian medicine.

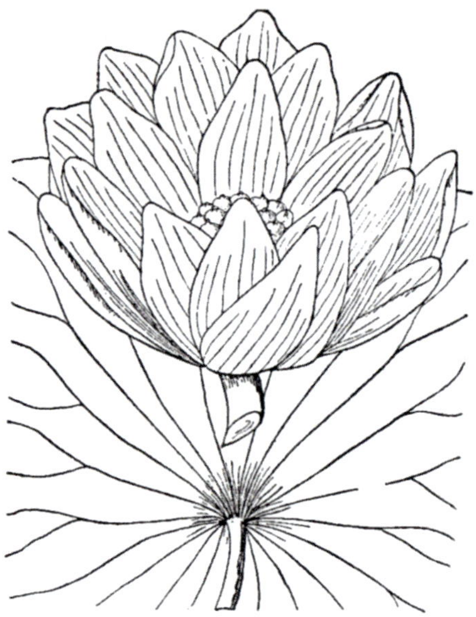

Nuphar — Nymphaeaceae
Pond lily

The Pond lilies, or Spatterdocks, are rooted, perennials with broad, leathery, exposed leaves (mostly floating, sometimes emersed) and submersed, membranous leaves. Foliage is generally heart-shaped, with rounded basal lobes, and a defined mid-vein/pinnate venation. Flowers are showy, spherical, and bright yellow, emersed singly atop a stout, rigid stalk. Flowers are bisexual with 5–6 petal-like sepals, inconspicuous scale-like petals, and numerous strap-like stamens surrounding a central, flattened stigmatic disk. Fruits are green to purplish, leathery, and berry-like.

Three species, all native, occur in New Jersey. The name *Nuphar lutea* (L.) Sm., belonging to a strictly Eurasian species, is often misapplied to Pond lilies of North America.

KEY TO SPECIES

1. Exposed leaf blades large (13–36 cm long), leaf stalks 4–12 mm wide; flowers large (2–4.5 cm wide) with 6 sepals and a yellow disk; rhizomes stout (2.5–7 cm diam.)........................2
1. Exposed leaf blades small (4–13 cm long); flowers small (1–2 cm wide) with 5 sepals and a dark red, deeply-lobed disk; rhizomes slender (0.5–2.5 cm diam.) ....*N. microphylla*
   2. Exposed leaves floating, leaf stalks flattened and laterally winged; inside surface of sepals purplish..*N. variegata*
   2. Exposed leaves emersed, sometimes floating, leaf stalks round in cross-section; inside surface of sepals usually green.. *N. advena*

N. variegata

N. microphylla
N. variegata

IMMIGRANT POND LILY *Nuphar advena* (Ait.) Ait. f.

Immigrant pond lily is a robust plant with stout rhizomes. Exposed leaves are usually emersed (sometimes floating), large (12–40 cm long) and broad (10–31 cm wide), green, with stout (4–11 mm wide) rounded stalks. Flowers (2–4.5 cm wide) have 6 sepals (inside surface green), long anthers (3–9 mm) and a yellow disk. Fruits are barrel-shaped (1.6–5 cm wide), green, and strongly vertically ribbed.

HABITAT & DISTRIBUTION

Nuphar advena is native to marshes, ponds, lakes, and tidal streams and rivers. It is widespread in New Jersey. Common along the lower Delaware River.

Notes: This species is very common in southeastern US. It reaches its northern limits in New England.

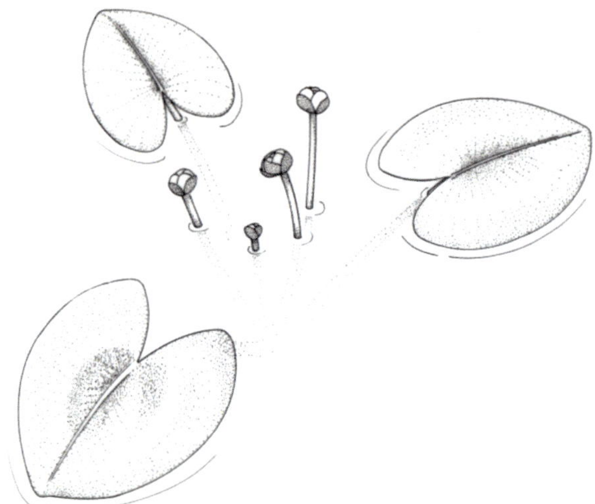

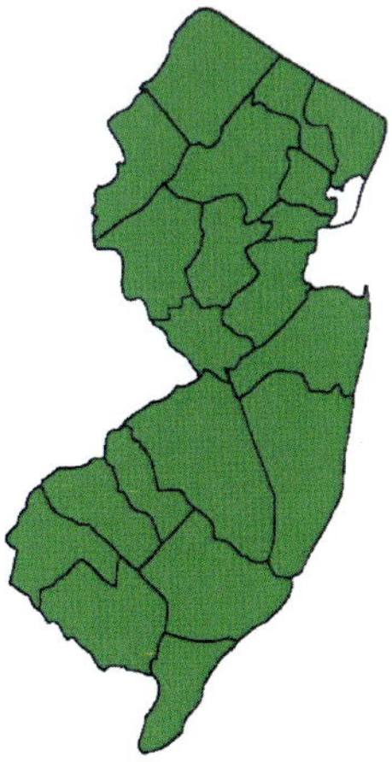

SMALL-LEAVED POND LILY *Nuphar microphylla* (Pers.) Fern.

Small-leaved pond lily, or Tiny cow lily, has floating leaves arising from slender, submersed rhizomes. Floating leaves (4–13 cm long, 3–8 cm wide), green to purple, typically have a deep sinus (up to half the blade length) with weak, compressed stalks (1–2.5 mm wide). Flowers (1–2 cm wide) have 5 sepals, short anthers (1–3 mm) and a dark red, deeply-lobed disk. Fruits are urn-shaped (1–2 cm wide), with an obvious neck and smooth wall.

HABITAT & DISTRIBUTION

Nuphar microphylla is a native species in lakes and ponds. At the southern end of its range, it is rare in New Jersey and state-listed as ***endangered***, considered *historic*.

Notes: This diminutive, quite distinctive, pond lily is imperiled throughout much of its range. In areas where it overlaps with *N. variegata*, the species naturally hybridize to yield plants—with largely intermediate features and limited fertility—recognized as *N.* ×*rubrodisca* Morong.

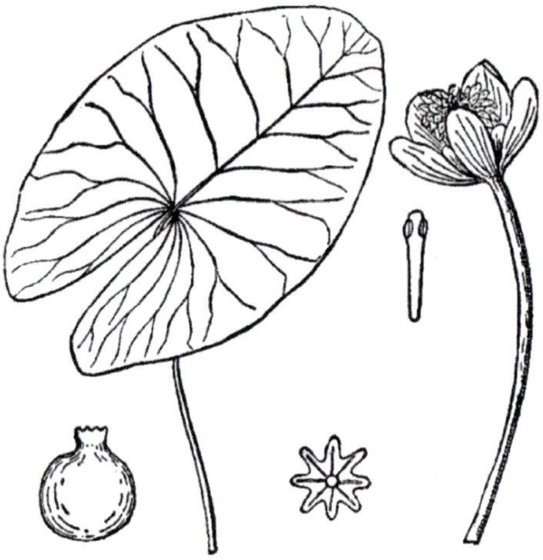

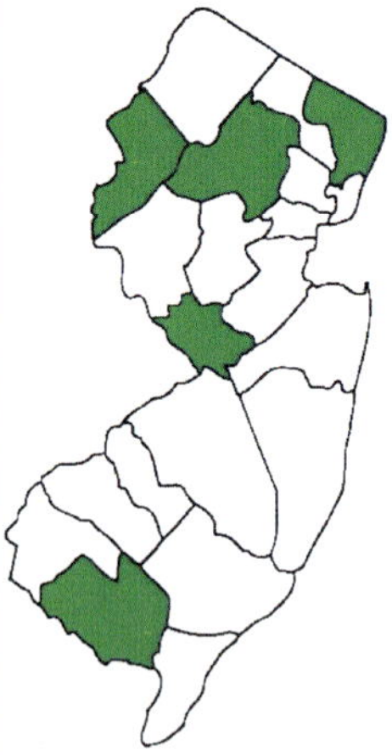

YELLOW POND LILY *Nuphar variegata* Dur.

Yellow pond lily, or Spatterdock, is a is a robust plant with stout rhizomes. Floating leaves are large (13–36 cm long) and broad (10–24 cm wide), green to purplish, with broad (4–10 mm wide), flattened, stalks that usually winged along their length. Flowers (2.5–4.5 cm wide) have 6 sepals (inside surface purple-tinged), long anthers (3–11 mm) and a yellow disk. Fruits are barrel-shaped (1.5–4 cm wide), green to purple, and strongly vertically ribbed.

HABITAT & DISTRIBUTION

Nuphar variegata is native to lakes, ponds, bogs, deep marshes, ditches, and slow-moving rivers. It is widespread in New Jersey, most common in the Pine Barrens.

Notes: This more northern species is ecologically tolerant and can colonize deeper (to 2 m) waters. Its long, stout, branched rhizomes can be uprooted by storms and beavers and subsequently float. It is known to naturally hybridize with *N. microphylla* to yield plants—with largely intermediate features and limited fertility—recognized as *N.* ×*rubrodisca* Morong.

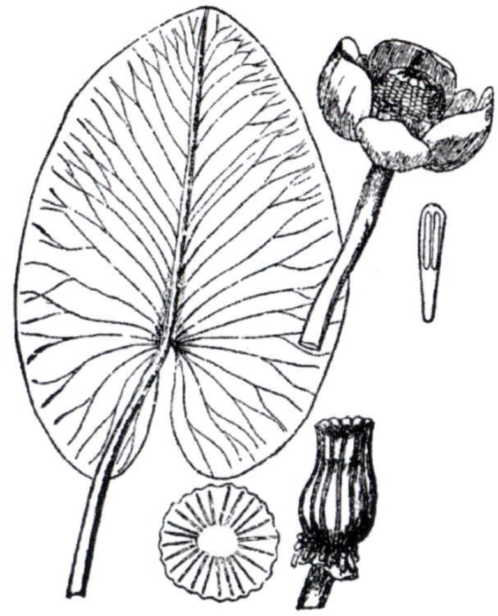

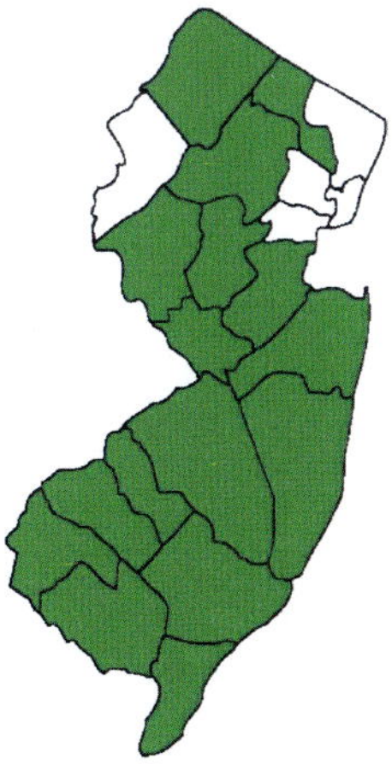

Nymphaea — Nymphaeaceae
Water lily

FRAGRANT WATER LILY *Nymphaea odorata* Ait.

Fragrant water lily is a rooted, perennial, with thick, elongated, horizontal rhizomes. Plants have broad, leathery, floating leaves with long, flexible, green or purple, leaf stalks. Leaves are generally circular in shape (8–40 cm wide), green above and usually purple below, with centrally radiating veins, and a closed sinus with pointed lobes. Flowers are large (5–19 cm wide), showy, fragrant, with yellow centers and numerous (17+), white to pale pink, petals. Flowers are bisexual and emersed just at the water surface (as if floating), borne singly atop stout stalks. Fruits are globose (4 cm), leathery, and berry-like, maturing underwater on coiled stalks.

HABITAT & DISTRIBUTION

Nymphaea odorata is a conspicuous, native species of still or slow waters of lakes, bogs, marshes, swamps, and rivers. It is widespread and common in New Jersey. It has broad tolerances of water depth (0.5–3 m), nutrients, and pH levels. Flowers are insect-pollinated and exhibit diurnal blooming (opening in early morning and closing late afternoon) over a 3-day period.

Notes: Two subspecies are represented in New Jersey. Unlike typical plants, the **rare** ssp. *tuberosa* (Paine) Wiersema & Hellquist is more robust with rhizomes forming numerous, detachable tubers. Its leaves have green leaf stalks with purplish stripes and blades mostly green underneath. This variant is critically imperiled in the state.

subsp. *odorata*

subsp. *tuberosa*

subsp. *tuberosa*

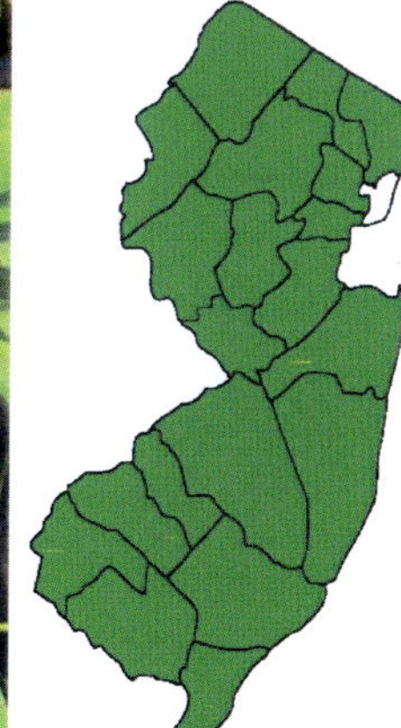

Nymphoides — Menyanthaceae
Floating-heart

The Floating-hearts are rooted, perennials of quiet waters with shiny, heart-shaped floating leaves which superficially resemble those of juvenile waterlilies (*Nuphar* or *Nymphaea*). Plants have slender, anchored rhizomes and long (to 2 m), buoyant, flexuous stems that bear leaves and flower clusters at their summit. Flowers are showy, with 5 united petals, emersed or floating, and borne in clusters from the base of the leafstalk—appearing as if borne on a long leaf stalk. Fruits are elliptical, green capsules.

Three species occur in New Jersey, including one non-native. All species are highly ornamental and cultivated for the water garden trade.

Key to Species

1. Flowers yellow, 20–25 mm wide; flowering stems with a pair of leaves (each 5–15 cm long) at base of flower cluster; usually lacking spur-like roots at base of leaves………… *N. peltata*
1. Flowers white, 5–14 mm wide; flowering stems with a single leaf at base of flower cluster; clusters of submersed spur-like roots present at the leaf base, near water surface…………2
   2. Floating leaves 3–5 cm long; stems 1 mm wide; sepal lobes green; fruits 4–5 mm long…………… *N. cordata*
   2. Floating leaves 4–15 cm long; stems to 2.5 mm wide; sepal lobes flecked with purple; fruits 10–14 mm long…………… *N. aquatica*

Big floating-heart is a submersed plant with floating leaves produced singly from the base of a flower cluster. The floating blades are heart-shaped (4–15 cm long), with rounded lobes. Submersed clusters of fleshy roots are sometimes produced at the leaf base, near water surface. Flowers (5–14 mm wide) are white with yellow centers, bloom above water, with conspicuously purple-flecked sepal lobes. Fruits are small (10–14 mm long) capsules.

HABITAT & DISTRIBUTION

Nymphoides aquatica is a native Coastal Plain species of lakes, ponds, and slow streams. It reaches its northern limit in southern New Jersey.

Notes: Very similar to Little floating-heart but with larger, courser leaves, thicker stems (1.5–2.5 mm thick), larger fruits, and purple-flecked flower stalks and sepals.

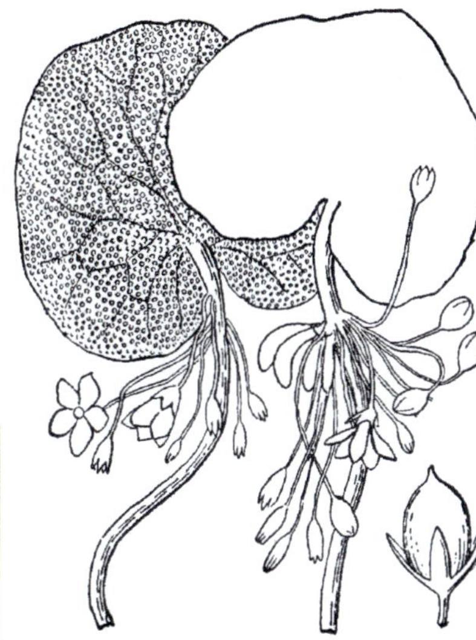

LITTLE FLOATING-HEART *Nymphoides cordata* (Ell.) Fern.

Little floating-heart is a submersed plant with narrow stems (1 mm thick) and floating leaves produced singly from the base of a flower cluster. The floating blades are heart-shaped (3–5 cm long), with rounded lobes, and usually mottled with purple. Submersed clusters of slender (2–4 mm thick), fleshy roots are produced at the leaf base, near water surface. Flowers (5–10 mm wide) are white with yellow centers, bloom above water, with green sepal lobes. Fruits are small (4–5 mm long) capsules.

HABITAT & DISTRIBUTION

Nymphoides cordata is a native species in lakes, ponds, and slow streams. It is **rare** in New Jersey, eligible for protection under the jurisdiction of the Highlands Preservation Area & Pinelands Commission.

Notes: Plants prefer shallow waters (<1 m) and are tolerant of either nutrient-poor or -rich systems. The clusters of tuber-like roots with attached floating leaves can detach as plantlets for dispersal purposes.

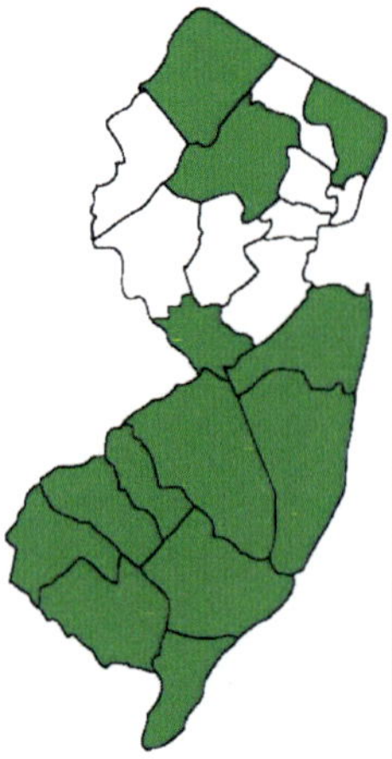

YELLOW FLOATING-HEART *Nymphoides peltata* (Gmel.) Ktze.

Yellow floating-heart is a submersed plant with floating leaves produced in pairs from the base of a flower cluster. The floating blades are heart-shaped (5–15 cm long), with rounded lobes, and wavy margins. Flowers (20–25 mm wide) are wholly bright yellow, and bloom above water. Fruits (12–25 mm long) are beaked, flattened, capsules containing seeds edged with stiff hairs.

HABITAT & DISTRIBUTION

Nymphoides peltata is a non-native species of lakes, ponds, and slow rivers. This Eurasian native—introduced for ornamental purposes—is **invasive** in southern New Jersey.

Notes: Plants are generally stout and highly productive, most common in nutrient-rich waters, and tolerant of waters to 4 m deep.

Orontium — Araceae
Golden Club

GOLDEN CLUB *Orontium aquaticum* L.

Golden Club is a highly distinctive perennial hydrophyte. Plants have a thick, rooted rhizome, and erect or floating leaves. Leaves are blue green, borne in a compact, basal cluster, with stout, long (10–40 cm), fleshy stalks and somewhat fleshy, oblong to elliptical, pointed, parallel-veined blades (10–30 cm). Flowers are minute, bright yellow, and borne in dense clusters at the end of long (2–10 cm long), thick (5–10 mm wide), white stalks, extending above water surface. Fruits are berry-like, slimy, spherical (6–10 mm), dark green, and 1-seeded.

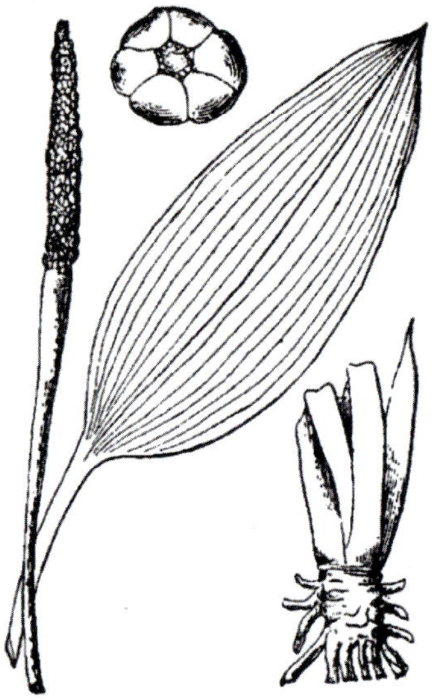

HABITAT & DISTRIBUTION

Orontium aquaticum is a native species of shallow waters (to 1 m) of ponds, swamps, freshwater tidal marshes, and shores of streams. Most common in southern New Jersey.

Notes: Its velvety & waxy leaf surfaces are resistant to wetting (hydrophobic). It is spring-flowering and produces buoyant fruits from which seeds can germinate while floating. It is cultivated as a water garden ornamental.

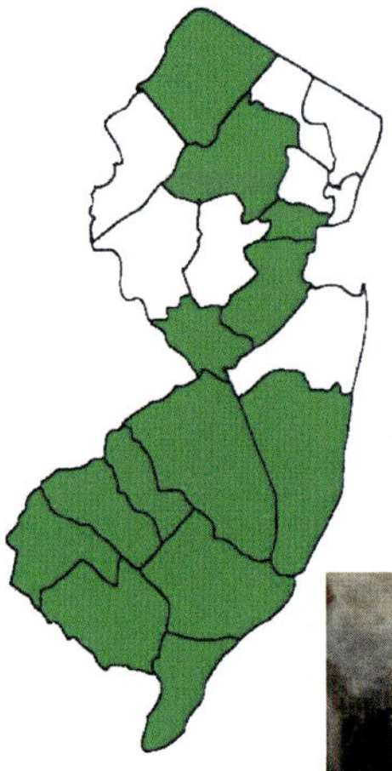

Persicaria — Polygonaceae
Smartweed

WATER SMARTWEED — *Persicaria amphibia* (L.) Gray

Water smartweed is a rooted, floating-leaved perennial with rhizomes that grow prostrate, and sprawling, branched stems. Leaves are alternate, floating, hairy to hairless, short-stalked, with elliptical blades (2–15 cm long, to 17–29 mm wide) and pointed or rounded tips. There is a cylindrical stipule (an ocrea) sheathing the stem at each node, sometimes flared at apex. Flowers are small (4–6 mm long), pink, 5-lobed, bisexual, and borne in an erect, dense, many-flowered spike-like cluster (10–30 mm long) that terminates the stem above water. Fruits are small (2–3 mm), flattened, dark brown, shiny, achenes.

HABITAT & DISTRIBUTION

Persicaria amphibia is a native species of shallow, still or slow-moving waters in marshes, lakes, and rivers. It is scattered in northern New Jersey.

Notes: It is sometimes referenced as *Polygonum amphibium* L. A very variable species, typically growing underwater or floating, but even emersed if water levels drop. It is similar to the more widespread emergent wetland species, Scarlet smartweed [*P. coccinea* (Muhl. ex Willd.) Greene], which can sometimes grow floating leaves if it becomes inundated. It has much wider leaves (32–63 mm) and longer (30–90 mm) flower clusters.

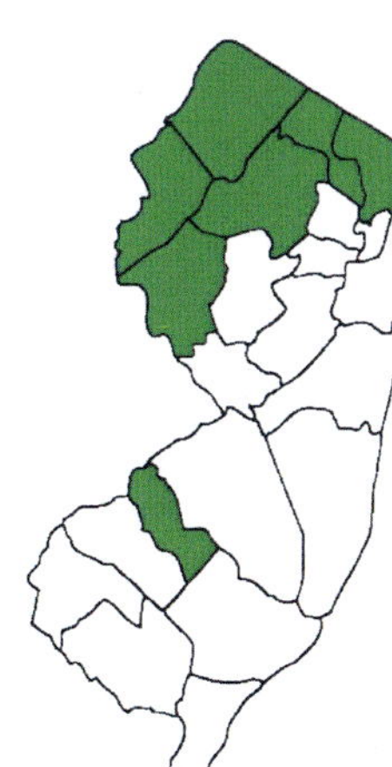

Pistia — Araceae
Water Lettuce

WATER LETTUCE *Pistia stratiotes* L.

Water lettuce, or Tropical duckweed, is a free-floating perennial with tufted leaves, long (to 50 cm) feathery roots hanging in water column, and short horizontal stems connecting plants. Leaves (2–15 cm long) are in a dense basal rosette, floating to emersed, light green, velvety hairy, parallel-veined, and spongy. Flowers, if present, enclosed in an erect, hairy, greenish, cluster at center of plant.

HABITAT & DISTRIBUTION

Pistia stratiotes is considered native to warmer regions of southern U.S. but introduced into the northeast in still or slow-moving waters of lakes and rivers. It has been sporadically introduced in New Jersey presumably as a water garden escape.

Notes: This plant can be aggressive and potentially problematic, but it is not known to over-winter in New Jersey.

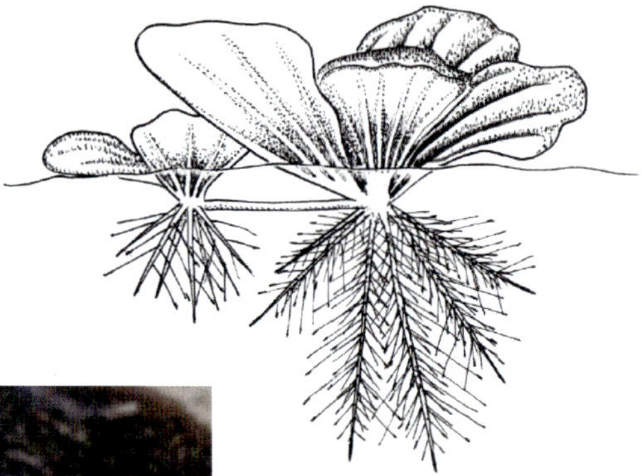

Podostemum — Podostemaceae
Riverweed

HORN-LEAVED RIVERWEED *Podostemum ceratophyllum* Michx.

Horn-leaved riverweed, or Threadfoot, is an olive-green, algal-like, submersed, perennial with flattened, leathery stems, and creeping, green roots adhering to hard substrates via fleshy disks. Leaves are alternate, long (2–142 mm), and repeatedly forked into linear or hair-like (0.05–0.8 mm wide) segments. Flowers are inconspicuous, water-pollinated, bisexual, and borne singly along stems. Fruits are small (1.5–3 mm long), 2-valved capsules.

HABITAT & DISTRIBUTION

Podostemum ceratophyllum is a native species of rocky, fast-flowing rivers and streams of good water quality. Usually growing in areas of rapids, attached to ledge, rocks, or boulders. It is **rare** and imperiled in New Jersey, but possibly overlooked.

Note: This is a highly unusual flowering plant—often mistaken for mosses or algae—occupying a highly specialized habitat. Plants become reproductive as water levels drop exposing them to air.

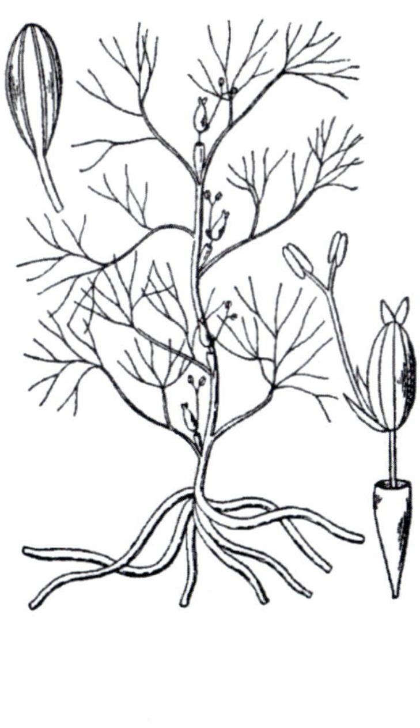

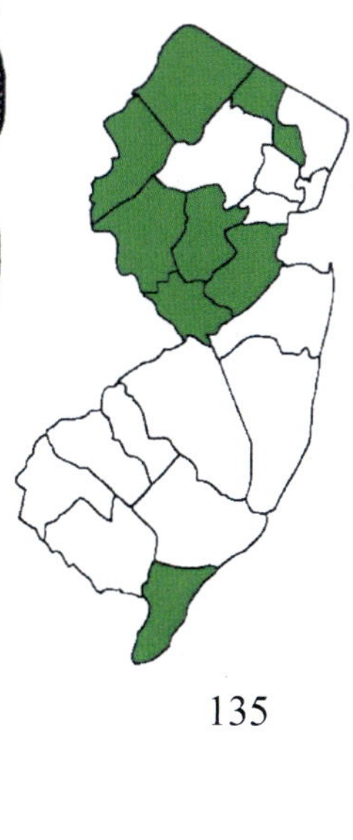

Pontederia — Pontederiaceae
Pickerelweed

PICKERELWEED *Pontederia cordata* L.

Pickerelweed is a submersed (or more commonly emersed) perennial with rhizomes rooted in mud. Leaves are submersed in a basal rosette when young. Blades are without stalks, linear, thin, ribbon-like (6–25 cm long, 4–6 mm wide), and with an observable midvein. Plants can sometimes have narrow emersed leaves.

HABITAT & DISTRIBUTION

Pontederia cordata is a native species of lake shores, ditches, and brackish tidal marshes. It is common throughout New Jersey. Plants are very variable in shape of leaves.

Notes: The young, submersed life-form of the species (f. *taenia* Fassett) is described here. Typically, the species exists as the larger, emergent, life-form. The emergent form, very common on muddy shores, is more robust overall and has stout, long-stalked (to 60 cm), glossy, heart-shaped leaf blades (to 12 cm wide) and dense spikes of showy, blue-purple flowers borne on upright stems. The submersed life-form is similar to Bur-reed (*Sparganium*) and Arrowhead (*Sagittaria*).

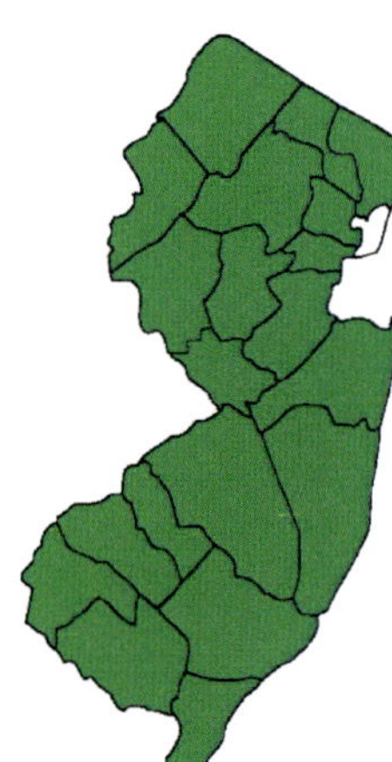

Potamogeton — Potamogetonaceae

Pondweed

The Pondweeds are mostly submersed, rooted perennials with simple or branched stems, regularly with slender, creeping rhizomes. Leaves are alternate (uppermost may appear opposite), mid-veined, and submersed and or floating. All species have submersed leaves, which are thin, ribbon-like or broader, and usually flaccid. Some species additionally have floating blades which are firmer, and elliptical in shape. At the base of each leaf, there is an open (margins unfused) or closed (fused) stipule that forms a cylindrical sheath around the stem. Sometimes a portion of the stipule is fused to base of leaf. Flowers are small, individually inconspicuous, and clustered mostly into narrow, cylindrical, wind-pollinated spikes held above water (or in submersed, few-flowered clusters). Fruits are small, hard, seed-like, achenes. Winter-buds (turions) are produced by some species at tips of branches or in leaf axils. Winter buds are firm, much-condensed stems with crowded stipules and reduced, thickened leaves.

Twenty-three species occur in New Jersey, including eight rare, and one introduced species. Pondweeds comprise the most diverse group of aquatic plants in New Jersey and collectively have high ecological importance as wildlife food. Identification is sometimes difficult and may require mature fruits. Vegetative features are highly variable and influenced by environmental conditions (water depth and flow). Pondweeds have a propensity for natural interspecific hybridization which can confound identification.

P. gramineus

P. natans

P. zosteriformis

P. obtusifolius

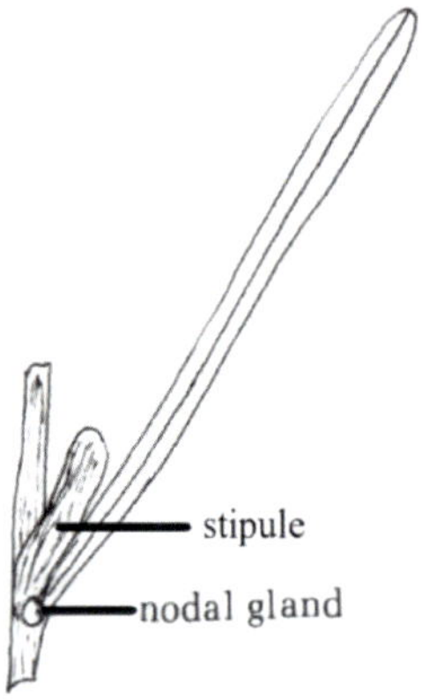

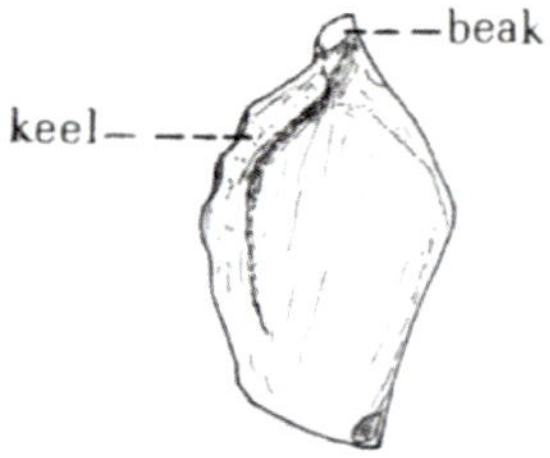

KEY TO SPECIES

1. Stipule fused to base of submersed leaves for about half of stipule length, remaining tip of stipule extending as a ligule.. 2
1. Stipule completely free from submersed leaf base..5
   2. Leaves conspicuously two-ranked (so that whole plant is flat), blades stiffish, with 20–60 veins, and a pair of round lobes at base; plants without floating leaves............ *P. robbinsii*
   2. Leaves not conspicuously two-ranked, blades lax, <20 veins, and not lobed at base; plants with or without floating leaves..3
3. Submersed leaves 0.1–0.6 mm wide, acute to long-tapering tips; floating leaves 3–7 veined, acute at tip ....*P. bicupulatus*
3. Submersed leaves 0.5–2 mm wide, tips blunt to acute; floating leaves 5–15 veined, rounded at tip..4
   4. Tips of submersed floating leaves blunt; fruit 1.5–2.5 mm wide, beak absent....... *P. spirillus*
   4. Tips of submersed floating leaves acute; fruit 1–2 mm wide, beak short (0.1 mm long)....... .... *P. diversifolius*

5. Plants with floating leaves 6
5. Plants without floating leaves 14
6. Submersed leaves linear, flattened or phyllodial (appearing as a bladeless leafstalk)..........7
6. Submersed leaves broadly linear-oblong, lance-shaped to elliptical. 9
7. Submersed leaves 2–10 mm wide, thin and transparent, 3–13 veined, with prominent lacunae band 1–2 mm wide on each side of mid-vein; fruits with distinct, acute keels on back and sides.. *P. epihydrus*
7. Submersed leaves 0.25–2.5 mm wide, thick and nearly opaque, phyllodial (appearing as a bladeless leaf stalk), 3–5 veined, lacking lacunae bands; fruit without keels on sides.......... 8
8. Floating blades 5–10 cm long, usually rounded or somewhat lobed at base, with 17–35 veins, leaf stalk pale and thin at blade end; stipules 4–10 cm long; fruit 3.5–5 mm wide, wrinkled on sides, keel inconspicuous... *P. natans*
8. Floating blades 2.5–6 cm long, rounded to tapering at base, with 7–23 veins, leaf stalk usually not pale at blade end; stipules 2.5–4 cm long; fruit 2–3.5 mm wide, not wrinkled on sides, with a prominent keel... *P. oakesianus*
9. Submersed leaves sessile, without a distinct stalk 10
9. Submersed leaves with a narrow stalk (petiole).. 11
10. Stems branched; submersed leaves green to brownish, tips usually pointed, margins with minute, 1-celled, teeth; fruit laterally compressed.. *P. gramineus*
10. Stems unbranched; submersed leaves usually reddish, tips blunt, margins smooth; fruit plump... *P. alpinus*
11. Floating leaves 19–49 veined; submersed leaf margins undulating (crisped); stems rusty spotted to black-spotted; fruits keeled...12
11. Floating leaves 11–29 veined; submersed leaf margins flat, rarely crisped; stem lacking spots 13
12. Stems black-spotted; submersed leaves with 7–19 veins, 10–25 mm wide, slightly arching; floating leaf blades with 15–19 veins; fruit 3.1–4.1 mm .... *P. pulcher*
12. Stems rusty-spotted; submersed leaves with 19–49 veins, 25–75 mm wide, distinctly arching; floating leaf blades with 27–49 veins; fruit 3.9–5.2 mm.................... *P. amplifolius*
13. Submersed leaves with long stalks (5–15 cm long), blades with 2–5 rows of lacunae on each side of mid-vein, larger leaves with blades 10–35 mm wide; leaf tips pointed; fruit red to red-brown, the lateral keels with blunt to sharp teeth... *P. nodosus*
13. Submersed leaves stalkless or with short stalks (0.5–4 cm long), larger leaves with blades 20–45 mm wide; leaf tip with an abrupt, short, stiff point; fruit gray-green to olive-green, the lateral keels without teeth... *P. illinoensis*
14. Leaf margins finely but distinctly and sharply toothed especially towards tip; fruit with prominent (2–3 mm long), curved, beak; turions commonly formed............................*P. crispus*
14. Leaf margins without distinct teeth; fruit beak <0.9 mm long; turions absent or rarely formed...15
15. Leaves linear, ribbon-like, thread-like, flattened or phyllodial (appearing as a bladeless leafstalk)..16
15. Leaves broadly linear-oblong, lance-shaped, or elliptical..25
16. Plants with obvious, elongated rhizomes...17
16. Plants lacking rhizomes or rhizomes not apparent 20
17. Leaves delicate, thread-like, 0.1–0.5 mm wide, 1-veined; flowering stalks 5–25 cm long...*P. confervoides*
17. Leaves flattened and ribbon-like or appearing as bladeless stalks, 2–11 mm wide, 3–13 veined; flowering stalks 1.5–8 cm long.. 18

18. Submersed leaves 2–10 mm wide, thin and transparent, 3–13 veined, with prominent lacunae band 1–2 mm wide on each side of mid-vein; fruits with distinct, acute keels on back and sides.. *P. epihydrus*

18. Submersed leaves 0.25–2 mm wide, thick and nearly opaque, phyllodial (appearing as a bladeless leaf stalk), 3–5 veined, lacking lacunae bands; fruit without keels on sides........19

19. Submersed leaves 0.7–2.5 mm wide, 3–5 veins; fruit 3.5–5 mm wide, wrinkled on sides, keel inconspicuous.. *P. natans*

19. Submersed leaves 0.25–1 mm wide, 3 veins; fruit 2–3.5 mm wide, not wrinkled on sides, with a prominent keel..*P. oakesianus*

20. Circular raised glands present on at least some nodes..21

20. Nodal glands absent.. 24

21. Stems conspicuously flattened, stiff, 0.6–3.2 mm wide; leaf blades with 15–35 veins; fruit 4–4.5 mm wide; stipules conspicuous, 15–35 mm long, firm, fibrous, white......*P. zosteriformis*

21. Stems not flattened, flexuous, <1 mm wide; leaf blades with 1–5 veins; fruit 1.5–3.5 mm wide; stipules inconspicuous, 3–18 mm long, delicate, not fibrous, green, brown, or white...... 22

22. Leaf blades 1–3.5 mm wide, bluntly pointed or rounded at tip, often reddish; fruit 2.5–3.5 mm wide; winter buds 3.5–7.8 cm long, 2.3–5.1 mm wide.................................. *P. obtusifolius*

22. Leaf blades 0.2–2.5 mm wide, pointed at tip, green; fruit 1.5–2.2 mm wide; winter buds 0.9–3.2 cm long, 0.3–1.8 mm wide 23

23. Stipules with mostly fused margins, forming a tube surrounding the stem; leaf blades with up to 2 rows of lacunae on each side of the midvein; flowering stalks 10–62 mm long, usually terminal, 1–3 per plant; spike usually of 2–4 distinct, interrupted whorls of flowers/fruits......... .... *P. pusillus*

23. Stipules wrapped around the stem, but with unfused, overlapping margins; leaf blades with up to 5 rows of lacunae on each side of the midvein; flowering stalks 5–30 mm long, axillary or terminal, more than 3 per plant; spike usually of 1–3 crowded whorls of flowers/fruits.. *P. berchtoldii*

24. Stems conspicuously flattened (to 3.2 mm wide); leaf blades with 15–35 veins; spikes cylindrical with 7–11 whorls of flower; flowering stems stout and long (20–50 mm); fruits 4–4.5 mm wide... *P. zosteriformis*

24. Stems rounded or slightly compressed (to 1 mm wide); leaf blades with 3–5 veins; spikes knob-like to cylindrical with 1–5 whorls of flowers; flowering stems short (3–11 mm); fruits 1.4–2.3 mm wide.. *P. foliosus*

25. Submersed leaf blades with a stalk...26

25. Submersed leaves without a stalk..29

26. Submersed leaf margins undulating (crisped); stems rusty-spotted to black-spotted.....27

26. Submersed leaf margins flat, rarely crisped; stems lacking spots..............................28

27. Stems black-spotted; submersed leaves with 7–19 veins, 10–25 mm wide, slightly arching; fruit 3.1–4.1 mm.. *P. pulcher*

27. Stems rusty spotted; submersed leaves with 19–49 veins, 25–75 mm wide, distinctly arching; fruit 3.9–5.2 mm.. *P. amplifolius*

28. Submersed leaves with long stalks (5–15 cm long), larger leaves with blades 10–35 mm wide; leaf tips pointed; fruit red to red-brown, the lateral keels with blunt to sharp teeth.... .... *P. nodosus*

28. Submersed leaves stalkless or with short stalks (0.5–4 cm long), larger leaves with blades 20–45 mm wide; leaf tip with an abrupt, short, stiff point; fruit gray-green to olive-green, the lateral keels without teeth.. *P. illinoensis*

29. Leaf blades not clasping the stem...30

29. Leaf blades with base conspicuously clasping the stem...32

30. Stems unbranched; submersed leaves reddish, tip usually blunt, margins without teeth; fruit plump.......... *P. alpinus*

30. Stems branched; submersed leaves green to brownish, tip usually pointed, margins with minute, 1-celled, teeth; fruit laterally compressed.......... 31

31. Leaves with 3–9 veins, with 1–2 rows of lacunae on either side of midvein; fruits 1.9–2.3 mm with beak 0.3–0.5 mm long.......... *P. gramineus*

31. Leaves with 7–19 veins, with 2–5 rows of lacunae on either side of midvein; fruits 2.5–3.6 mm with beak 0.5–0.8 mm long.......... *P. illinoensis*

32. Stipules conspicuous and persistent; leaf blades often >10 cm long, toothless, the tips boat-shaped (hood-like); rhizomes rusty-red spotted; fruit 4–5.7 mm wide with a prominent keel; flowering stems usually >18 cm long.......... *P. praelongus*

32. Stipules inconspicuous or soon disintegrating; leaf blades usually <10 cm long, with minute, 1-celled teeth on margins, the tips flat; rhizomes unspotted; fruit 1.6–4.2 mm wide with an inconspicuous keel or without a keel; flowering stems usually <10 cm long.......... 33

33. Leaf blades egg-shaped to near circular, rarely to 5 cm long, delicately 7–15 veined; stipules delicate, disintegrating and absent on lower part of stem; fruit 1.6–3 mm wide.... *P. perfoliatus*

33. Leaf blades narrowly egg-shaped to narrowly lance-shaped, mostly 3–10 cm long, coarsely 13–21 veined; stipules disintegrating into coarse, white fibers; fruit 2.2–4.2 mm wide.......... *P. richardsonii*

ALPINE PONDWEED *Potamogeton alpinus* Balb.

Alpine pondweed, or Red pondweed, is a submersed, rooted, perennial, with round, slender, unbranched stems (to 200 cm long) and creeping rhizomes. Leaves of two types: all submersed or occasionally both submersed and floating. Submersed leaves are alternate, lax, toothless, linear to lance-shaped (4.5–18+ cm long, 5–20 mm wide), without stalks, reddish green, 7–9 veins, with 0–6 rows of lacunae on either side of midvein, and blunt at tip. Stipules are inconspicuous (1.5–2.5 cm long), light brown to reddish, sheathing, and completely free from leaf base, blunt at tip. Floating leaves are stalked (stalks 0.1–1.2 cm long, continuous in color to blade junction), blades reddish green, elliptic to oblong (4–7 cm long, 10–25 mm wide), 9–13 veins, and tapering at base. Flower clusters are dense, cylindrical (1–3.5 cm long) and emersed above water (flowering stem 3–10 cm long, erect, axillary or terminal). Fruit plump, olive brown, 3–3.5 mm long, with a keel on back and possibly on sides, and a curved beak (0.5–0.9 mm). Turions are not produced.

HABITAT & DISTRIBUTION

Potamogeton alpinus is a native boreal species of shallow to deep, alkaline, cold-water pools, ponds, and slow streams. Based on a collection from the Musconetcong River it is reported from northwest New Jersey, which would represent its southernmost limit.

Notes: A distinctive feature of this plant is its often strong reddish color, especially in upper portions and flowering stems. The dark red color becomes more evident when plants are dried.

Similar to Grassy pondweed but differs by having red-tinged, longer (to 18 cm), submersed leaves, unbranched stems, and larger, plump fruits.

BIG-LEAVED PONDWEED *Potamogeton amplifolius* Tuck.

Big-leaved pondweed is a robust, submersed, rooted, perennial, with round, often rusty-spotted, few-branched stems (6–110 cm long) and creeping rhizomes. Leaves of two types: all submersed or both submersed and floating. Submersed leaves are alternate, with narrow, black-spotted stalks (0.5–4.5 cm long), lax, distinctly arching, often folded, broadly elliptic (5–12.5 cm long, 2.5–7.5 cm wide), undulating margins, green, often turning reddish-brown, 19–49 veins, lacunae absent, and pointed at tip. Stipules are conspicuous (1.5–11.7 cm long), light brown, sheathing, and completely free from leaf base. Floating leaves are stalked (stalks 2.3–22.6 cm long), blades light green, elliptic to narrowly egg-shaped (4.3–9.2 cm long, 2.5–3.8 cm wide), 27–49 veins, and rounded to lobed at base. Flower clusters are dense, cylindrical (3.4–6.5 cm long) and emersed above water (flowering stem 4.5–22 cm long, erect, axillary or terminal). Fruit reddish brown, 3.9–5.2 mm wide, with a keel on back and sides, and an erect beak (0.5–0.8 mm). Turions are not produced.

HABITAT & DISTRIBUTION

Potamogeton amplifolius is a native species of shallow to deep, lakes, ponds, and rivers. It is most common in northern New Jersey. An easily recognized pondweed with its large, often reddish, strongly arching, many-veined, submerged leaves, and ability to colonize deeper waters.

Notes: Similar to Spotted pondweed (*P. pulcher*) but with rusty-spotted stems and larger, arching, many-veined, submersed blades. When floating leaves are absent, plants can be confused with Illinois pondweed (*P. illinoensis*).

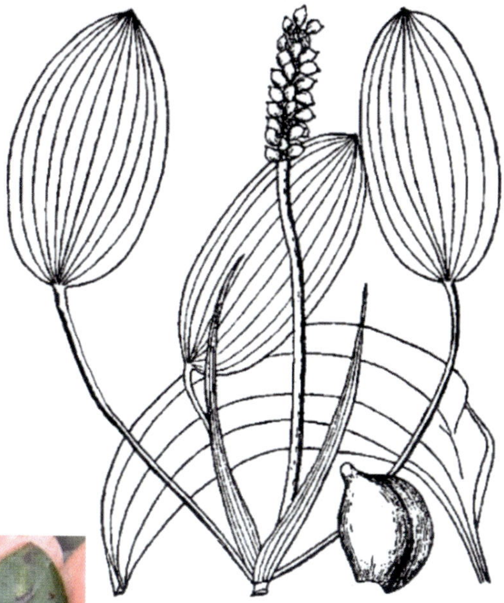

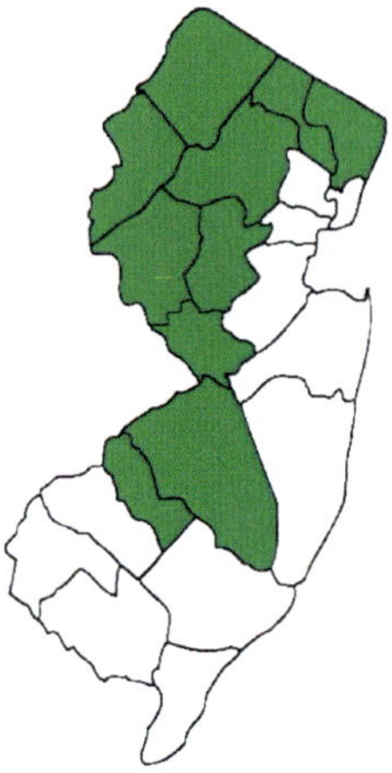

BERCHTOLD'S PONDWEED *Potamogeton berchtoldii* Fieber

Berchtold's pondweed is a delicate, submersed, rooted, perennial, with slender stems (18–150 cm long). Leaves are all submersed, alternate, flaccid, linear (0.9–5.4 cm long, 0.2–2.5 mm wide), pale green to olive-green, 1–5 veins, lacunae present in 1–5 rows on each side of vein, and pointed at tip. Paired, circular, raised glands (–0.5 mm wide), green (same as stem), are inconspicuous at a few nodes. Stipules are inconspicuous, 3.1–9.2 mm long, brown to green or white, delicate, not shredding at tip, wrapped around the stem with overlapping (unfused) margins, and completely free from leaf base. Flower clusters are mostly knob-like (1.5–10 mm long), with 1–3 crowded whorls of flowers/fruits, emersed above water or submersed, at end of cylindric stems (0.5–3.0 cm long), more than 3 per plant. Fruit green to brown, 1.5–2.2 mm wide, not keeled, sides rounded, and with an erect beak (0.1–0.6 mm). Turions are common, slender (0.9–3.2 cm long, 0.3–1.8 mm wide), soft, and leaves two-ranked, with inner leaves modified into a hardened structure.

HABITAT & DISTRIBUTION

Potamogeton berchtoldii is a native species of shallow lakes, pools, and streams. It is presumed widespread in New Jersey.

Notes: This is our most common narrow-leaved pondweed. It is similar to Small pondweed (*P. pusillus*), but with more (1–5 rows) lacunae per side of leaf midrib, >3 flowering stems per plant, and uninterrupted flowering spikes. It is called *P. pusillus* subsp. *tenuissimus* (Mertens & Koch) Haynes & Hellquist in some references.

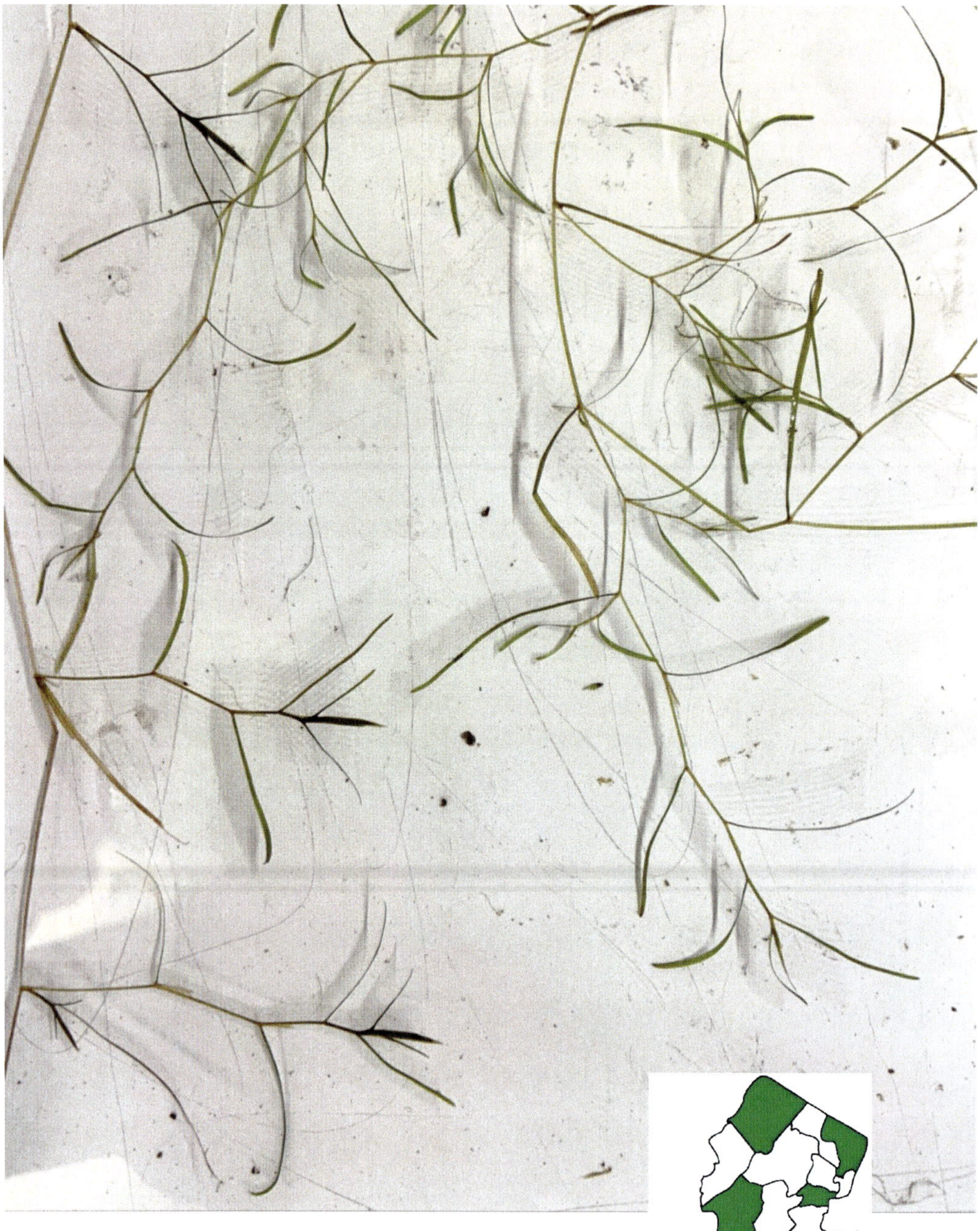

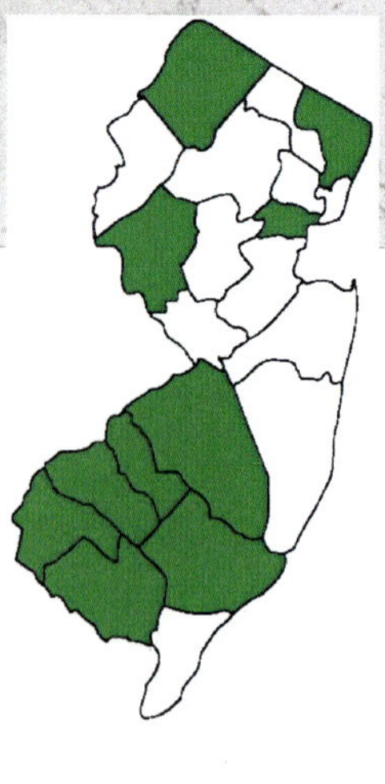

SNAIL-SEED PONDWEED *Potamogeton bicupulatus* Fern.

Snail-seed pondweed is a submersed, rooted, perennial, with compressed, highly branched, slender stems (10–25 cm long) and creeping rhizomes. Leaves of two types: all submersed or both submersed and floating. Submersed leaves alternate, linear and thread-like (1.5–11 cm long, 0.1–0.4 mm wide), light green, 1 vein, lacunae absent, and pointed or long-tapering at tip. Stipules are inconspicuous, light green, fused to base of submersed leaves for <½ of stipule length, with remaining tip of stipule free (usually greater than fused portion). Floating leaves are stalked (stalks 3–35 mm long), blades elliptic to lance-shaped (6–23 mm long, 1–11 mm wide), 3–7 veins, with acute to long-tapering leaf tips. Flower clusters of two types: either globular (1.5–7 mm long) and submersed (flowering stem 1–10 mm long, somewhat recurved, axillary) or short-cylindrical (3–14 mm long) and emersed above water (flowering stem 4–22 mm long, erect or recurved, axillary or terminal). Fruit greenish brown, 1–1.5 mm wide (including keel), with well-developed bumpy keel and usually lacking a beak. Embryo distinctly coiled with more than a full spiral. Turions are not produced.

HABITAT & DISTRIBUTION

Potamogeton bicupulatus is a native, northeastern species of shallow, usually acidic, lakes and streams. It is ***rare*** in New Jersey, eligible for protection under the jurisdiction of the Highlands Preservation Area.

Notes: Similar to Northern snail-seed pondweed (*P. spirillus*) which has ribbon-like submersed leaves, fused portion of stipules about half stipule length, and rounded floating blades.

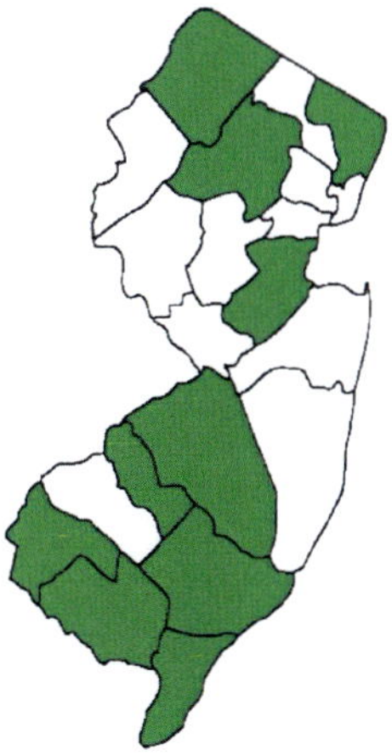

ALGA PONDWEED *Potamogeton confervoides* Rchb.

Alga pondweed is a very delicate submersed, rooted, perennial, with round, much-branched stems (10–80 cm long) and obvious, elongated, creeping rhizomes. Leaves alternate, submersed, thread-like (2–6.5 cm long, 0.1–1 mm wide), flaccid, pale green, 1 vein, and long-tapering and bristly at tip. Stipules are inconspicuous, pale green, and completely free from leaf base. Flower clusters short (5–12 mm long), emersed above water, at end of unusually long stems (5–25 cm long). Fruit light green, 2–3 mm long, 1.7–2.8 mm wide, with keels and erect beak (0.5 mm). Turions (0.7–2 cm long) present in leaf axils of old leaves.

HABITAT & DISTRIBUTION

Potamogeton confervoides is a northern, native species of shallow, acidic, lakes and ponds. It is ***rare*** in New Jersey, eligible for protection under the jurisdiction of the Highlands Preservation Area. **Notes:** This plant is found in our most acidic waters (≤ pH 5) including boggy ponds. Its leaves are so delicate and hair-like that when the plant is removed from the water, they collapse onto each other. Easy to overlook if not flowering.

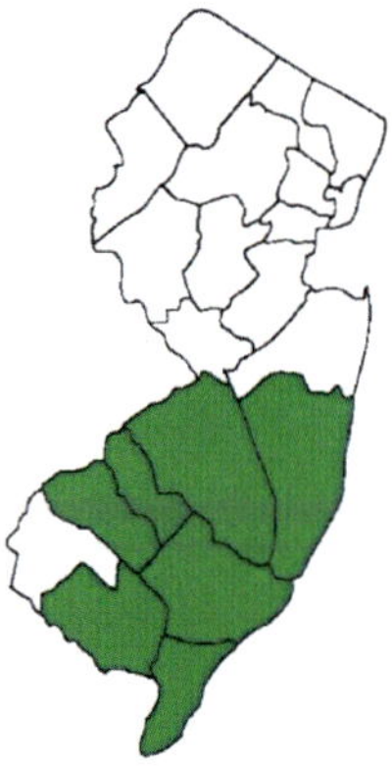

CURLY PONDWEED *Potamogeton crispus* L.

Curly pondweed is a submersed, rooted, perennial, with flattened, few-branched, slender stems. Leaves are all submersed, alternate, bright green, slightly stiff, linear-oblong (12–90 cm long, 4–10 cm wide), round at tip, with 3–5 veins and 2–5 rows of lacunae on each side of midvein. Leaf margins are wavy and conspicuously sharp toothed especially towards tip. Stipules are brown, inconspicuous, and completely free from leaf base. Flowers are borne above water in cylindrical spikes (10–15 mm long) with 6–20 flowers. Fruits (6 mm long, 2.5 mm wide) are brown to red brown, with a prominent (2–3 mm long) curved beak and wavy keel. Turions (1.5–3 cm long, 2 cm wide), consisting of hard, rolled leaves, are commonly formed in leaf axils or at stem tips.

HABITAT & DISTRIBUTION

Potamogeton crispus is a non-native species of alkaline, often polluted, lakes and slow, freshwater to brackish rivers. It is **invasive** in New Jersey.

Notes: Introduced from Europe, this species can be a problematic weed. It is an unusually early blooming species and produces turions in early summer. Plants typically go dormant and decay in late summer as turions germinate into small plants.

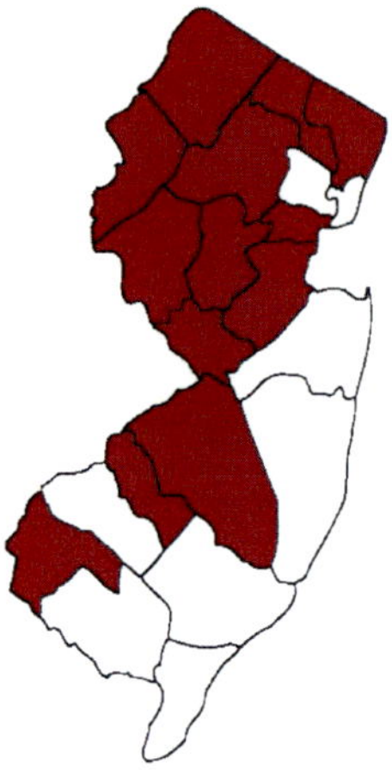

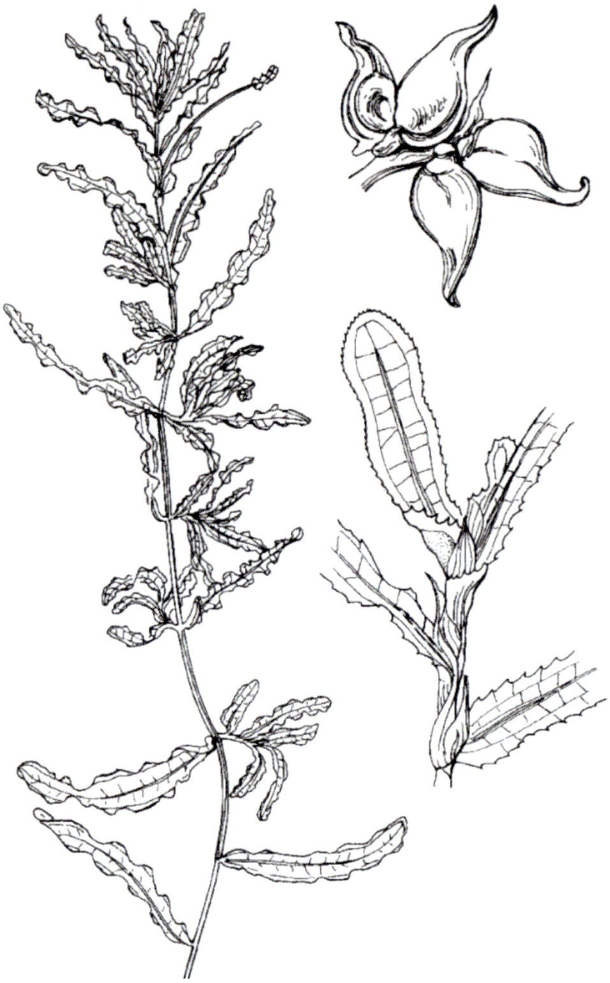

WATER-THREAD PONDWEED *Potamogeton diversifolius* Raf.

Water-thread pondweed is a submersed, rooted, perennial, with compressed, branched, slender stems (10–35 cm long) and creeping rhizomes. Leaves of two types: all submersed or both submersed and floating. Submersed leaves alternate, linear (2–6 cm long, 0.5–1.5 mm wide), red brown to light green, 1–3 veins, with a narrow lacunar band along each side of the midrib, and pointed at tips. Stipules are inconspicuous, reddish brown to light brown, fused to base of submersed leaves for ½ of stipule length, with remaining tip of stipule free (usually equal to or longer than fused portion). Floating leaves are stalked (stalks 1–8 mm long), blades elliptic to lance-shaped (1–5 cm long, 3–8.5 mm wide), 5–17 veins, with rounded leaf tips. Flower clusters of two types: either globular (2–3 mm long) and submersed (flowering stem 3–5 mm long, recurved, axillary) or cylindrical (5–10 mm long) and emersed above water (flowering stem 6–40 mm long, erect or slightly recurved, axillary or terminal). Fruit greenish brown, 1–1.5 mm wide (including keel), 3-keeled, with a minute beak (0.1 mm long). Embryo distinctly coiled in more than one full spiral. Turions are not produced.

HABITAT & DISTRIBUTION

Potamogeton diversifolius is a native, southern species of lakes, pools, and rivers. It is approaching its northern limit in New Jersey, where it is distributed state-wide.

Notes: This is the most common pondweed of southeastern US. It is one of three species in our flora that produce two types of flowering spikes (emersed and submersed). The other species are Snail-seed pondweed (*P. bicupulatus*) and Northern snail-seed pondweed (*P. spirillus*).

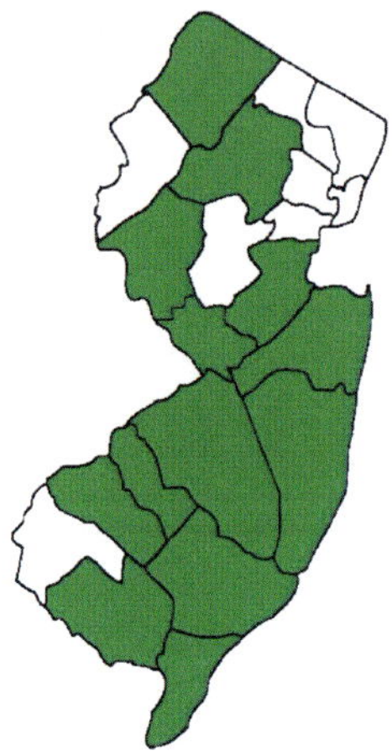

RIBBONLEAF PONDWEED *Potamogeton epihydrus* Raf.

Ribbonleaf pondweed is a submersed, rooted, perennial, with slightly flattened, slender stems (10–90 cm long) and creeping rhizomes. Leaves of two types: all submersed or both submersed and floating. Submersed leaves alternate, flat, linear (5–22 cm long, 2–10 mm wide), red-brown to light green, thin and transparent, 3–13 veined, with prominent lacunae bands 1–2 mm wide on each side of mid-vein, and rounded at tip. Stipules are inconspicuous, reddish brown to light green, sheathing, completely free from leaf base. Floating leaves are stalked (stalks 2–13 cm long), blades light green, elliptic (2.5–9 cm long, 4–20 mm wide), 11–41 veins, with rounded leaf tips. Flower clusters are dense, cylindrical (0.8–4 cm long) and emersed above water (flowering stem 1.5–5 cm long, erect, and axillary). Fruit greenish brown, 2.5–4.5 mm wide, with acute keels on back and sides and an erect beak (0.5 mm). Turions are not produced.

HABITAT & DISTRIBUTION

Potamogeton epihydrus is a native species of shallow, acidic or alkaline, lakes, ponds, and slow rivers. It is widespread in New Jersey.

Notes: Probably our most common pondweed. It is known to hybridize with Snailseed pondweed (*P. bicupulatus*).

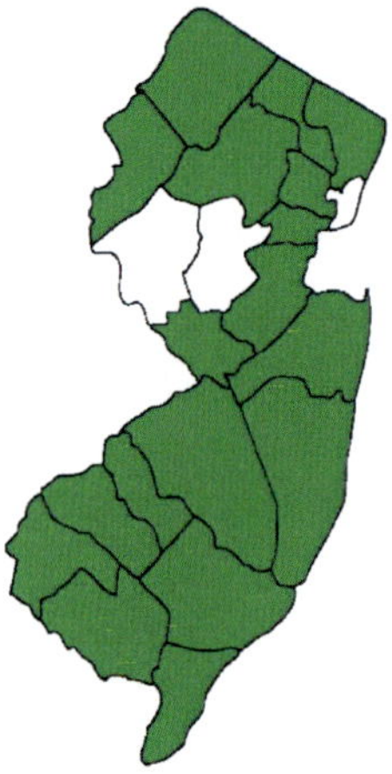

LEAFY PONDWEED *Potamogeton foliosus* Raf.

Leafy pondweed is a delicate, submersed, rooted, perennial, with much-branched, slightly compressed stems (4–75 cm long). Leaves are all submersed, alternate, flaccid, linear (1.3–8.2 cm long, 0.3–2.3 mm wide), pale green to olive-green, 3–5 veins, lacunae rarely present in 0–2 rows on each side of midvein, and pointed at tip (rarely with bristle). Circular glands (to 0.3 mm wide), black to gold, are rarely present at nodes. Stipules are inconspicuous, 2–22 mm long, brown to green, delicate, wrapped around the stem with overlapping margins, and completely free from leaf base. Flower clusters are knob-like to cylindric (1.5–7 mm long), emersed above water, at end of axillary, short (3–11 mm long) stems. Fruit olive-green to brown, 1.4–2.3 mm wide, with a wing-like, undulating keel on back, and erect beak (0.2–0.6 mm). Turions are uncommon, slender (0.9–2.5 cm long, 0.6–2 mm wide), soft, with inner leaves modified into a hardened structure.

HABITAT & DISTRIBUTION

Potamogeton foliosus is a native species of shallow lakes and streams. It is widespread in New Jersey.

Notes: This is the only narrow-leaved pondweed with an undulating, wing-like keel along back of the fruit. It is known to hybridize with *P. pusillus*.

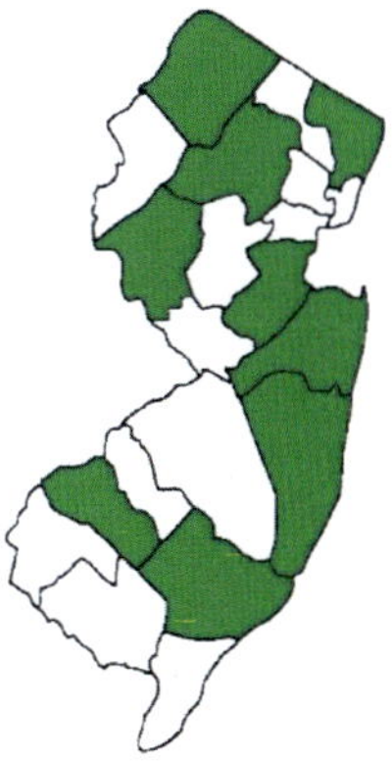

GRASSY PONDWEED *Potamogeton gramineus* L.

Grassy pondweed is a submersed, rooted, perennial, with round to flattened, slender, branching stems (to 150 cm long) and creeping rhizomes. Leaves of two types: all submersed or both submersed and floating. Submersed leaves are alternate, lax, elliptic (3.1–9.1 cm long, 3–27 mm wide), without stalks, light to brownish green, 3–9 veins, with 1–2 rows of lacunae on either side of midvein, and pointed at tip. Stipules are inconspicuous (1.3–1.6 cm long), pale green to brown, sheathing, and completely free from leaf base. Floating leaves are stalked (stalks 3–5.5 cm long, continuous in color to blade junction), blades yellow green to dark green, elliptic to egg-shaped (3.5–4 cm long, 16–20 cm wide), 11–13 veins, and rounded at base. Flower clusters are dense, cylindrical (1.5–3.5 cm long) and emersed above water (flowering stem 3.2–7.7 cm long, erect, axillary and terminal). Fruit greenish brown, 1.9–2.3 mm wide, with a keel on back and on sides, and an erect beak (0.3–0.5 mm). Turions are not produced.

HABITAT & DISTRIBUTION

Potamogeton gramineus is a native species of shallow lakes, ponds, and rivers. This northern species reaches its southern limit in northern New Jersey.

Notes: Leaf shape, size, and arrangement can be highly variable in relation to water depth. Similar to Alpine pondweed (*P. alpinus*). Alpine pondweed differs by having red-tinged, longer (to 18 cm), submersed leaves, unbranched stems, and larger, plump fruits. Grassy pondweed is known to naturally hybridize with *P. illinoensis*, *P. natans*, *P. nodosus*, *P. oakesianus*, and *P. perfoliatus* in parts of its range.

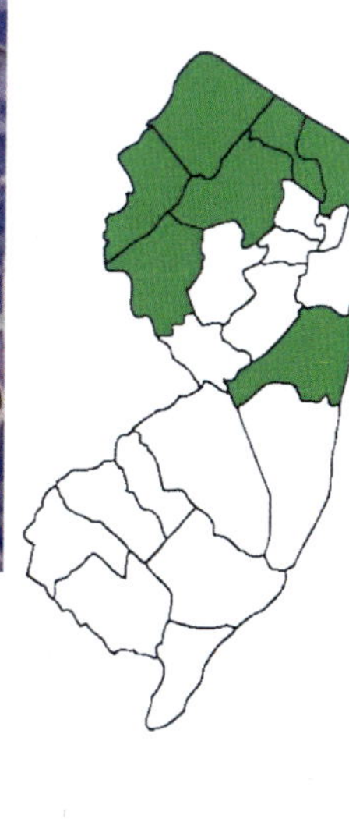

Illinois pondweed is a submersed, rooted, perennial, with round, few-branched, stems (28–120 cm long), and creeping rhizomes. Leaves of two types: all submersed or both submersed and floating. Submersed leaves are alternate, stalkless or with short stalks (0.5–4 cm long), lax, flat to undulating, lance-shaped to elliptic (5–20 cm long, 20–45 mm wide), red-brown to light green, 7–15 veins, with 2–5 rows of lacunae on each side of a prominent mid-vein, and abruptly tapered to a short (to 4 mm), stiff point at tip. Stipules are conspicuous (1–8 cm long), light brown to red-brown, sheathing, and completely free from leaf base. Floating leaves are stalked (stalks 2–9 cm long), blades light green, elliptic to oblong (4–19 cm long, 2.0–6.5 cm wide), 13–29 veins, and tapering at base. Flower clusters are dense, cylindrical (2.5–7 cm long) and emersed above water (flowering stem 4–30 cm long, erect, axillary or terminal). Fruit gray green to olive-green, 2.5–3.6 mm wide, with well-developed keels and an erect to slightly curved beak (0.5–0.8 mm). Lateral keels without teeth. Turions are not produced.

HABITAT & DISTRIBUTION

Potamogeton illinoensis is a stout, native species of shallow, mostly alkaline, lakes, ponds, rivers, and streams. It is critically imperiled and state-listed as ***endangered*** in New Jersey.

Notes: Floating leaves are often not produced, especially in deeper water. It is similar to Long-leaf pondweed (*P. nodosus*), but with stalkless or shorter-stalked, wider, submersed leaves and green fruits. When submersed blades are stalkless, plants resemble Grassy pondweed (*P. gramineus*) but have more numerous veins and larger fruits. It is known to hybridize with both Grassy pondweed and Big-leaved pondweed (*P. amplifolius*) at times.

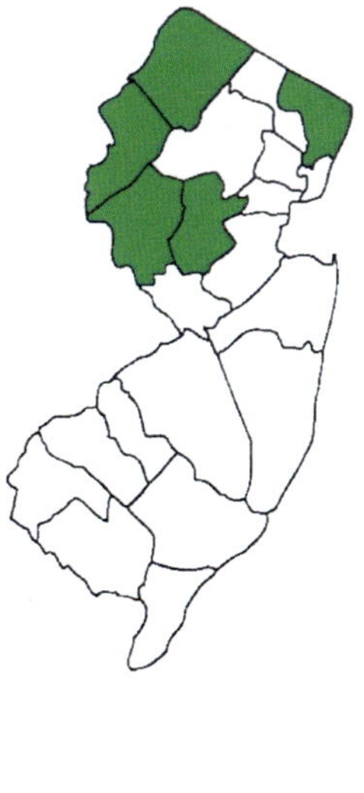

Floating pondweed is a submersed, rooted, perennial, with round, mostly unbranched, slender stems (30–90 cm long) and creeping rhizomes. Leaves both submersed and floating. Submersed leaves are alternate, stiff, linear (9–20 cm long, 0.7–2.5 mm wide), phyllodial (appearing as a bladeless leaf stalk), light to dark green, 3–5 obscure veins, lacking lacunae bands, and blunt at tip. Stipules are conspicuous (4–10 cm long), whitish, sheathing, and completely free from leaf base. Floating leaves are long-stalked (stalks 5–29 cm long, with a distinctly bent and lighter area at blade junction), blades light green, oval-elliptic to egg-shaped (5–10 cm long, 1.5–6 cm wide), 17–35 veins, usually rounded or heart-shaped at base. Flower clusters are dense, cylindrical (2.5–5 cm long) and emersed above water (flowering stem 4.5–9.5 cm long, erect, and terminal). Fruit greenish brown, 3.5–5 mm wide, wrinkled on sides, with an inconspicuous keel on back and an erect to curved beak (0.4–0.8 mm). Turions are not produced.

HABITAT & DISTRIBUTION

Potamogeton natans is a native species of acidic to alkaline lakes, ponds, rivers and streams, including tidally influenced waters. This more northern species is approaching its southern limit in New Jersey.

Notes: This plant is easily identified by its phyllodial submersed leaves (when persisting), a band of paler green tissue on end of leaf stalk where it meets a floating blade, and usually lobed base of floating blades. In non-flowing waters, the apex of leafstalks on floating leaves are noticeably bent at a 90° angle where it meets the blade. The floating leaf blade shape and degree of lobing at base is influenced by water currents. It is similar to Oakes' pondweed (*P. oakesianus*).

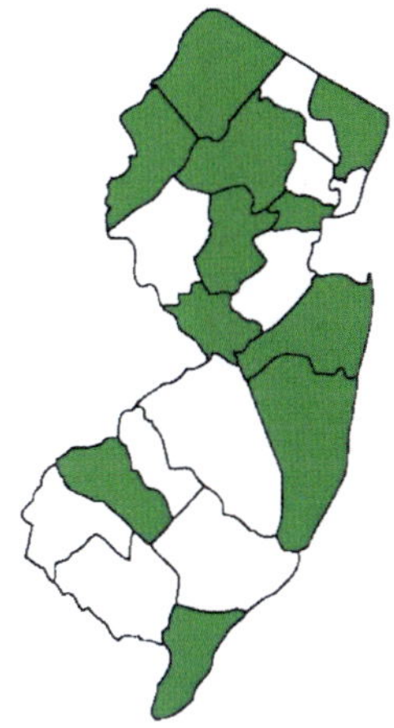

LONG-LEAF PONDWEED *Potamogeton nodosus* Poir.

Long-leaf pondweed is a submersed, rooted, perennial, with round, few-branched, stems (to 100 cm long), and whitish rhizomes. Leaves of two types: all submersed or both submersed and floating. Submersed leaves are alternate, with long stalks (5–15 cm long), lax, flat, narrowly lance-elliptic (9–20 cm long, 10–35 mm wide), light to dark green, 7–15 veins, with 2–5 conspicuous rows of lacunae on each side of a prominent mid-vein, and pointed at tip. Stipules are conspicuous (3–9 cm long), light brown, sheathing, and completely free from leaf base. Floating leaves are stalked (stalks 3.5–26 cm long), blades light green, elliptic (3–11 cm long, 1.5–4.5 cm wide), 11–21 veins, and tapering to rounded at base. Flower clusters are dense, cylindrical (2–7 cm long) and emersed above water (flowering stem stout, 3–15 cm long, erect, terminal). Fruit reddish brown, 2.7–4.3 mm wide, with well-developed keels and an erect beak. Lateral keels with blunt to sharp teeth. Turions are not produced.

HABITAT & DISTRIBUTION

Potamogeton nodosus is a native species of shallow to deep lakes, rivers, and streams. It is more common in northern New Jersey.

Notes: Plants are easily distinguished by the large, long-stalked submersed leaves and long-stalked, elliptic floating leaves, each tapering at both ends. It is similar to Illinois pondweed (*P. illinoensis*), but with longer-stalked, narrower, submersed leaves and reddish fruits. Submersed leaves often senesce before fruiting, so plants then can resemble Floating pondweed (*P. natans*). This species is known to hybridize with Grassy pondweed (*P. gramineus* and Illinois pondweed (*P. illinoensis*) in parts of its range.

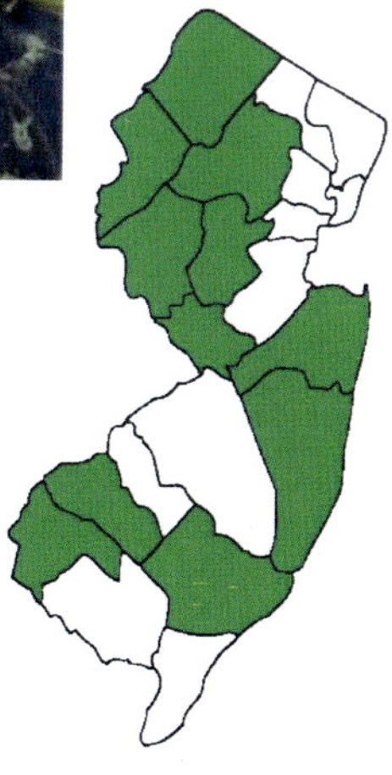

Oakes' pondweed is a submersed, rooted, perennial, with round, much-branched, red-spotted, slender stems (7–75 cm long) and creeping rhizomes. Leaves both submersed and floating. Submersed leaves are alternate, delicate and lax, linear (5–16 cm long, 0.25–1 mm wide), phyllodial (appearing as a bladeless leaf stalk), pale green, 3 veins, lacking lacunae bands, and pointed at tip. Stipules are conspicuous (2.5–4 cm long), whitish, sheathing, and completely free from leaf base. Floating leaves are stalked (stalks 3.2–7.5 cm long, continuous in color to blade junction), blades light to dark green, lance- to egg-shaped (2.5–6 cm long, 1–2 cm wide), 7–23 veins, and rounded or tapering at base. Flower clusters are dense, cylindrical (1–3.5 cm long) and emersed above water (flowering stem 2.5–8 cm long, erect, and terminal). Fruit greenish brown, 2–3.5 mm wide, not wrinkled on sides, with a prominent keel on back and keels on sides, and an erect beak (0.4–0.8 mm). Turions are not produced.

HABITAT & DISTRIBUTION

Potamogeton oakesianus is a native species of shallow, acidic, bogs, lakes, ponds and occasionally streams. It is ***rare*** in New Jersey, eligible for protection under the jurisdiction of the Highlands Preservation Area.

Notes: As our only other pondweed with submersed, phyllodial leaves, it is similar to Floating pondweed (*P. natans*), but these leaves in Oakes' pondweed are much narrower (delicate and soon deteriorating too) as are the floating blades, which are not lobed at base. It is known to hybridize with Grassy pondweed (*P. gramineus*).

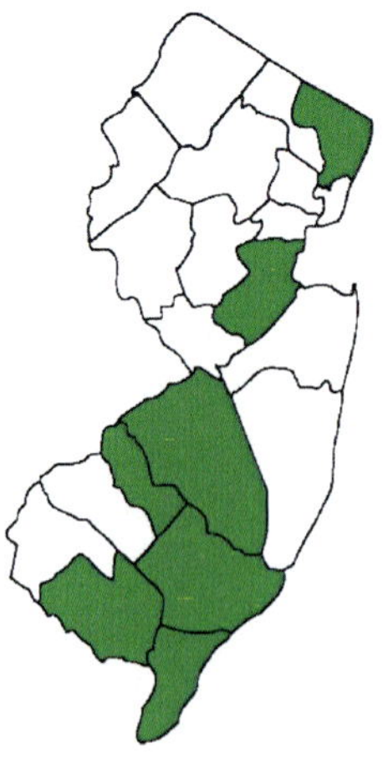

BLUNT-LEAVED PONDWEED *Potamogeton obtusifolius* Mert. & Koch

Blunt-leaved pondweed is a delicate, submersed, rooted, perennial, with slender, slightly compressed stems (35–90 cm long). Leaves are all submersed, alternate, flaccid, linear (3–8.2 cm long, 1–3.5 mm wide), green to reddish, 3 veins, lacunae present in 1–3 rows on each side of vein, and bluntly pointed or rounded at tip. Paired, circular, raised glands (0.3–1 mm wide), are yellowish green to gold, are common at nodes. Stipules are inconspicuous, 6–18 mm long, white, delicate, rarely shredding at tip, sheathing the stem, and completely free from leaf base. Flower clusters are cylindrical (8–13 mm long), emersed above water, at end of rounded stems (0.8–2 cm long). Fruit olive green to brown, 2.5–3.5 mm wide, sometimes keeled, and with an erect beak (0.8–1 mm). Turions are abundant, slender (3.5–7.8 cm long, 2.3–5.1 mm wide), soft, and leaves two-ranked, flattened, with inner and outer leaves in same plane.

HABITAT & DISTRIBUTION

Potamogeton obtusifolius is a native species of shallow, moderately calcareous waters of lakes and slow streams. It is at the southernmost limit of its range in New Jersey, where it is critically imperiled and state-listed as ***endangered***.

Note: This unusually wide narrow-leaved pondweed is very similar to the more common Berchtold's pondweed (*P. berchtoldii*), but with wider, blunt tipped leaves often flushed with maroon.

CLASPING-LEAVED PONDWEED *Potamogeton perfoliatus* L.

Clasping-leaved pondweed is a submersed, rooted, perennial, with round stems (to 2.5 m long) and unspotted rhizomes. Leaves submersed, alternate, lax, egg-shaped to near circular (1–7.6 cm long, 0.7–4 cm wide), with minute (1-celled) teeth on margins, blade base rounded and conspicuously clasping stem, olive green, 7–15 delicate veins, lacking lacunae, and with a flat, rounded tip. Stipules are inconspicuous (3.5–6.5 cm long), delicate, disintegrating into fibers, absent on lower part of stem, light brown to green, sheathing the stem, and completely free from leaf base. Flower clusters are cylindrical (0.4–4.8 cm long) and emersed above water, on cylindric stems (1–7.3 cm long). Fruit greenish brown, 1.6–3 mm wide, without keels, and an erect beak (0.4–0.6 mm). Turions are not produced.

HABITAT & DISTRIBUTION

Potamogeton perfoliatus is a native species of lakes, bays, and rivers, including brackish, tidal rivers. It is widespread in New Jersey. Known to hybridize with *P. berchtoldii*, *P. epihydrus*, *P. gramineus*, and *P. richarsonii* in parts of its range.

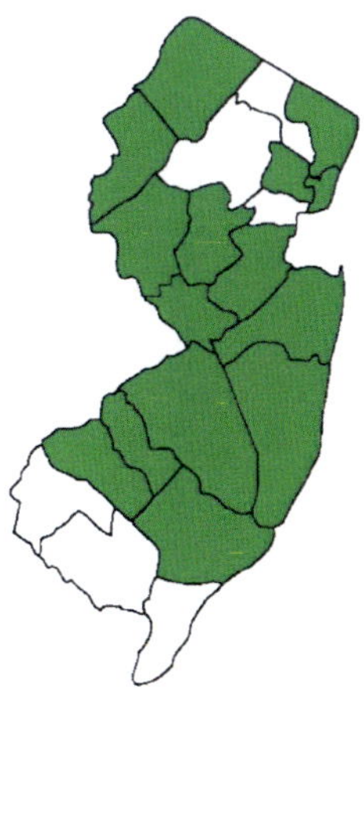

White-stemmed pondweed is a submersed, rooted, perennial, with round, zig-zagged stems (to 2 m long) and red spotted, white rhizomes. Leaves submersed, alternate, lax, linear to lance-shaped (6–28 cm long, 1–4.6 cm wide), blade base conspicuously clasping stem (without lobes), pale green, 11–33 veins, lacking lacunae, and with a hood-like, boat-shaped tip. Stipules are conspicuous (3–8 cm long), mostly white, fibrous, shredding at tip, sheathing the stem, and completely free from leaf base. Flower clusters are cylindrical (3.4–7.5 cm long) and emersed above water, on long (9.5–53 cm) stems. Fruit greenish brown, 4–5.7 mm wide, with a prominent, sharp keel on back, and an erect beak (0.6–0.1 mm). Turions are not produced.

HABITAT & DISTRIBUTION

Potamogeton praelongus is a native northern species of, shallow to deep, neutral to alkaline, waters of lakes and rivers. It is at its southernmost limit in New Jersey, where it is critically imperiled and state-listed as ***endangered***.

Notes: White-stemmed pondweed is distinctive with its large white stipules, submersed leaves clasping zig-zagged stems, and boat-shaped leaf tips (that split when pressed flat).

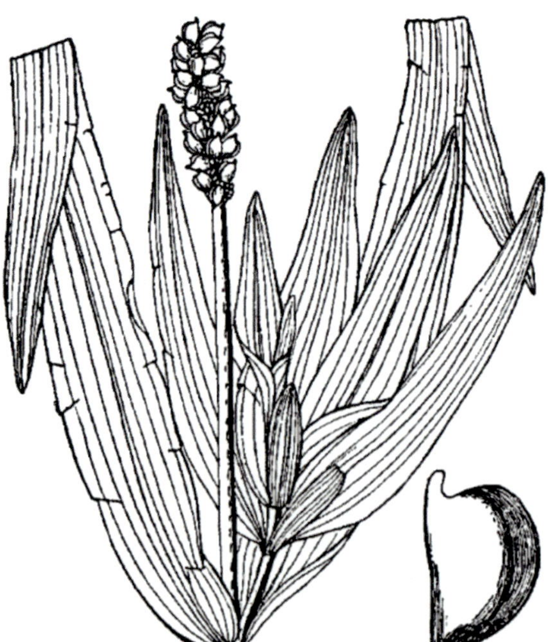

Spotted pondweed is a submersed, rooted, perennial, with round, conspicuously black-spotted, unbranched stems (8–95 cm long) and creeping rhizomes. Leaves both submersed and floating. Submersed leaves are alternate, with narrow, black-spotted stalks (0.5–4.5 cm long), lax, slightly arching, narrowly lance-shaped (3.5–13.8 cm long, 10–25 mm wide), undulating margins, dark green, 7–19 veins, with 2–5 rows of lacunae on either side of midvein, and pointed at tip. Stipules are inconspicuous (0.7–1.2 cm long), light to dark brown, sheathing, and completely free from leaf base. Floating leaves are stalked (stalks stout, 1–16.5 cm long, black-spotted), blades light to dark green, broadly elliptic (2.5–8.5 cm long, 1.1–4.4 cm wide), 15–19 veins, and rounded at base. Flower clusters are dense, cylindrical (1.7–3.6 cm long) and emersed above water (flowering stem 3.3–9.4 cm long, erect, axillary and terminal). Fruit dark greenish brown, 3.1–4.1 mm wide, with a keel on back and sides, and an erect beak (0.5 mm). Turions are not produced.

HABITAT & DISTRIBUTION

Potamogeton pulcher is a native, eastern species of shallow, acidic lakes and rivers. It is widespread in New Jersey.

Note: The conspicuously black-spotted stems and leaf stalks are distinctive. Similar to Big-leaved pondweed (*P. amplifolius*) but with black-spotted stems, less-broad submersed blades with fewer veins, and floating blades with fewer veins. It is known to hybridize with *P. amplifolius* in parts of its range.

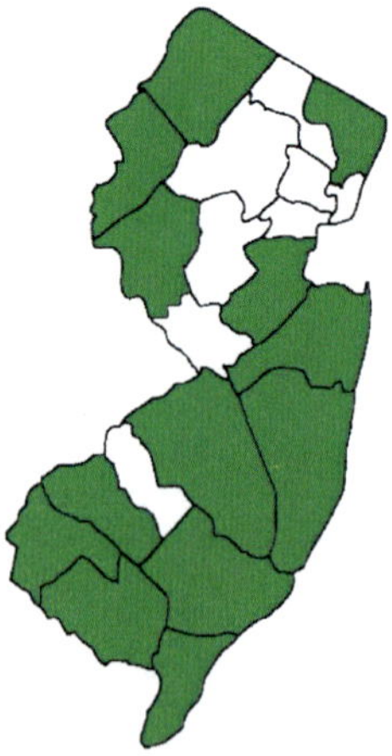

SMALL PONDWEED *Potamogeton pusillus* L.

Small pondweed is a delicate, submersed, rooted, perennial, with slender stems (18–150 cm long). Leaves are all submersed, alternate, flaccid, linear (1.4–6.5 cm long, 0.5–1.9 mm wide), pale green to olive-green, 1–5 veins, lacunae absent or present in 1–2 rows on each side of vein, and pointed at tip. Paired, circular, raised glands (to 0.5 mm wide), green (same as stem), are inconspicuous at a few nodes. Stipules are inconspicuous, 3.1–9.2 mm long, brown to green or white, delicate, not shredding at tip, with fused margins, forming a tube surrounding the stem, and completely free from leaf base. Flower clusters are cylindrical (1.5–10 mm long), usually with 2–4 interrupted whorls of flowers/fruits, emersed above water or submersed, at end of narrow, mostly terminal, stems (0.1–6.2 cm long), only 1–3 per plant. Fruit green to brown, 1.5–2.2 mm wide, not keeled, sides concave, and with an erect beak (0.1–0.6 mm). Turions are common, slender (0.9–3.2 cm long, 0.3–1.8 mm wide), soft, and leaves two-ranked, with inner leaves modified into a hardened structure.

HABITAT & DISTRIBUTION

Potamogeton pusillus is a native species of lakes, pools, and slow streams. It is statewide in New Jersey.

Notes: This narrow-leaved pondweed is distinctive with its narrow, 1–5 veined leaves, collar-like stipules, and interrupted fruit spikes (up to 3 per plant). It is similar to Berchtold's pondweed (*P. berchtoldii*).

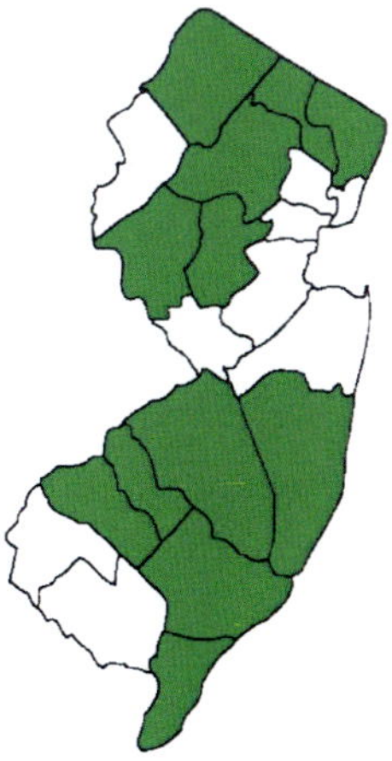

RICHARDSON'S PONDWEED *Potamogeton richardsonii* (Benn.) Rydb.

Richardson's pondweed is a submersed, rooted, perennial, with round stems (to 1 m long) and rhizomes. Leaves submersed, alternate, lax, narrowly egg-shaped to narrowly lance-shaped (1.6–13 cm long, 0.5–2.8 cm wide), with minute teeth on margins, blade base rounded and conspicuously clasping stem, olive green, 13–21 coarse veins, lacking lacunae, and with a flat, pointed tip. Stipules are conspicuous (1.2–1.7 cm long), firm, disintegrating into coarse, white fibers, sheathing the stem, and completely free from leaf base. Flower clusters are cylindrical (1.3–3.7 cm long) and emersed above water, on cylindric stems (1.5–14.8 cm long). Fruit greenish brown, 2.2–4.2 mm wide, usually without keels, and an erect beak (0.4–0.7 mm). Turions are not produced.

HABITAT & DISTRIBUTION

Potamogeton richardsonii is a native northern species of shallow, mostly calcareous, lakes and streams. Old records have it limited to northwest New Jersey, which would represent its southernmost occurrence in the northeast. Its current status is uncertain.

Notes: It is similar to the closely related and more widespread Clasping-leaved pondweed (*P. perfoliatus*) with which it is known to hybridize.

ROBBINS' PONDWEED *Potamogeton robbinsii* Oakes

Robbins' pondweed, or Fern pondweed, is a submersed, rooted, perennial, with round, branched, slender stems (to 1 m long) and creeping rhizomes. Leaves are all submersed, alternate, strongly two-ranked (attached on opposite sides of the stem so that whole plant is flat), closely spaced, dark green to reddish, stiff, lance-shaped (20–120 mm long, 3–8 mm wide), sharply pointed, and with pair of round lobes at base (where leaf meets stipule) that protrude past the stem. Leaves are often arching, with a conspicuous midvein, and finely toothed edges. A conspicuous, translucent, greenish brown to white, stipular sheath is fused to base of leaves for ¼ of stipule length, with remaining tip of stipule free and shredding. Flowers are borne just above water in slender spikes (7–20 mm long) on branching stems. Fruits (3–5 mm long, 2–3 mm wide), rarely produced, are brown, with an erect beak (0.7–0.9 mm long) and wavy keel. Turions are not produced.

HABITAT & DISTRIBUTION

Potamogeton robbinsii is a northern native species of lakes and slow rivers. It is reaching the southern end of its range in New Jersey where it is ***rare***, eligible for protection under the jurisdiction of the Highlands Preservation Area.

Notes: Plants are often in deep waters (5–7 m) where populations are dense (to 1000 plants per m^2). It is the only pondweed to have branched flowering stems and lobed leaf bases. It rarely flowers or sets fruit.

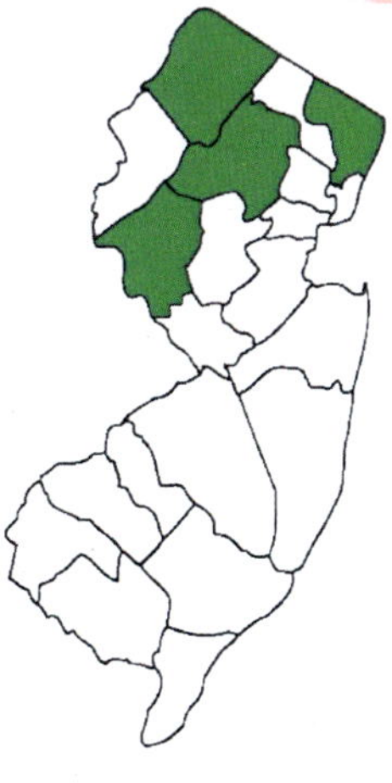

NORTHERN SNAIL-SEED PONDWEED *Potamogeton spirillus* Tuck.

Northern snail-seed pondweed is a submersed, rooted, perennial, with compressed, branched, slender stems (5–40 cm long) and creeping rhizomes. Leaves of two types: all submersed or both submersed and floating. Submersed leaves alternate, linear (0.7–8 cm long, 0.5–2 mm wide), red brown to light green, 1–3 veins, commonly with a broad lacunar band along each side of the midrib, and blunt-tipped. Stipules are inconspicuous, reddish brown to light green, fused to base of submersed leaves for ½ of stipule length, with remaining tip of stipule free (usually equal to or shorter than fused portion). Floating leaves are stalked (stalks 5–25 mm long), blades elliptic to lance-shaped (6–35 mm long, 2–13 mm wide), 5–15 veins, with rounded leaf tips. Flower clusters of two types: either globular (2–5 mm long) and submersed (flowering stem 0.5–3 mm long, recurved, axillary) or short-cylindrical (4–13 mm long) and emersed above water (flowering stem 4–27 mm long, erect or recurved, axillary or terminal). Fruit greenish brown, 1.5–2.5 mm wide (including keel), with blunt keel and lacking a beak. Embryo distinctly coiled in a full spiral. Turions are not produced.

HABITAT & DISTRIBUTION

Potamogeton spirillus is a native, northeastern species of lakes and rivers. It is widespread in New Jersey where it is at the southernmost end of its range.

Notes: This is one of three species in our flora that produce two types of flowering spikes (emersed and submersed). The other species are Snail-seed pondweed (*P. bicupulatus*) and Water-thread pondweed (*P. diversifolius*).

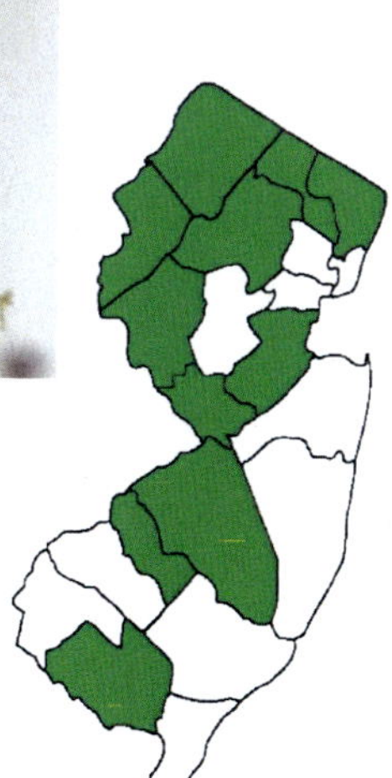

FLAT-STEM PONDWEED *Potamogeton zosteriformis* Fern.

Flat-stem pondweed is a submersed, rooted, perennial, with conspicuously flattened (appearing winged), stiff, stems (60–120 cm long, 0.6–3.2 mm wide). Leaves are all submersed, alternate, linear (10–20 cm long, 2–5 mm wide), light green, 15–35 veins, lacunae absent, and blunt to tapering at tip. Circular glands (to 0.3 mm wide), gold, are sometimes present at nodes. Stipules are conspicuous, 15–35 mm long, firm, fibrous, white, shredding at tip, sheathing the stem, and completely free from leaf base. Flower clusters are cylindrical (15–30 mm long), emersed above water, at end of stout, cylindric stems (2–5 cm long). Fruit olive green to green, 4–4.5 mm wide, sharp keeled on back, and with an erect beak (0.6–1 mm). Turions are common, flattened, large (4–7.5 cm long, 2–4.5 mm wide), firm, with leaves two-ranked, the inner and outer leaves oriented in the same plane, and the inner leaves undifferentiated.

HABITAT & DISTRIBUTION

Potamogeton zosteriformis is a native species of shallow calcareous lakes and streams. It is approaching its southernmost limit in New Jersey, where it is critically imperiled and state-listed as ***endangered***.

Notes: It is a distinctive pondweed with its flat, winged stems and many-veined, parallel-sided, linear leaves to 5 mm wide. Leaves hold their shape when removed from water.

Proserpinaca — Haloragaceae

Mermaid-weed

The Mermaid-weeds are amphibious, rooted, perennials that can be mostly or entirely submersed. Stems, rooted from the lower nodes, grow out of water from rhizomes. Leaves are alternate, and their form varies greatly by water depth: blades range from smaller and deeply pinnately divided (submersed) to larger and merely toothed (emergent). Flowers are small, purplish-greenish, and borne 1–3 in the emergent leaf axils. Fruit is a 3-seeded, 3-angled nutlet.

Two species occur in New Jersey, both native. A rare putative hybrid, long recognized as *P. ×intermedia* MacKenzie, was first described from specimens collected from the Pine Barrens in 1910.

Key to Species

1. Emersed leaves (20–40 mm long) sharply-toothed, submersed leaves (5–30 mm long) deeply divided into 7–14 pairs of segments; fruits 2.3–6 mm wide............................*P. palustris*
1. All leaves (10–30 mm long) deeply divided, submersed leaves with 6–9 pairs of segments; fruits 2–2.8 mm wide.. *P. pectinata*

Marsh mermaid-weed *Proserpinaca palustris* L.

Marsh mermaid-weed is a submersed plant (10–40 cm long) with flowering portions emergent. Leaves are alternate (20–40 mm long), emersed ones sharply-toothed and submersed ones deeply-divided into 7–14 pairs of narrow segments 5–30 mm long. Flowers are borne in axils of emersed leaves, each with a toothed leaf-like bracts below. Fruits are 2.3–6 mm wide and sharply angled.

Habitat & Distribution

Proserpinaca palustris is native to shallow ponds and slow streams. It is widespread in New Jersey.

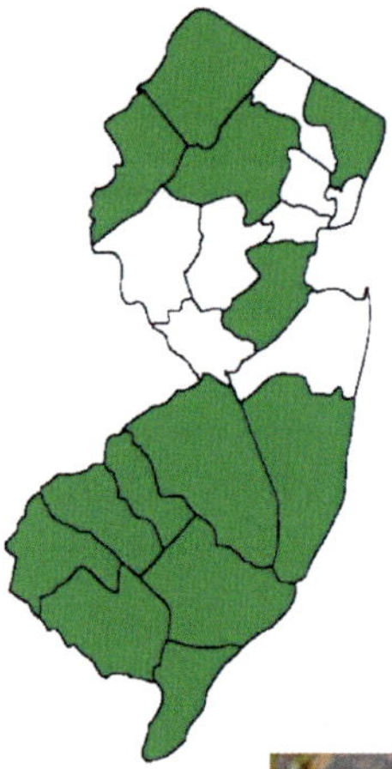

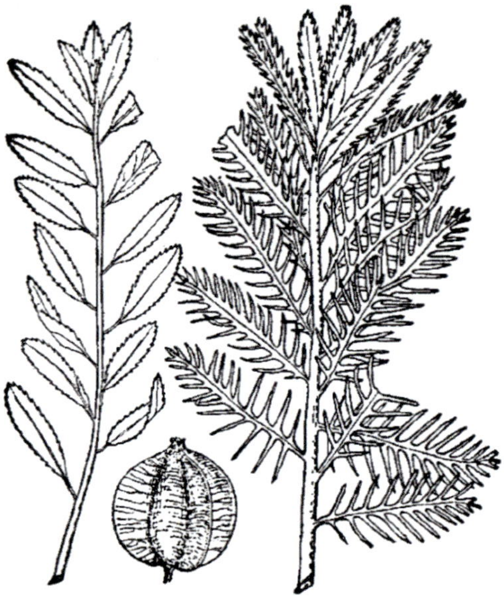

Comb-leaved mermaid-weed is usually a submersed plant with flowering portions emergent. Leaves are alternate (10–30 mm long) and deeply divided into 6–9 pairs of narrow segments 2–7.5 mm long. Flowers are borne in axils of emersed leaves, each with a deeply divided leaf-like bract. Fruits are 2–2.8 mm wide and bluntly angled.

HABITAT & DISTRIBUTION

Proserpinaca pectinata is native to shallow ponds, bogs, and ditches. This Coastal Plain species is common in southern New Jersey.

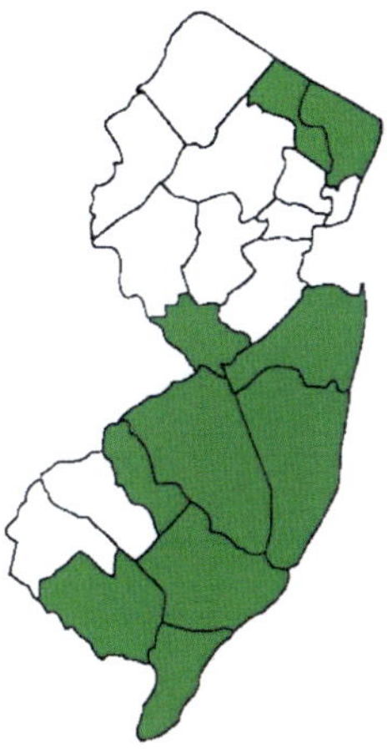

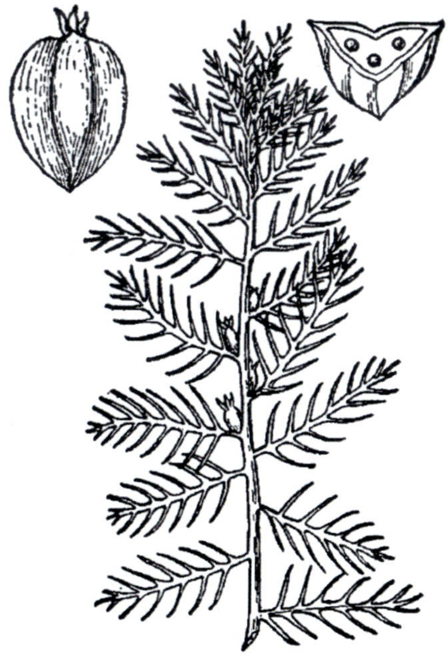

Ranunculus — Ranunculaceae
Crowfoot

The Crowfoots, or Buttercups, have just a few truly aquatic species with highly dissected, submersed leaves (or deeply lobed floating leaves). Leaves are evidently stalked and expanded at base sheathing the stem. Flowers are conspicuous and held above water, each with 5 colored petals, and numerous stamens and pistils. Fruits are clusters of small, seed-like achenes.

Four aquatic species occur in New Jersey, all native and highly variable in terms of leaf shape depending on conditions. Additionally, there are several other species of Buttercups (e.g., *R. hispidus* Michx., *R. recurvatus* Poir., *R. repens* L.) that occupy wetland edges or moist woods in New Jersey. These emergent species (not detailed here) have mostly erect stems and simple, broad leaves held above water.

Key to Species

1. Leaves all arising from base of plant (basal) on long stalks, blades floating (or emersed), flat, and deeply lobed............ *R. sceleratus*
1. Leaves alternate along stems, mostly submersed and highly divided into very narrow segments............ 2
   2. Leaf segments flat and ribbon-like; petals yellow; fruits smooth............ *R. flabellaris*
   2. Leaf segments thread-like, petals white (with yellow blotch at base); fruits transversely wrinkled............ 3
3. Leaves flaccid and collapsing when out of water, leafstalk evident above sheathing base..... .... *R. trichophyllus*
3. Leaves firmer and holding shape when out of water, leafstalk absent with leaves branching immediately above sheathing base............ *R. longirostris*

R. longirostris

R. flabellaris

R. sceleratus

YELLOW WATER CROWFOOT *Ranunculus flabellaris* Raf.

Yellow Water crowfoot is a submersed perennial with floating, hollow, stems rooted at lower nodes. Leaves are alternate, mostly submersed, kidney-shape to semicircular in outline (1.5–7 cm long), highly divided into flat, ribbon-like segments (1–2 mm wide), with expanded, sheathing stalks. Flowers are bisexual, emersed above water, borne 1-few on a stout stalk, with 5–6, shiny, yellow petals (7–12 mm long), and green centers. Fruit small (2.5–3.5 mm long), smooth, with a winged margin, and beak (1–2 mm long).

HABITAT & DISTRIBUTION

Ranunculus flabellaris is a native species of open, shallow (30–100 cm deep), acidic or alkaline, quiet waters of ponds, bogs, and swamps. It is **rare** in New Jersey, eligible for protection under the jurisdiction of the Highlands Preservation Area.

Note: Leaves near stem tips are sometimes emersed or floating. These leaves can be merely lobed, rather than the highly divided submersed leaves.

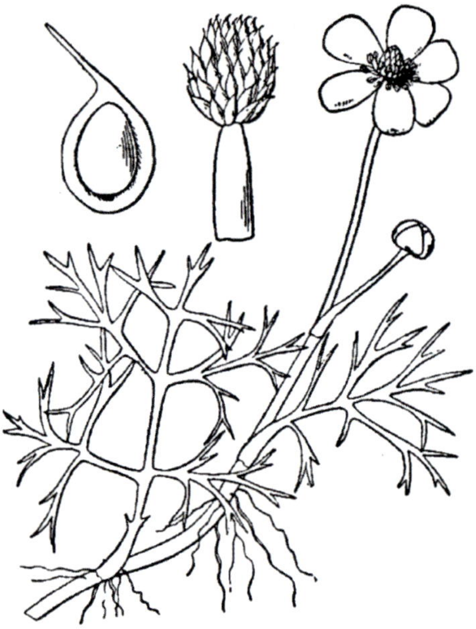

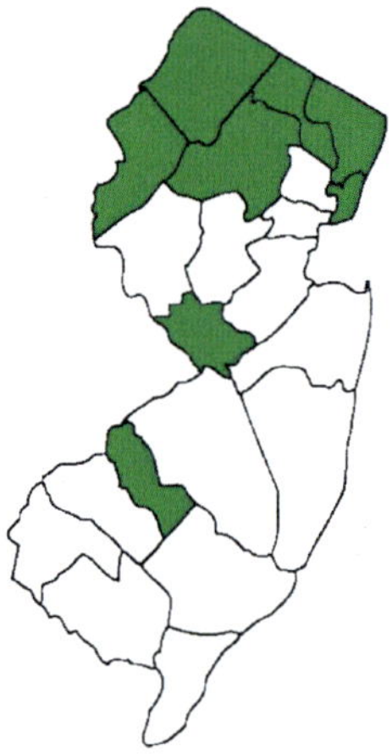

WHITE WATER CROWFOOT *Ranunculus longirostris* Godr.

White Water crowfoot is a submersed perennial with elongate, branched stems rooted at lower nodes. Leaves are alternate, submersed, round to semicircular in outline (1.5–3 cm long), rigid, branching immediately above expanded, sheathing base, and highly divided into thread-like segments. Flowers are bisexual, emersed above water, borne singly on a long stalk from a leaf axil, with five white petals (6–8 mm long), and yellow centers. Fruit small (2 mm long), transversely wrinkled, and with persistent beak (1 mm long).

HABITAT & DISTRIBUTION

Ranunculus longirostris is a native species of cold, deep (2–5 m), ponds and slow streams. It is critically imperiled and **rare** in New Jersey, eligible for protection under the jurisdiction of the Highlands Preservation Area. Restricted to mostly alkaline waters.

Notes: Due to differences of taxonomic opinion, this plant has often been combined with the Eurasian *R. aquatilis* L. in other references. It is similar to *R. trichophyllus*.

Cursed crowfoot is a submersed annual with floating hollow stems rooted at base. Leaves are all basal (arising from submersed base of plant), with long stalks, and floating, deeply lobed blades (divided into 3–5 main segments). Flowers are bisexual, emersed above water on branching clusters, with five, small (2–5 mm long), yellow petals, and green centers. Fruit small (1.5–2 mm long), transversely finely wrinkled, with a minute beak.

HABITAT & DISTRIBUTION

Ranunculus sceleratus is a presumed native of shallow, fresh to brackish waters of marshes, swamps, springs, and tidal marshes. It is scattered throughout New Jersey.

Note: This species is highly variable and adaptable. Described here is the submersed form of the species. More often, plants will be erect, largely emergent, with alternate leaves supported on a hollow stem.

WHITE WATER CROWFOOT *Ranunculus trichophyllus* Chaix

White Water crowfoot is a submersed perennial with elongate, branched stems rooted at lower nodes. Leaves are alternate, submersed, round to semicircular in outline (2–6 cm long), highly divided into thread-like segments (sometimes hairy), and leafstalks (5–20 mm long) with expanded, sheathing bases. Flowers are bisexual, emersed above water, borne singly on a long stalk from a leaf axil, with five white petals (3–5 mm long), and yellow centers. Fruit small (2 mm long) and transversely wrinkled.

HABITAT & DISTRIBUTION

Ranunculus trichophyllus is a native northern species of springs, ponds, and slow streams. It is imperiled and **rare** in New Jersey, eligible for protection under the jurisdiction of the Highlands Preservation Area.

Notes: Due to differences of taxonomic opinion, this plant has often been combined with the Eurasian *R. aquatilis* L. in other references. It is similar to *R. longirostris*.

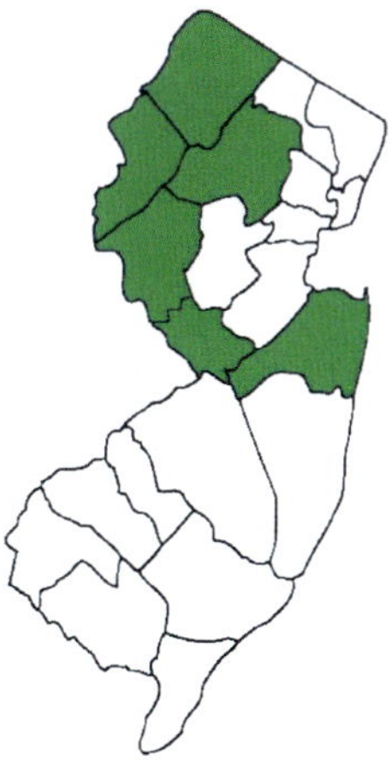

Rorippa — Brassicaceae
Yellow Cress

LAKE YELLOW CRESS *Rorippa aquatica* (Eat.) Palmer & Steyerm.

Lake yellow cress, or Lake cress, is a rooted, perennial with mostly submersed, flaccid stems or with upper ends emergent. Leaves are highly variable, alternate, and of two types (2–6 cm long, 7–15 mm wide): emergent with oval to oblong, simple blades, and submersed leaves highly dissected into fine thread-like divisions. Flowers are bisexual, each with four, white petals (6–10 mm long) and borne on elongated clusters above water. Fruit, if made, are oblong (4–7 mm long, 3 mm wide).

HABITAT & DISTRIBUTION

Rorippa aquatica is a native species of streams, lakes, ponds. It is state-listed as ***endangered*** in New Jersey, but considered *historic.* It occupies clean, calcareous, slow-moving waters that experience natural water level fluctuations. Plants exhibit high levels of vegetative reproduction whereby easily detached submersed leaves (or stems fragments) float, root, and develop into plantlets.

Ruppia — Ruppiaceae
Wigeon-grass

WIGEON-GRASS *Ruppia maritima* L.

Wigeon-grass, or Beaked ditch-grass, is a delicate, rooted, entirely submersed, marine perennial with rhizomes and thread-like stems (<1 mm wide). Leaves are alternate, thread-like (6–10 cm long, <0.5 mm wide), green, blunt-tipped, and fused to translucent stipules which sheath the stems at nodes. Flowers are bisexual, underwater, borne in pairs within a leaf sheath when young. Fruits ovoid (2 mm long), fleshy, short-beaked, each borne on a long stalk (1–2 cm long), in clusters of four at end of a stalk (<25 mm long) which can sometimes coil.

HABITAT & DISTRIBUTION

Ruppia maritima is a native, salt-tolerant plant of ponds, streams, ditches, and tidal pools. Common in shallow, brackish and saline waters of coastal New Jersey.

Note: Can be confused with Horned-pondweed (*Zannichellia palustris*).

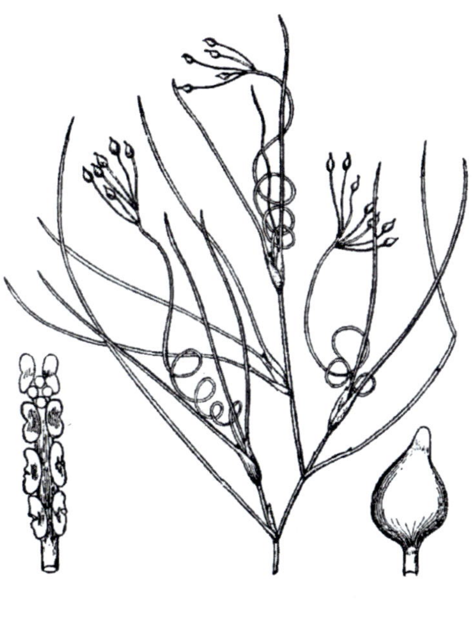

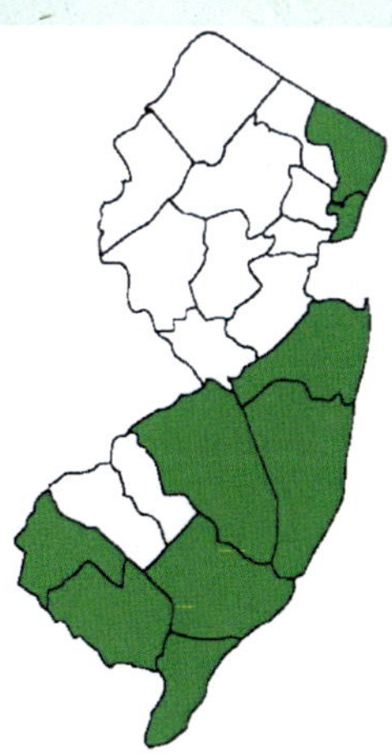

Sagittaria — Alismataceae
Arrowhead

The Arrowheads are rooted, submersed, floating-leaved, or emersed perennials, often with two leaf types on same plant. Leaves arise from a basal rosette and are highly variable in shape, influenced by water depth. Roots are fibrous and bear distinctive cross-walls (septate). Flowers are showy, insect-pollinated, with three white petals, and mostly unisexual (grouped on same plant), clustered in bracted whorls of three around a usually upright stem. The upper whorls are male flowers and lower female/fruiting (or bisexual). Flattened, winged, seed-like fruits (achenes) are crowded into a spherical cluster with persistent sepals at the base.

Seven truly aquatic species, all native, occur in New Jersey. Other Arrowheads (i.e., *S. latifolia* Willd., *S. engelmanniana* J.G. Sm., and *S. australis* (J.G. Sm.) Small) occupy shallow pond margins and wetlands in New Jersey. These emergent species (excluded here), some of which can be very common, have firm, erect, foliage with obvious blades, commonly lobed at their bases.

Key to Species

1. Sepals closely appressed in fruit, enclosing the fruit head; stalk of fruit head recurved........2
1. Sepals spreading or recurved in fruit, not enclosing the fruit head; stalk of fruit head ascending to spreading..4
   2. Leaves thick and spongy (5–10 mm wide), phyllodial; flowering stem emersed with 1–2 whorls of flowers, lower flowers bisexual........................ *S. montevidensis*
   2. Leaves flattened or lens-shaped in cross-section (1–4 mm wide), phyllodial; flowering stem usually floating with 2–10 whorls of flowers, lower flowers female...................3
3. Leaves flattened, ribbon-like, and flexuous (>30 cm long); flowering stems 10–200 cm long; plants often in swift freshwater rivers........................*S. filiformis*
3. Leaves lens-shaped in cross-section, often firm (5–30 cm long); flowering stem 5–40 cm long; plants coastal, mostly in tidal brackish waters........................*S. subulata*
   4. Stamens with filaments covered in short hairs; leaf blades (if present) without lobes......5
   4. Stamens with hairless filaments; leaf blades with basal lobes........................*S. cuneata*
5. Leaves all phyllodial, essentially round in cross-section, generally tapering from near the base to tip.. *S. teres*
5. Leaves either phyllodial and flattened with parallel margins that taper somewhat abruptly to the apex, or with a flattened, expanded blade at tip........................6
   6. Lowest whorl of female flowers borne on 1–3 cm long stalks; flowering stem straight, without a distinct bend; fruits 1.5–2 mm long........................*S. graminea*
   6. Lowest whorl of female flowers stalkless or short-stalked (≤0.5 cm long); flowering stem often with a conspicuous bend at the lowest whorl of flowers; fruits 2.5–4 mm long.........
   .... *S. rigida*

S. graminea

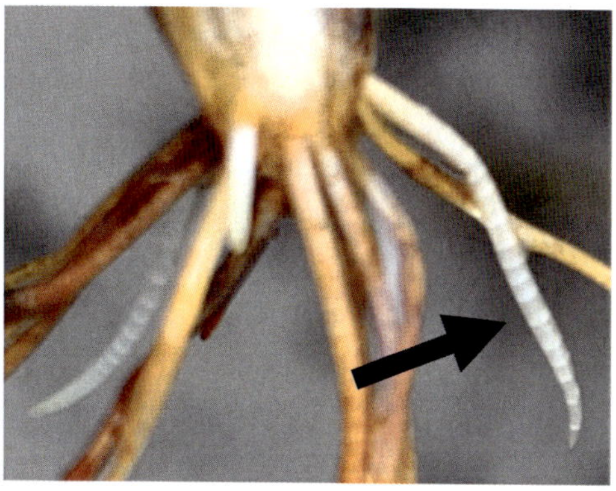

S. teres
S. graminea

S. cuneata

NORTHERN ARROWHEAD *Sagittaria cuneata* Sheldon

Northern arrowhead is a variable species with submerged, flattened (2.5–45 cm long, 1.5–11 cm wide), phyllodial leaves and floating (or emersed) leaves. Floating leaves have expanded blades (75–90 mm long, 35–40 mm wide), usually with basal lobes (shorter than the rest of blade), and 3-sided petioles. Flowers (to 25 mm wide) are emersed, with short petals (7–10 mm long), and recurved sepals that do not enclose the flower or fruit head. Stamens have linear, hairless filaments. Fruit (1.8–2.6 mm, 1.3–2.5 wide) is keeled with a diagnostic short (0.1–0.5 mm long), erect beak at the apex.

HABITAT & DISTRIBUTION

Sagittaria cuneata is a native, northern, perennial species of cold (often calcareous), pools, lakes, and sluggish streams. It is critically imperiled and state-listed as ***endangered*** in New Jersey. Often occurs in open, deep waters (>1 m), and when flowing, plants take on a growth form with mostly long, broad, ribbon-like submersed leaves and relatively few floating leaves.

Notes: Our only arrowhead with truly floating leaves. Similar to the widespread Common arrowhead (*S. latifolia*), but the submersed leaves, floating blades, shorter petals (≤10 mm), and ascending, short (≤5 mm) fruit beak of *S. cuneata* distinguish it. When plants are sterile, its ribbon-like leaves may be difficult to distinguish from *Vallisneria* and *Sparganium*.

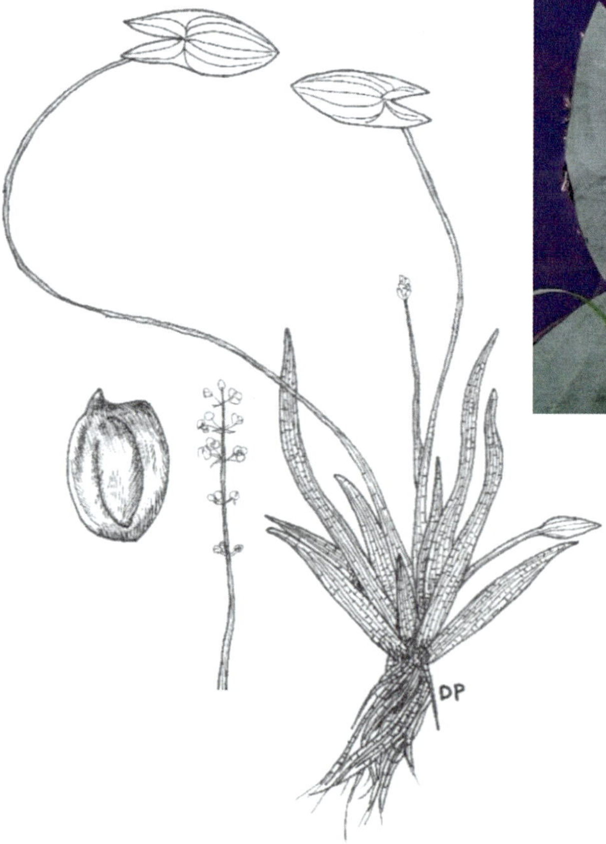

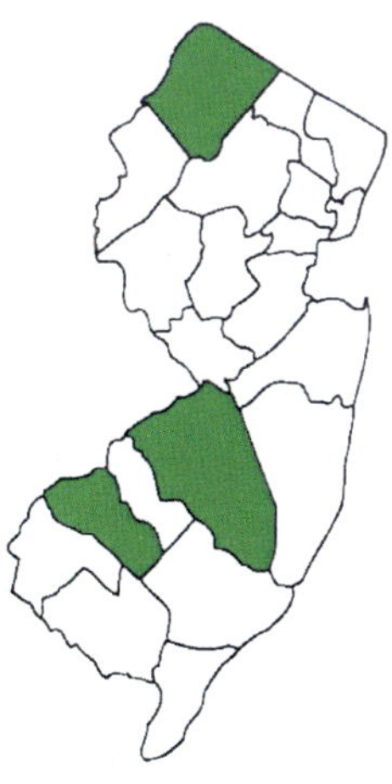

NARROW-LEAVED ARROWHEAD *Sagittaria filiformis* JG Sm.

Narrow-leaved arrowhead is a submerged perennial riverine plant. Leaves are submersed, ribbon-like, and long (30–250 cm long, 0.1–1.5 cm wide), or sometimes floating at ends with a dilated linear-ovate blade (to 0.5 cm wide). Flowers (to 30 mm wide) borne on a long (10–200 cm), usually floating, stem with 4–10 whorls of flowers. Sepals are erect and closely appressed in female flowers, enclosing the flower (or fruit head). Stamens have dilated, hairless filaments. Stalk of fruit head recurved, 1.5–4.5 cm long. Fruits have an erect (1 mm) lateral beak.

HABITAT & DISTRIBUTION

Sagittaria filiformis is a native Coastal Plain species. It occupies shallow to deep reaches of slow to swift flowing waters. Rare and state-listed as ***endangered*** in New Jersey, considered *historic*. **Notes**: This species is frequently found sterile and not known to produce fruit in our area.

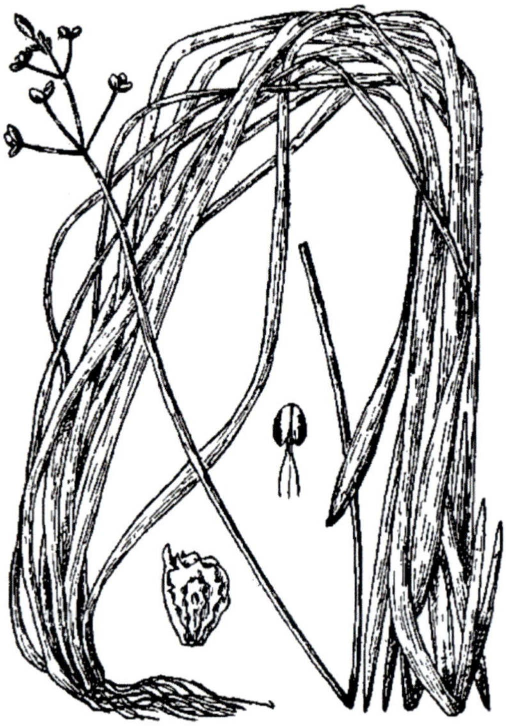

GRASS-LEAVED ARROWHEAD *Sagittaria graminea* Michx.

Grass-leaved arrowhead is a submerged (or emergent) rhizomatous perennial. Leaves are submersed, flattened, and phyllodial (6.5–35 cm long, 0.5–1 cm wide) with parallel margins that taper somewhat abruptly to the tip, or can have emersed leaves with a flattened, expanded blade (linear to linear-oval in shape, 2.5–17.5 cm long, 0.2–4 cm wide) lacking lobes. Flowers (to 23 mm wide) borne on an emergent, straight (without a distinct bend), stem with 1–12 whorls of flowers. Sepals are spreading or recurved in fruit, not enclosing the fruit head. Lowest whorl of female flowers borne on stalks (1–3 cm long). Stamens have dilated filaments covered in short hairs. Stalk of fruit head ascending to spreading. Fruits have an erect (0.2 mm) lateral beak.

HABITAT & DISTRIBUTION

Sagittaria graminea is a native species of ponds, rivers, and freshwater tidal marshes. Widespread in New Jersey. In our region, it often occurs as submerged rosettes without flowers/fruit.

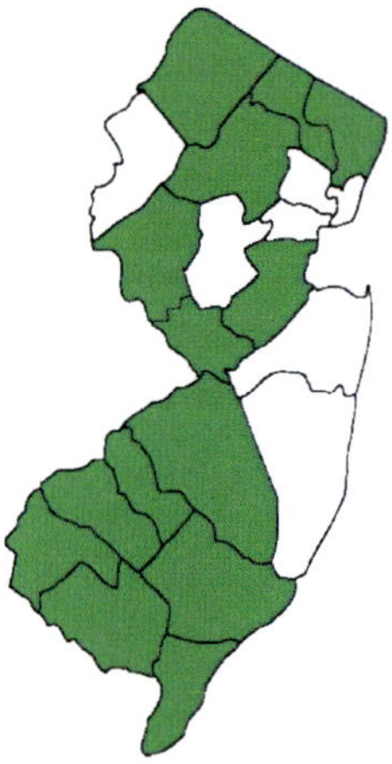

SPONGY-LEAVED ARROWHEAD *Sagittaria montevidensis* Cham. & Schlecht.

Spongy-leaved arrowhead, or Estuary arrowhead, is a submersed, diminutive, annual plant. Leaves are submersed, thick, spongy, and strap-like (4–17 cm long, 0.5–1 cm wide). Leaves sometimes have expanded, spongy, lance-shaped blades. Flowers (ca. 20 mm wide) borne on an emersed stem, shorter than the leaves, singly or with 1–2 whorls of flowers. The lowest flowers are bisexual (with ring of sterile stamens). Sepals are erect and closely appressed in female flowers, enclosing the flower (or fruit head). Stamens have linear, hairless filaments. Stalk of fruit head thickened and recurved, 0.5–4.2 cm long. Fruits have a horizontal lateral beak (0.4–0.8 mm).

HABITAT & DISTRIBUTION

Sagittaria montevidensis is a native, coastal plant found on mudflats and shores of freshwater tidal rivers, typically exposed on mud at low tide. It is **rare** in New Jersey coastal areas, eligible for protection under the jurisdiction of the Highlands Preservation Area.

Note: The plants described here represent ssp. *spongiosa* (Engelm.) Bogin. (= *S. calycina* var. *spongiosa*) of brackish tidal waters. Hooded Arrowhead is the closely related non-tidal freshwater subsp. *calycina* (Engelm.) Bogin. (= *S. calycina* var. *calycina*) which is also rare in New Jersey. It is typically more emergent in growth, not exposed at low tides, with broad, non-spongy, leaf blades.

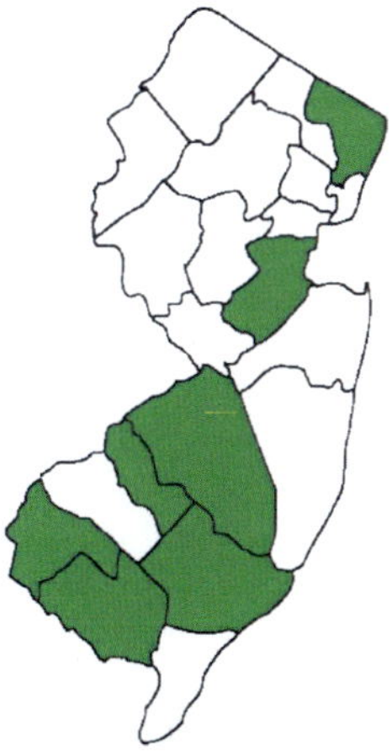

SESSILE-FRUITED ARROWHEAD *Sagittaria rigida* Pursh

Sessile-fruited arrowhead is a submerged (or emergent) perennial with slender stolons. Leaves are submersed, stiff, flattened, and phyllodial (30–70 cm long, 0.5–1 cm wide) with parallel margins that taper somewhat abruptly to the tip, or can be emersed with an expanded blade (linear to oval in shape, 5–15 cm long, 0.6–12 cm wide) commonly lacking lobes. Flowers (to 30 mm wide) borne on an emergent stem, conspicuously bent at the lowest whorl of flowers, with 2–8 whorls of flowers. Sepals are recurved and not enclosing the flower or fruit head. Lowest whorl of female flowers stalkless or borne on very short stalks (≤0.5 cm long). Stamens have dilated filaments covered in short hairs. Fruits have a recurved, lateral beak (0.8–1.4 mm).

HABITAT & DISTRIBUTION

Sagittaria rigida is a native species with highly variable leaves (influenced by water depth) which occurs in shallow to deep, fresh or brackish, waters of rivers, ponds, and pools.

Note: When plants occur only as submersed, sterile rosettes it is impossible to distinguish from Grass-leaved arrowhead (*S. graminea*).

AWL-LEAVED ARROWHEAD *Sagittaria subulata* (L.) Buch.

Awl-leaved arrowhead is a submerged perennial, low-growing, tidal plant. Leaves are submersed, phyllodial (5–30 cm long, 0.1–0.4 cm wide), and lens-shaped in cross-section (i.e., two convex surfaces), sometimes with a linear-ovate blade (to 1.5 cm wide). Flowers (to 12 mm wide) borne on a floating stem (5–40 cm long), with 2–7 whorls of flowers. Sepals are erect and closely appressed in female flowers, enclosing the flower (or fruit head). Stamens have dilated, hairless filaments. Stalk of fruit head recurved. Fruits have an erect (0.4 mm) lateral beak.

HABITAT & DISTRIBUTION

Sagittaria subulata is a native coastal species, often submersed at high tide and exposed during low tides. It occupies shallow, estuarine brackish waters (salinity 0.5–18 ppt) and can be mat-forming.

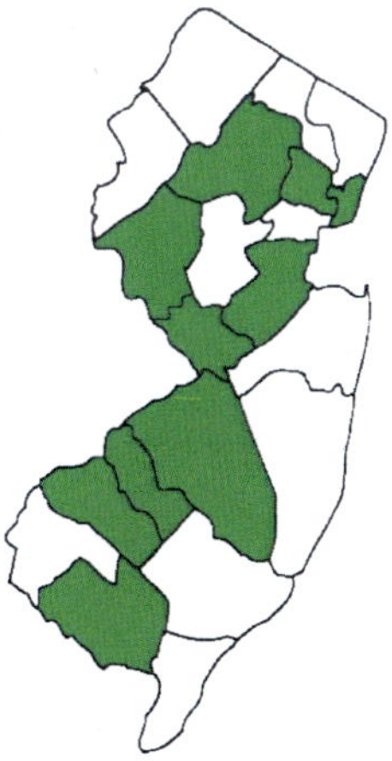

Quill-leaved arrowhead is a submerged (or emergent) perennial with slender stolons. Leaves are submersed, rigid, linear (3.5–18.5 cm long, 0.15–0.4 cm wide), and essentially round in cross-section, thickest at base generally tapering to the tip, or can have longer leaves (to 60 cm) with emersed tips. Flowers (to 15 mm wide) borne on an emergent, straight (without a distinct bend), stem with 1–4 whorls of flowers. Sepals are spreading or recurved in fruit, not enclosing the fruit head; Lowest whorl of female flowers borne on stalks (1–3 cm long). Stamens have dilated filaments covered in short hairs. Stalk of fruit head ascending to spreading. Fruits have an erect (0.3–0.4 mm) to horizontal beak.

HABITAT & DISTRIBUTION

Sagittaria teres is a native Coastal Plain species of mostly sandy, acidic ponds. It is imperiled in New Jersey, state-listed as ***endangered***. Plants can be locally abundant and often inconspicuous as non-flowering, submersed rosettes.

Notes: Most similar to Grass-leaved arrowhead (*S. graminea*), especially when occurring as submersed basal rosettes, but leaves are always round in cross-section and never form blades.

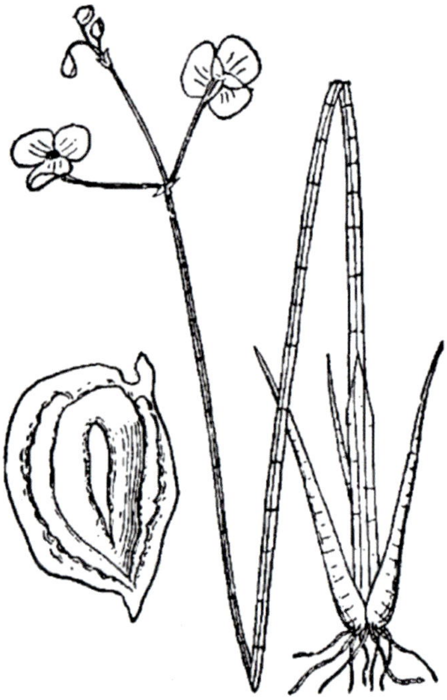

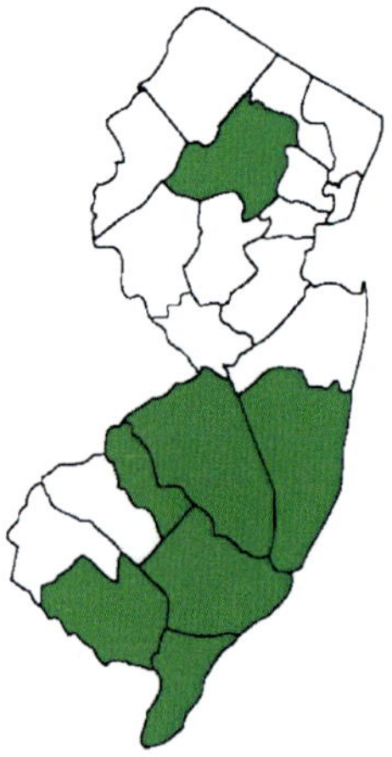

Salvinia — Salviniaceae
Water Spangles

WATER SPANGLES *Salvinia minima* Baker

Water Spangles, or Watermoss, is a small, free-floating, aquatic fern with horizontal hairy stems (to 6 cm long), and spreading leaves, some of which resemble branched roots. Floating leaf blades are round (1–1.5 cm long), flat, dark green, covered in stiff, branched hairs, and appear opposite (a third feathery root-like leaf is submerged). Plants reproduce by spores, borne on submersed leaves.

HABITAT & DISTRIBUTION

Salvinia minima is a non-native, tropical fern that may be sporadically **introduced** or escaped into stagnant waters. This mat-forming species is commonly cultivated as a water garden or aquarium plant.

Notes: This plant can rapidly colonize a site but cannot survive winter in our area. The branched surface hairs make the floating leaves highly hydrophobic.

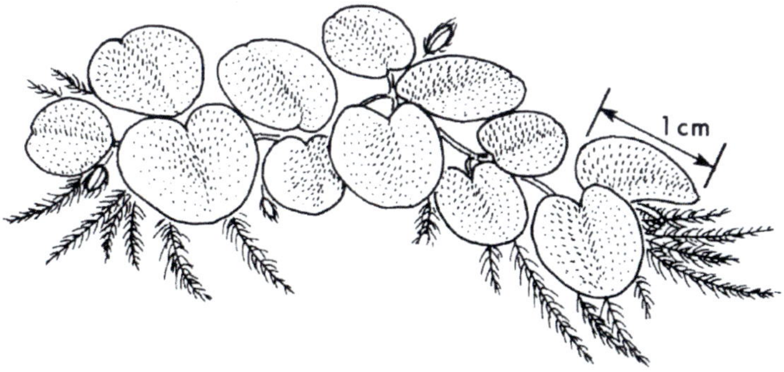

Schoenoplectus — Cyperaceae
Bulrush

WATER BULRUSH *Schoenoplectus subterminalis* (Torr.) Soják.

Water bulrush is a rooted, grass-like, perennial, with submerged, flaccid, thread-like leaves clustered along slender (1 mm diameter), soft rhizomes and erect flowering stems. Leaves are alternate, submerged (or tips floating), 3–20, thin (to 1 mm wide), flexuous, with sheathing bases. Flowers are minute, borne in a small (4–5 mm long), straw-colored cluster at tip of a slender, upright stem (20–150 cm long), extending above water surface. A single, leaf-like (2–20 mm long) bract is attached below flower cluster, appearing like a continuation of the stem. Fruit is a seed-like (2.5 mm long), 3-sided achene.

HABITAT & DISTRIBUTION

Schoenoplectus subterminalis is a native species of ponds, bogs, and slow-moving streams. It is widespread in New Jersey.

Notes: This plant typically forms dense colonies and can colonize water to 1 m deep. Sometimes leaves can be erect and C-shaped in cross-section. Similar to Robbins' spikerush (*Eleocharis robbinsii*).

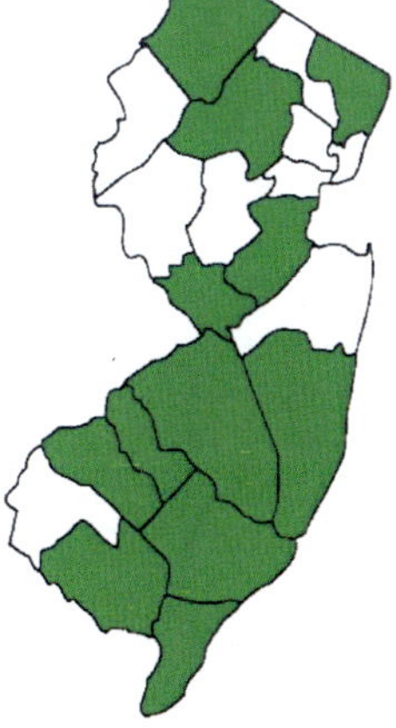

Sclerolepis — Asteraceae
Bogbutton

PINK BOGBUTTON — *Sclerolepis uniflora* (Walt.) Britt., Sterns & Poggenb.

Pink bogbutton is a rooted, perennial, with creeping, flexuous, submerged or floating (erect and emersed if stranded), sparingly branched stems (to 60 cm long) and slender rhizomes. Leaves are whorled (in groups of 3, 4, or 6), stalkless, linear (7–23 mm long, 0.3–2 mm wide), toothless, 1-veined, and tipped with a tiny callus. Flowers are borne, above water, in a single, round, pink to white, cluster (head) at end of an erect, flowering stem (2–6 cm long).

HABITAT & DISTRIBUTION

Sclerolepis uniflora is a native species of shallow pools, lakes, ditches, or bogs. It is **rare** and imperiled in New Jersey.

Notes: This mat-forming plant is typically submerged and only vegetative, but when stranded on exposed sandy or peaty shores it becomes upright, more condensed, and flowers. Plants may also be found free-floating.

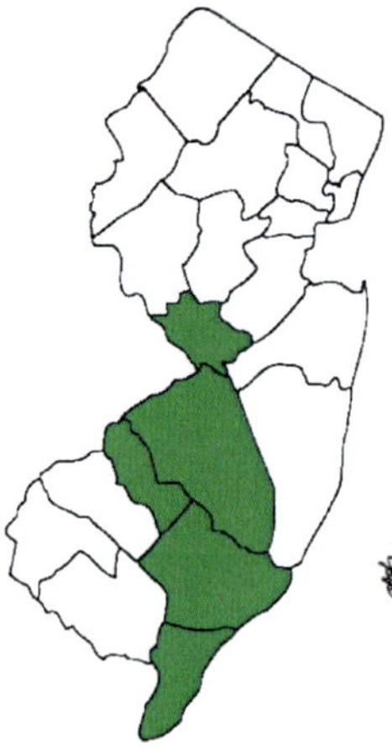

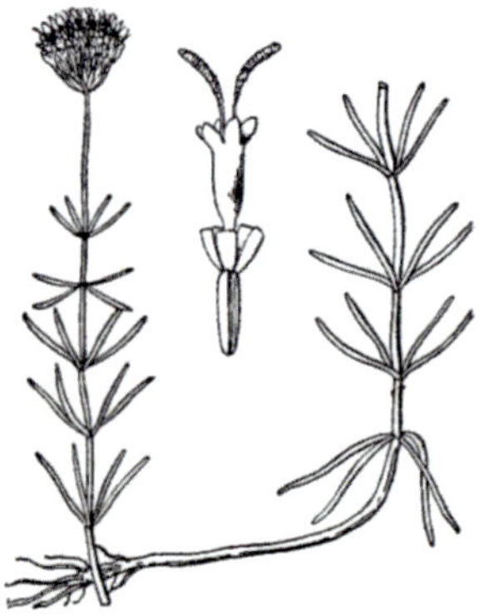

Sparganium — Typhaceae
Bur-reed

The Bur-reeds are rooted, perennials with buried rhizomes and long (10–50+ cm), floating stems. Leaves are submersed or partially floating, long (0.5–1+ m), linear (2–10 mm wide), flaccid, and generally flattened. Flowers are small, wind-pollinated, and unisexual (both on same plant), grouped into dense, spherical clusters (heads) held above water. Female flowers occupy the lower positions on the flowering stem and male flowers the uppermost positions. Fruits are a spherical aggregate of small, hard, beaked drupes.

Three aquatic species, all native, with leaves and flower structures usually floating occur in New Jersey. Mature fruits are needed for correct identification. Several other Bur-reed species (e.g., *S. americanum* Nutt., *S. androcladum* (Engelm.) Morong, *S. emersum* Rehmann, and *S. eurycarpum* Engelm.) also occur in New Jersey and occupy wet shores or shallow waters. These emergent wetland species (not detailed here), however, are generally stout, with mostly stiff, erect, and emersed stems, and emersed, distinctly keeled leaves.

Key to Species

1. Flowering stems with 1 cluster of male flowers; fruit clusters 5–12 mm in diam.; beak of fruit 0.5–1.5 mm long... *S. natans*
1. Flowering stems with 3+ clusters of male flowers; fruit clusters 15–25 mm in diam.; beak of fruit 1.5–3.5 mm long..2
   2. Flowering stems branched; beak of mature fruit flattened and strongly curved; leaves 4–10 mm wide and flat...*S. fluctuans*
   2. Flowering stems unbranched; beak of mature fruit generally rounded and straight; leaves 2–5 mm wide with surface slightly convex.. *S. angustifolium*

S. angustifolium

NARROW-LEAVED BUR-REED *Sparganium angustifolium* Michx.

Narrow-leaved bur-reed is a submersed, rooted perennial. Leaves are submersed, with floating ends, long (to 1 m), ribbon-like (2–5 mm wide), with a slightly rounded surface. Flowering stems are unbranched with 2–5 female flower clusters, the lowest one on a stalk arising from the axil of a leafy bract. Male flower clusters number 4–10+. Fruit clusters 15–25 mm in diam. Fruits dull, reddish to brown (3–7 mm long) with a straight or slightly curved beak 1.5–2 mm long.

HABITAT & DISTRIBUTION

Sparganium angustifolium is a native species of shallow lakes and slow streams. It is state-listed as ***endangered*** in New Jersey, considered *historic*.

Note: Similar to the rare Simple-stemmed bur-reed (*S. emersum*) which on occasion can have flaccid and floating leaves. Usually *S. emersum* has broader (6–12 mm wide), erect and emergent leaves which have a prominent keel along the lower surface of distal portions. Its fruit beak is also longer (2–6 mm).

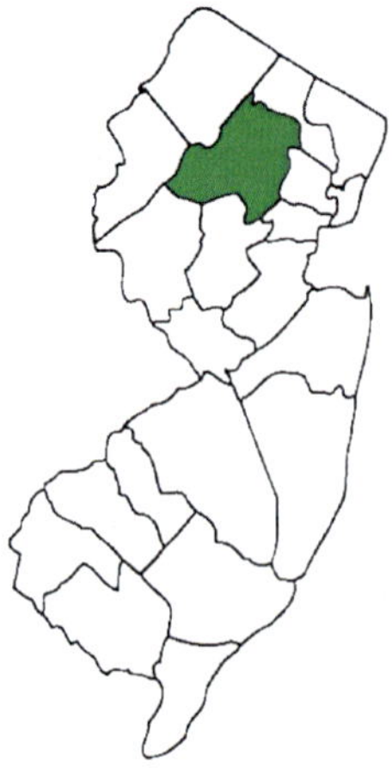

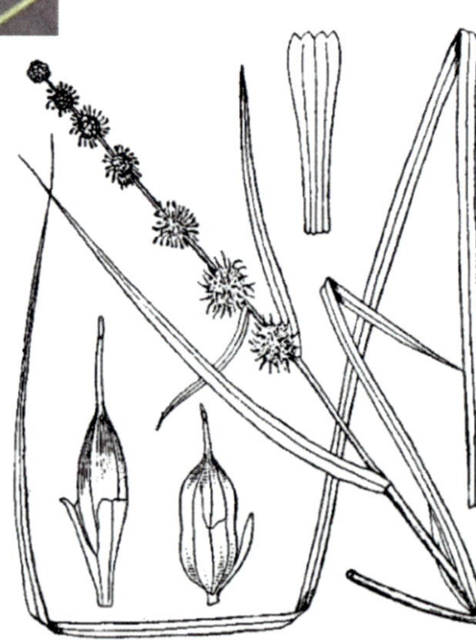

FLOATING BUR-REED *Sparganium fluctuans* (Morong) Robinson

Floating bur-reed is a submersed, limp, rooted perennial. Leaves are submersed, with floating ends, strap-shaped (to 1.5 m long, 4–10 mm wide), and flat (but slightly keeled at base). Flowering stems are branching with 2–4 female flower clusters and 3–6 male flower clusters. Fruit clusters 15–23 mm in diam. Fruits dull, dark reddish-brown (3–5 mm long) with a flattened, strongly curved beak 2–3.5 mm long.

HABITAT & DISTRIBUTION

Sparganium fluctuans is a native species of shallow, still lakes or slow rivers. It is reported to reach the southern limit of its range in New Jersey. Occurrences are poorly documented.

Notes: Its branched flowering stem is similar to that of both *S. americanum* and *S. androcladum*. These two species, however, typically have emersed, erect leaves that are strongly keeled on undersides.

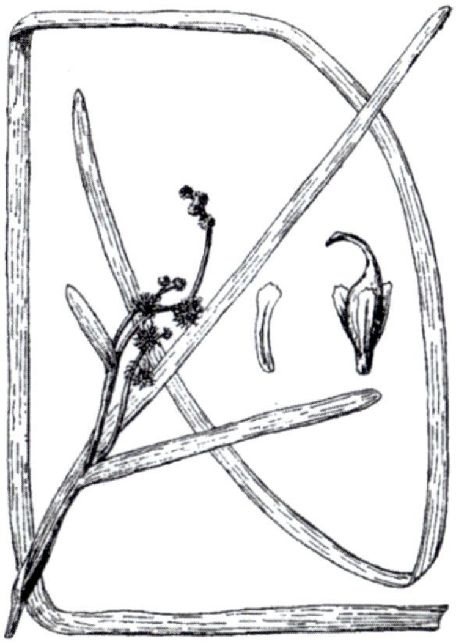

ARCTIC BUR-REED *Sparganium natans* L.

Arctic bur-reed is a submersed, rooted perennial. Leaves are submersed, with floating ends, grass-like (to 1.5 m long, 2–7 mm wide), and flat. Flowering stems are unbranched with 1–3 female flower clusters and only 1 male flower cluster. Fruit clusters 5–12 mm in diam. Fruits dull, greenish or brown (3–4 mm long) with a slender beak 0.5–1.5 mm long.

HABITAT & DISTRIBUTION

Sparganium natans is a native, northern species of shallow lakes, peatlands, and slow streams. It is critically imperiled in New Jersey and state-listed as ***endangered***. This plant has been called *S. minimum* (Hartm.) Wallr. in some references.

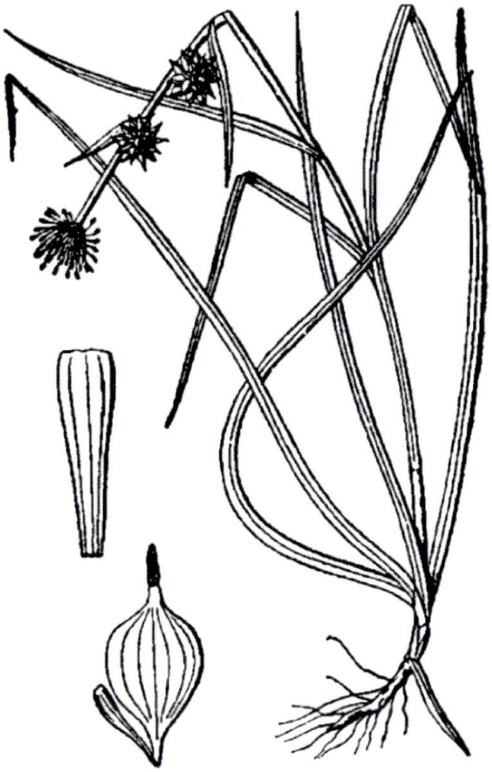

Spirodela — Araceae
Duck-meal

COMMON DUCK-MEAL *Spirodela polyrhiza* (L.) Schleid.

Common duck-meal is a diminutive, perennial, floating on water surface. Its body, or thallus (not differentiated into stem and leaf), is small (2–10 mm long, 1.3–10 mm wide), flattened, rounded to egg-shaped, with 5–21 veins and often a purple dot on top surface, and solid red-purple beneath. Slender, 7–21, unbranched roots (to 30 mm long) are clustered on lower surface extending into water. Flowers and fruits are minute, rarely seen. Turions formed late in season.

HABITAT & DISTRIBUTION

Spirodela polyrhiza is a native species of ditches, ponds, lakes, and slow rivers. It is widespread in New Jersey.

Notes: Like most duckweeds, vegetative reproduction is extensive. Usually, multiple plants are connected and intermixed with other duckweeds (*Lemna* and *Wolffia*).

Similar to the non-native Spotted duck-meal [*Landoltia punctata* (GFW Mey.) Les & Crawford)] which has only 2–5 roots, 5–7 obscure veins, and a smaller thallus (2–5 mm long) lacking a purple spot. This introduced species is not recorded for New Jersey but is in waters of nearby Pennsylvania and Delaware.

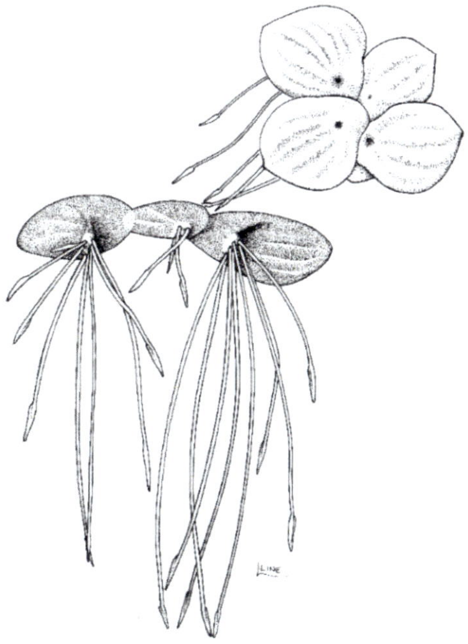

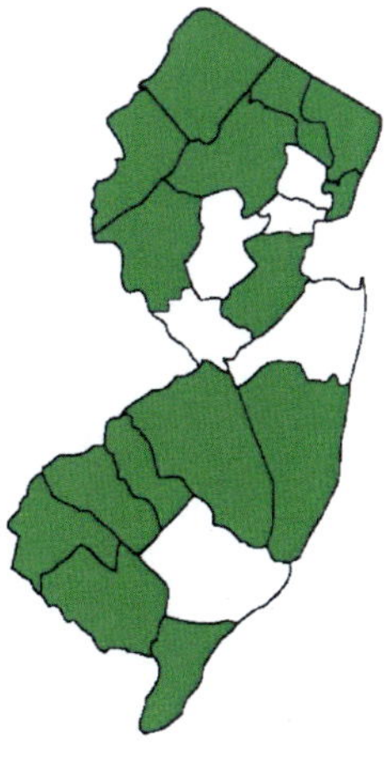

Stuckenia — Potamogetonaceae
False pondweed

The False pondweeds are submersed, rooted, perennials with slender, flexuous, much-branched, stems, and slender, creeping rhizomes bearing white tubers (1–2 cm long) at ends. Leaves are submersed, alternate, very narrow (≤1 mm wide), mostly 1-veined, channeled, opaque, and rigid. At the base of each leaf, there is a stipule that forms a cylindrical sheath around the stem. A portion of the stipule (greater than two-thirds of its length) is fused to base of leaf, with the remaining unfused portion extending as a ligule. Flowers are small, individually inconspicuous, and clustered in cylindrical spikes at ends of long (to 15 cm), flexible, stems floating on water surface. Fruits are small, hard, seed-like, achenes.

Two species are reported for New Jersey, both typical of alkaline, calcareous waters. The abundant underground tubers and fruits are an important food for waterfowl.

Key to Species

1. Leaves sharp pointed; stipular sheaths open with overlapping edges; fruit yellow-brown to brown (mostly 3–4.5 mm long) with a distinct beak (1 mm) .... *S. pectinatus*
1. Leaves minutely blunt or notched; stipular sheaths with margins fused at base; fruit dark brown (mostly 2–3 mm long) beakless.. *S. filiformis*

THREAD-LEAF FALSE PONDWEED *Stuckenia filiformis* Pers.

Thread-leaf false pondweed has leaves narrowly linear (1–15 cm long, 0.2–0.5 mm wide), channeled, mid-veined, stiff, and tapered to a more or less blunt tip. Stipules (0.2–0.5 mm wide) are attached to base of leaf for most of their length, forming a tightly closed sheath (10–40 mm long) around the stem, the free tip extending as a ligule 2–20 mm long. Flowers are clustered in a cylindrical spike (1–5 cm long) of 2–6 interrupted whorls of flowers, at end of a slender, flexuous, submersed stalk (2–15 cm). Fruits are mostly 2–3 mm long, dark brown, beakless, with a low round keel.

HABITAT & DISTRIBUTION

Stuckenia filiformis is a native plant of cold, shallow (<1 m) or deep, calcareous or brackish waters of lakes, ponds, and slow streams. More common in regions to the north, it reportedly reaches the southern end of its range in New Jersey where it is poorly documented.

Note: Plants growing in deep water with a strong current can be more robust than those in still water. This species is sometimes referenced as *Potamogeton filiformis* Pers.

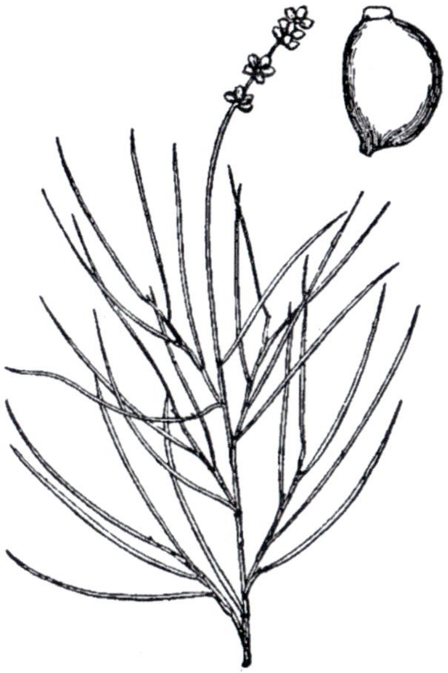

Sago false pondweed *Stuckenia pectinata* (L.) Böerner

Sago false pondweed has much-branched stems with numerous fan-like sets of leaves. Leaves linear (3–15 cm long, 0.2–1 mm wide), channeled, mid-veined, stiff, and tapered to a sharp-pointed tip. Stipules (1–2 cm long) are attached to base of leaf for most of their length, forming an open sheath (0.8-1.1 cm) around the stem, the free tip extending as a small ligule (0.8 mm long). Flowers are clustered in a floating, cylindrical spike (1.5–3 cm long) of 3–5 interrupted whorls of flowers, at end of a slender, flexuous, submersed stalk (3–12 cm). Fruits are mostly 3–4.5 mm long, distinctly beaked (0.5–1 mm long), brown to yellow-brown, with a round keel.

Habitat & Distribution

Stuckenia pectinata is a native plant of shallow streams, rivers, including tidal brackish waters, and calcareous lakes.

Note: Colonies can form dense, bushy masses. This species is sometimes referenced as *Potamogeton pectinatus* L.

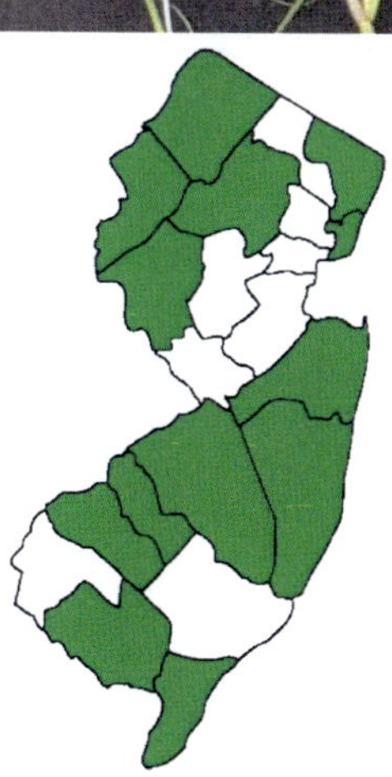

Trapa — Lythraceae
Water-chestnut

WATER-CHESTNUT *Trapa natans* L.

Water-chestnut, or Caltrop, is a rooted, annual plant with elongated (to 1 m), flexuous stems terminating with a floating rosette (to 50 cm diam.) of triangular leaves. Leaves are of two types: floating leaves are alternate, green (4–6 cm long, 4–8 cm wide), with triangular to diamond-shaped, broadly toothed blades, and swollen and spongy stalks. Submersed leaves are alternate or opposite, pinnately divided into linear (2–18 cm long), root-like segments. Flowers are bisexual, borne singly, above water, from a floating leaf axil, with 4 white petals. Fruit is dark, dry, nut-like (2–3 cm long, 2–4.5 cm wide) with 4 stout, spreading spines.

HABITAT & DISTRIBUTION

Trapa natans is a non-native species of lakes and margins of slow rivers. It is widespread in northern New Jersey where it is **invasive**. Native to Eurasia, it was first introduced into North America as an ornamental plant in the late 1800s.

Notes: This is a highly distinctive plant with its inflated, buoyant, rosette of leaves and hard, black, spiny fruits. It prefers nutrient-rich, shallow (<2 m) waters and can reach high densities. This species is highly fecund, grows rapidly, and exhibits long seed dormancy. Floating rosettes can detach and float freely.

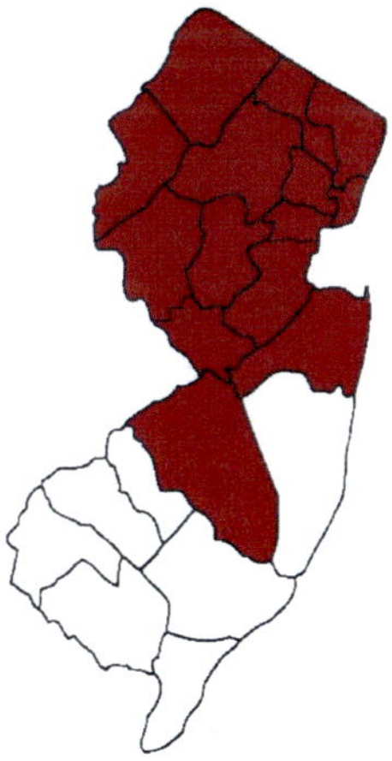

Utricularia — Lentibulariaceae
Bladderwort

The Bladderworts are delicate, mostly submersed, carnivorous perennials or annuals with narrow, rootless, green stems. Plants are mostly free-floating in water or in some cases anchored to a saturated substrate by buried branches. Leaves (actually branches simulating leaves) are green, mostly divided into narrowly linear segments, and bearing tiny, sac-like, animal traps (i.e., bladders). Flowers are showy, mostly yellow, or white to pink-purple in a few species, and borne singly or clustered at end of an elongated, unbranched stalk (peduncle) elevated above water surface. Petals are asymmetrical, united, parted to form an upper and lower (larger) lip, and a spur (i.e., elongated hollow, sac-like appendage). Fruits are rounded capsules. Many species form compact winter buds (turions) late in the season.

Fourteen species occur in New Jersey, of which one is non-native. Without flowers present, proper species identification can be difficult.

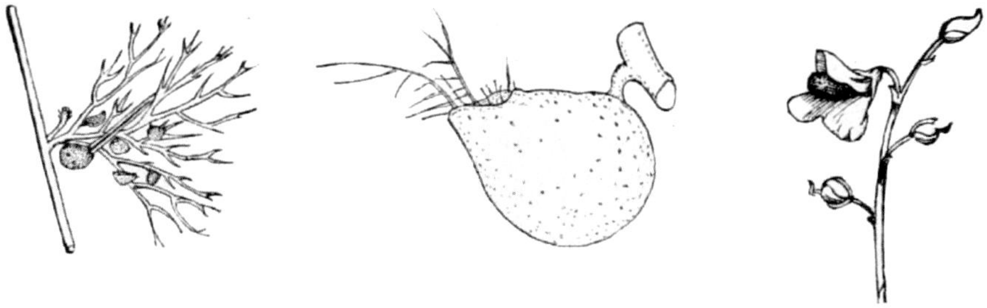

Key to Species

1. Flowers creamy white, 1–2.5 mm long; flower stalks very reduced (2–10 mm long), usually curved; stems thread-like and branched, lacking leaves, but bearing bladders........*U. olivacea*
1. Flowers yellow, pink, or purple, 5–20 mm long; flower stalks well-developed, supporting a 1–many flowers; stems with leaves present (sometimes absent in the terrestrial species) with or without bladders..........2
   2. Leaves few, unbranched and thread-like (or very narrowly linear), completely or mostly hidden in substrate; plants appearing terrestrial and only apparent when flowering; bladders few, 0.2–1.1 mm long..........3
   2. Leaves numerous, finely forked 1-many times, all or mostly on stems floating under water, conspicuous; bladders numerous, 1–5 mm long.......... 6
3. Petals purple; one flower per stem; scale-like bracts on flowering stem paired and fused; leaves with ≥1 transverse partitions.......... *U. resupinata*
3. Petals yellow, 2–15 flowers per stem; scale-like bracts on flowering stem alternate; leaves without transverse partitions..........4
   4. Flower stalk 4–15 mm long; petal spur usually reddish, up to 5 mm long, pressed against lower lip; fruits 1–1.5 mm long.......... *U. subulata*
   4. Flower stalk 1–2 mm long; petal spur never reddish, up to 14 mm long, pointing downward; fruits 2–5 mm long..........5
5. Flower spur 7–14 mm long, and lower lip 9–16 mm long; flowers (2–6) are crowded towards end of a stout, green to yellowish-green, peduncle; capsules 4–5 mm long.......... *U. cornuta*
5. Flower spur 2–8 mm long, and lower lip 7–12 mm long; flowers (2–15) not crowded on wiry, greenish purple to purple, peduncle; capsules 2–3.5 mm long.......... *U. juncea*

6. Flowering stem with a whorl of spongy, inflated branches near water surface functioning as floats..........7

6. Flowering stem without strongly inflated branches..........8

7. Flowering stem 10–30 cm tall with 9–14 bright yellow flowers; floats 3–8 cm long and up to 8 mm wide, gradually tapered toward base.......... *U. inflata*

7. Flowering stem 3–5 cm tall with 1–7 dull yellow flowers; floats 1–4 cm long and 2–4 mm wide, with mostly parallel sides.......... *U. radiata*

8. Leaves all whorled; bladders borne at tips of leaf segments and lacking external hairs; flowers pink-purple.......... *U. purpurea*

8. Leaves mostly alternate or crowded at base; bladders scattered on sides of leaf segments and with whisker-like hairs at the mouth; flowers yellow..........9

9. Leaf segments distinctly flat, with a visible midrib; floral bracts lobed at base..........10

9. Leaf segments fine and hair-like, without a midrib; floral bracts not lobed..........11

10. Green leaf-like branches (above substrate) lacking bladders and whitish branches (buried in substrate) bearing bladders; leaf segments spine-toothed; bladders 1.5–4 mm long.......... *U. intermedia*

10. Green leaf-like branches (above substrate) bearing some bladders; leaf segments not spine-toothed; bladders 1–2 mm.......... *U. minor*

11. Plants small and simple, <15 cm long; principal leaves mostly forked 1–4 times, up to 1 cm long, the leaf segments without marginal spines; flowering stem 1–6 flowered..........12

11. Plants stout and bushy, 30–100 cm long; principal leaves mostly forked 5–17 times, 1–6.5 cm long, the leaf segments with minute marginal spines; flowering stem 2–14 flowered..........13

12. All leaf-like branches green and bladder-bearing.......... *U. gibba*

12. Leaf-like branches of two types: those in water are green, with few bladders, and those buried in the substrate are whitish, bearing many bladders.......... *U. striata*

13. Leaves 1.5–6.5 cm long, coarse, usually forked 6–17 times; bladders up to 6 mm long; flowering stem 6–14 flowered, with 1–3 scales below the lowest flowers; underwater flowers lacking; turions 5.5–13.5 mm thick.......... *U. vulgaris*

13. Leaves 1–2 cm long, extremely delicate and limp, forked 5–9 times; bladders up to 2 mm long; flowering stem 2–8 flowered, without scales below the lowest flowers; bud-like, underwater flowers also borne singly on short, submersed stalks; turions 2–5 mm thick.......... *U. geminiscapa*

U. geminiscapa

U. vulgaris

U. purpurea

U. gibba

U. purpurea

HORNED BLADDERWORT *Utricularia cornuta* Michx.

Horned bladderwort is an inconspicuous perennial. Leaves are alternate, few, slender and unbranched (needle-like), and mostly hidden within the surface of a wet soil substrate. Leaves bear few, tiny (0.2–1.1 mm long) bladders also buried in the substrate. Flowers are bright yellow, very fragrant, each with a short stalk (1–2 mm long), a long (7–14 mm) spur pointed downward, and a lower lip 9–16 mm long. Flowers are crowded 2–6 on an upright, stout, green to yellowish-green, peduncle (10–25 cm tall) with a few, widely spaced, alternate, scale-like bracts. Capsules are 4–5 mm long. No turions are produced.

HABITAT & DISTRIBUTION

Utricularia cornuta is a native species of acidic waters of bogs, pond shores, and river margins. In New Jersey, it is most frequent in Pine Barrens.

Note: One of the so-called "terrestrial" species of bladderwort, it is only apparent when flowering. Plants can be abundant, and form thin, tangled mats on a substrate which can dislodge and float.

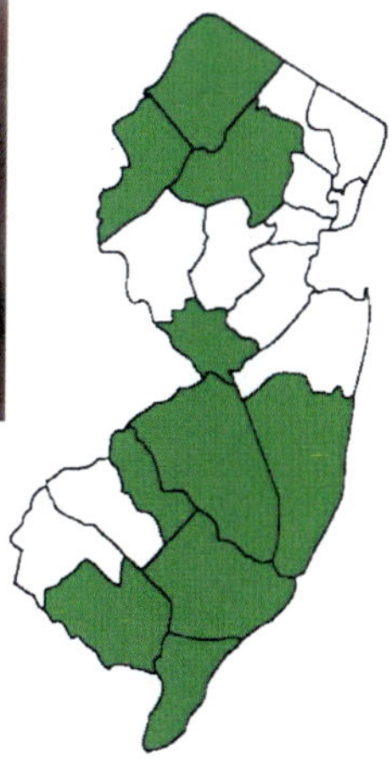

MIXED BLADDERWORT *Utricularia geminiscapa* Benj.

Mixed bladderwort is a submersed, bushy, perennial with slender, elongated stems. Leaves are alternate, delicate (1–2 cm long), usually forked 5–9 times into limp, hair-like segments, with a few minute, marginal spines. Leaves bear numerous bladders (1–2 mm long). Flowers are yellow, with lower lip 5–8 mm long, and borne 2–8 on an upright peduncle (5–15 cm tall). In late summer, bud-like, petal-less flowers are also borne singly at the tips of short (2.5–7.5 mm long), submersed stems. Turions are small (2–5 mm wide), loose, green, and lacking hairs.

HABITAT & DISTRIBUTION

Utricularia geminiscapa is a native species of, usually shallow, acidic, peatlands, pools, ponds, lakes, and streams. It is widespread in New Jersey.

Note: Similar to smaller plants of Common bladderwort (*U. vulgaris*) but overall reduced and finer, with submersed flowers, fewer emersed flowers, and smaller turions.

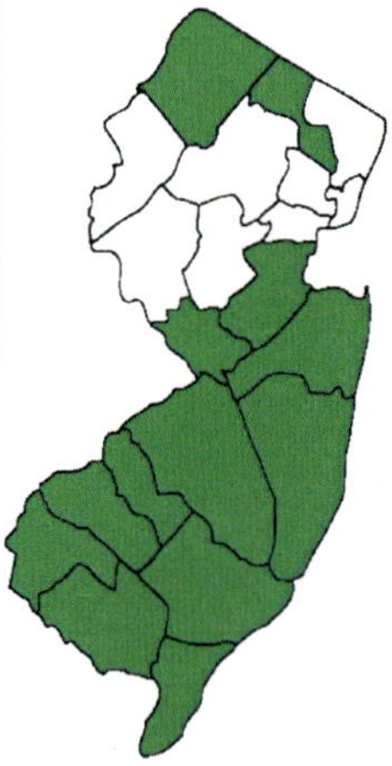

CREEPING BLADDERWORT *Utricularia gibba* L.

Creeping bladderwort is a delicate, submersed (or creeping), annual or perennial, with slender, short (to 10 cm long), intertwined, green stems. Leaves are alternate, short (rarely >5 mm long), mostly forked 1–2 times, and bear few, small (1 mm), bladders on sides. Flowers are yellow, with a blunt spur about half the length of the lower lip (5–6 mm long) and borne 1–2 on an upright peduncle (5–10 cm tall). Capsules are 2–3 mm long. Turions are not produced.

HABITAT & DISTRIBUTION

Utricularia gibba is a native species of shallow lakes and ponds. It is **rare** in New Jersey, eligible for protection under the jurisdiction of the Highlands Preservation Area and Pinelands Commission.

Notes: Commonly found as free-floating, intricately tangled, masses, but flowering is usually limited to plants in very shallow water (2–3 cm deep) or those stranded on wet, exposed shores. Two-flower bladderwort (*U. biflora* Lam.), which is state-listed as an *endangered* species in New Jersey, is combined here.

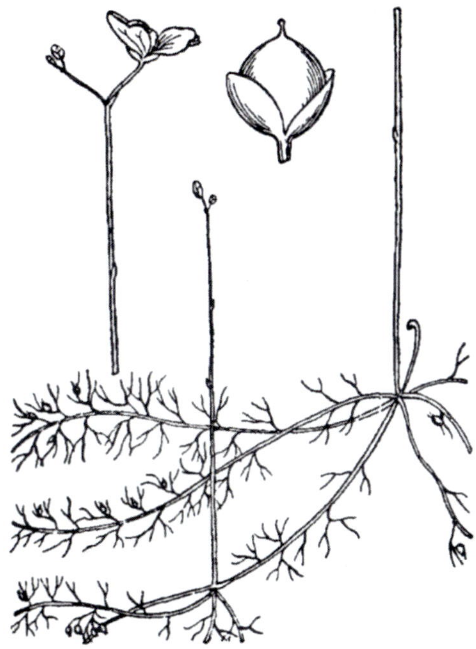

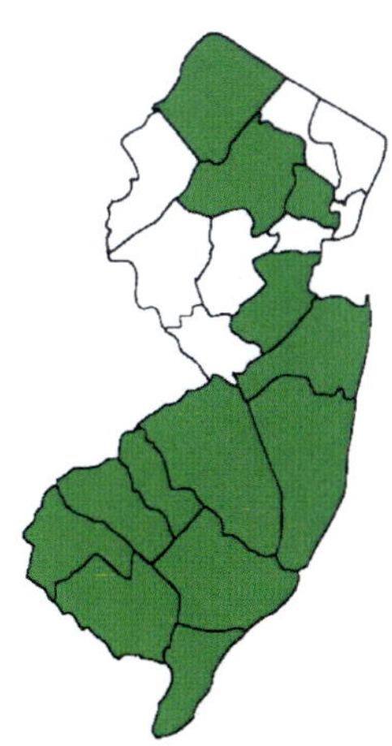

SWOLLEN BLADDERWORT *Utricularia inflata* Walt.

Swollen bladderwort is a submersed, perennial with slender, elongated stems. Submersed leaves (to 18 cm long) are alternate, bushy, repeatedly forked into thread-like segments bearing bladders on the sides. Uppermost leaves are whorled (5–10) around base of peduncle and noticeably inflated, floating at water surface. Floats (3–8 cm long, to 8 mm wide) are spongy, gradually tapered toward peduncle, with branching along half its length. Flowers are bright yellow, stalked (10–35 mm long), spur about half the length of the lower lip (20–25 mm long), and borne 9–14 (usually 10–11) on an upright peduncle (10–30 cm tall).

HABITAT & DISTRIBUTION

Utricularia inflata is a native southeastern Coastal Plain species of shallow to deep, clear, lakes and ponds. It reaches the northern limit of its native range in New Jersey, introduced farther north. This species can reproduce vegetatively by stem fragmentation and tuber formation and has potential to become weedy.

Note: Similar to *U. radiata*, but is much more robust, has tapering floats, and larger flowers.

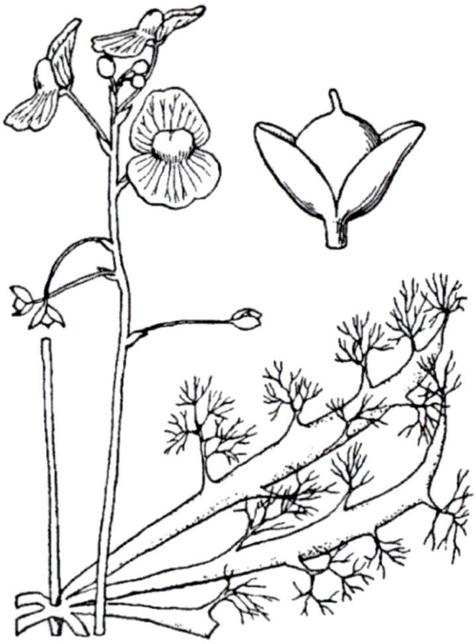

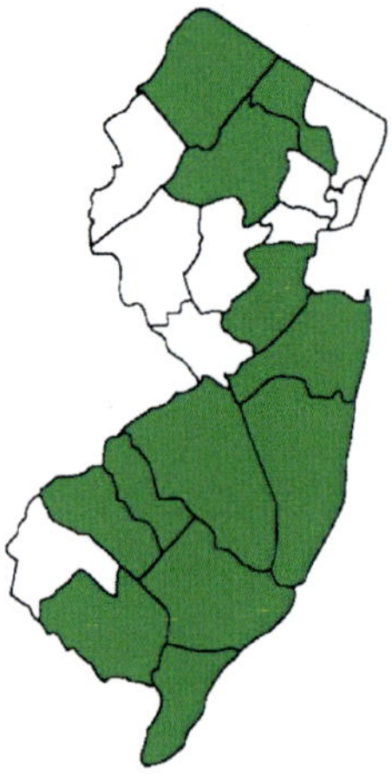

FLAT-LEAVED BLADDERWORT *Utricularia intermedia* Hayne

Flat-leaved bladderwort is a delicate, submersed (or creeping on substrate under water), perennial with slender stems. Leaves (above substrate) are alternate, green, fan-like, forked into strongly flattened, minutely spine-toothed, segments (5–20 mm long), lacking any bladders. Separate, whitish, leaf-like shoots (usually embedded in substrate) bear bladders (1.5–4 mm long). Flowers are bright yellow, with a long (8–12 mm) lower lip, well-developed spur (to 12 mm), and borne 2–5 on an upright peduncle (6–20 cm tall). Turions are oval (3–10 mm long).

HABITAT & DISTRIBUTION

Utricularia intermedia is a native species of shallow waters of ponds, bogs, and marshes. This northern species is at the southern limit of its range in New Jersey where it is **rare**, eligible for protection under the jurisdiction of the Highlands Preservation Area.

Notes: The species is intolerant of eutrophication. Similar to Lesser bladderwort (*U. minor*), but with green bladder-less leaves and larger, bright yellow flowers.

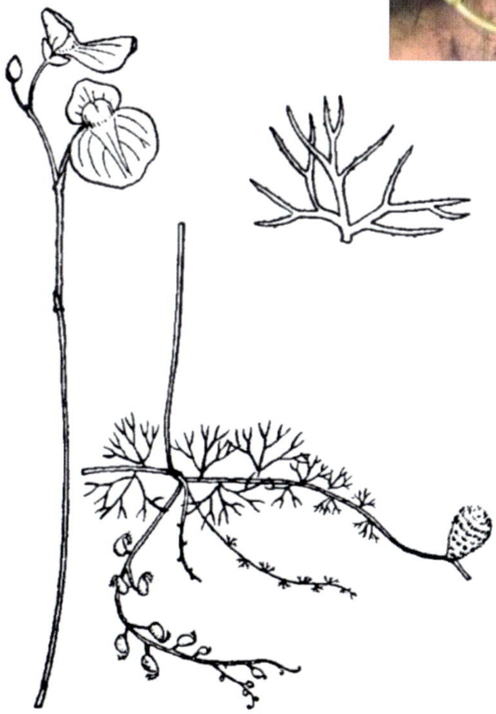

© M. Graziano

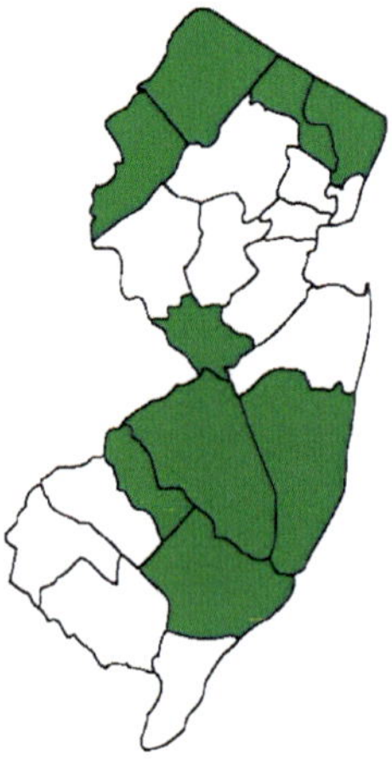

Southern bladderwort is an inconspicuous subterranean perennial. Leaves are alternate, few, somewhat straplike, unbranched, and mostly hidden within the surface of a wet peat or sand substrate. Leaves bear few, tiny (0.2–1.1 mm long) bladders also buried in the substrate. Flowers are bright yellow, each with a short stalk (1–2 mm long), prominent spur 2–8 mm long (pointing downward or backward), and a lower lip 7–12 mm long. Flowers 2–15, not crowded on an upright, wiry, greenish purple to purple, peduncle (10–40 cm tall) with a few, widely spaced, alternate, purple, scale-like bracts. Capsules are 2–3.5 mm long. No turions are produced.

HABITAT & DISTRIBUTION

Utricularia juncea is a native, Coastal Plain species of bogs, pond shores, and wet peaty ditches. This southern plant is nearing the northern limits of its range in New Jersey.

Note: One of the so-called "terrestrial" species of bladderwort, it is only apparent when flowering. Vegetative parts are intermixed in the substrate. It is similar to *U. cornuta* but with smaller and more numerous, less crowded, flowers.

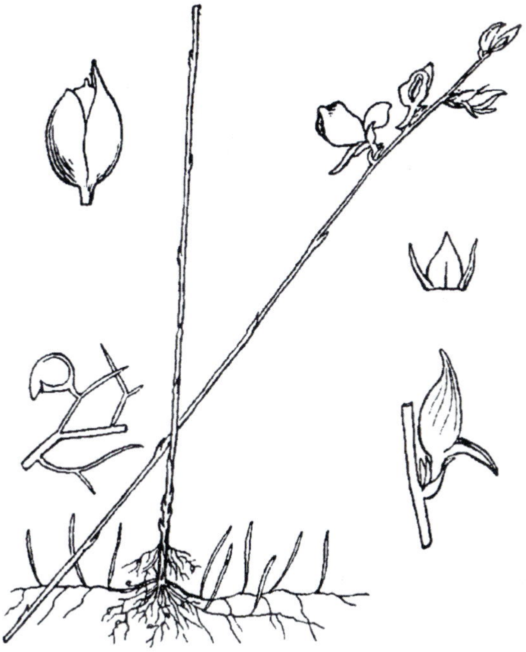

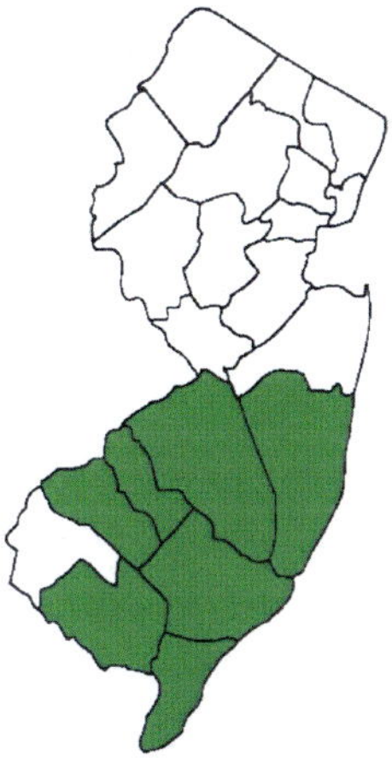

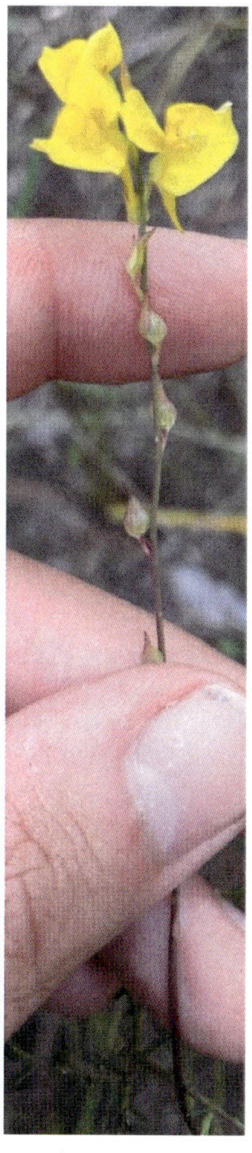

Lesser bladderwort is a delicate, submersed (or creeping on wet substrate), perennial with slender stems. Leaves are alternate, numerous, fan-like, and usually forked 3–4 times into distinctly flattened segments (3–10 mm long). Green leaves bear few, small (1–2 mm long) bladders while whitish leaves embedded in substrate bear most bladders. Flowers are pale yellow, small (petals 6–8 mm long), with an obscure (almost absent) spur, and borne 2–8 on an upright peduncle (4–15 cm tall). Turions are tiny (<3 mm), reddish-green, and rounded.

HABITAT & DISTRIBUTION

Utricularia minor is a diminutive, native species of shallow (<0.5 m deep), typically nutrient-poor, water of ponds, lakes, and rivers. This northern species reaches the southern limit of its range in New Jersey, where it is critically imperiled and state-listed as ***endangered***.

Notes: Plants are rarely found in flower, so they can be easily overlooked. Flattened aspect of leaves easily seen under hand lens. Similar to Flat-leaved bladderwort (*U. intermedia*), but with green leaves bearing bladders and smaller, pale flowers.

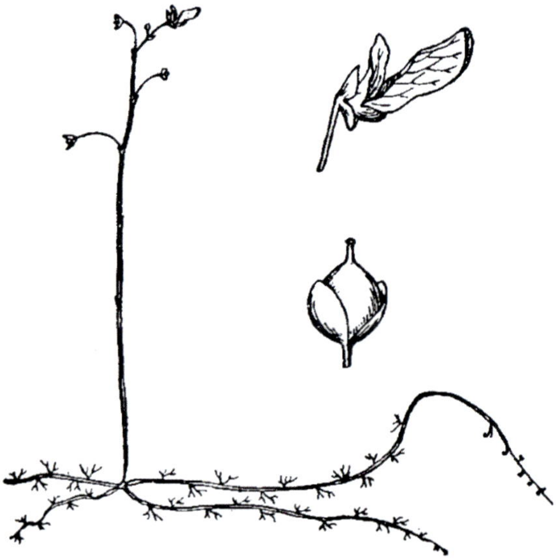

PIEDMONT BLADDERWORT *Utricularia olivacea* Wright ex Griseb.

Piedmont bladderwort, or Pygmy bladderwort, is an inconspicuous, diminutive floating annual. Stolons are greenish, delicate (0.05–0.1 mm wide), branched, coiled at tips, and lacking leaves. Leaves all modified into bladders (0.3–0.8 mm long) which are numerous, borne on short stalks, positioned alternately along the stem. Flowers are tiny (1–2.5 mm long), white to creamy-white, borne 1–2 on a short (2–10 mm), usually curved, flowering stem. Petals are fused to form two lips, lower lip to 0.5 mm long, not spurred. Capsules 1 mm long. No turions are produced.

HABITAT & DISTRIBUTION

Utricularia olivacea is a native, Coastal Plain species of shallow ponds and lakes with fluctuating water levels. This southern species reaches the northern limit of its range in southern New Jersey, where it is critically imperiled and state-listed as ***endangered***.

Note: Plants are extremely tiny and delicate, suspended or floating, and often entangled in other floating vegetation. Sometimes plants are stranded on muck as water recedes. This is the only bladderwort species in North America to completely lack leaves. Outside of Florida, records of occurrence for this species are very scarce as it is more than likely overlooked in the field.

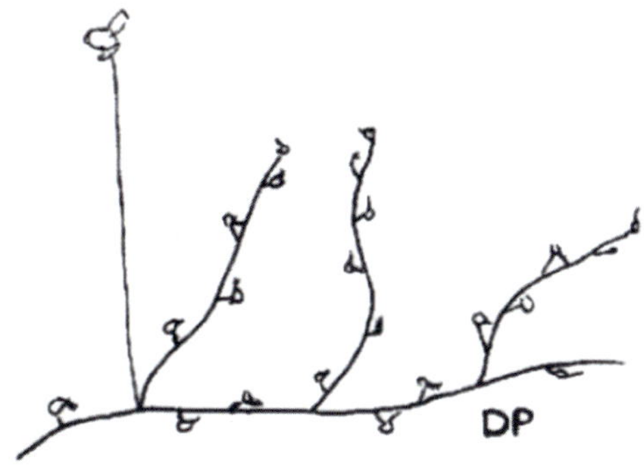

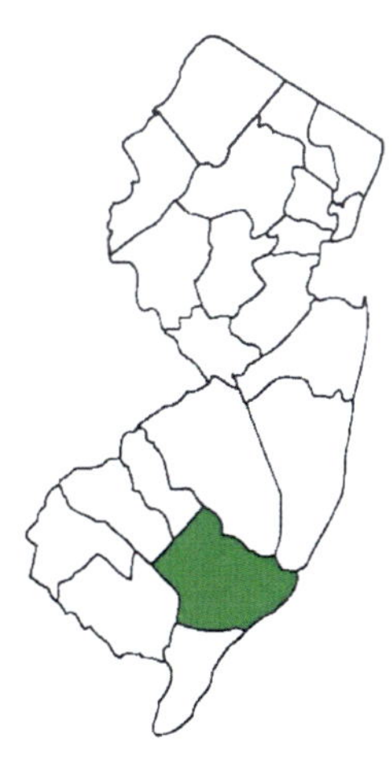

PURPLE BLADDERWORT *Utricularia purpurea* Walt.

Purple bladderwort is a submersed, perennial, with slender, elongated (to 1 m), much-branched stems. Leaves are in whorls of 5–7, conspicuous, stalked (1–1.5 cm long), forked several times into thread-like segments that bear bladders at their tips. Bladders are without external guide hairs. Flowers are pink-purple, with a blunt spur (2–5 mm long) pressed against the yellow-blotched lower lip, and borne 2–5 on an upright peduncle (5–15 cm tall). Turions are not produced.

HABITAT & DISTRIBUTION

Utricularia pupurea is a native species of lakes, ponds, and slow streams. It is **rare** in New Jersey, eligible for protection under the jurisdiction of the Highlands Preservation Area and Pinelands Commission.

Notes: Plants are free-floating and when conditions are optimal often become abundant. This species is found mostly in acidic, low nutrient waters and considered a good indicator species of phosphorous-poor water bodies.

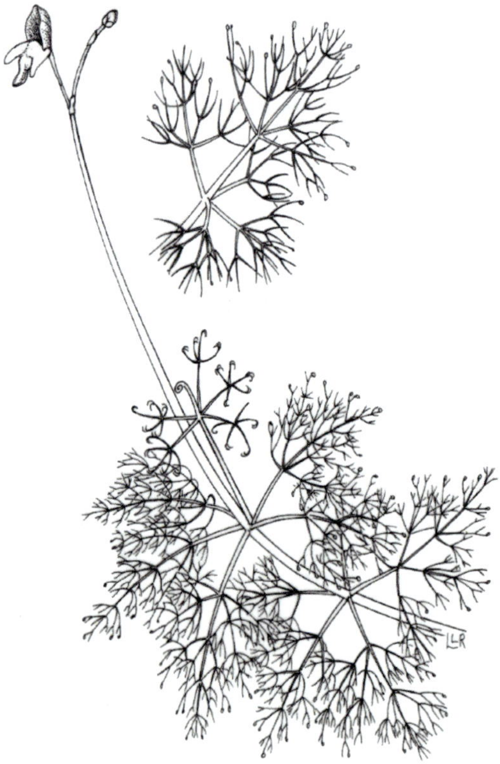

© M. Graziano

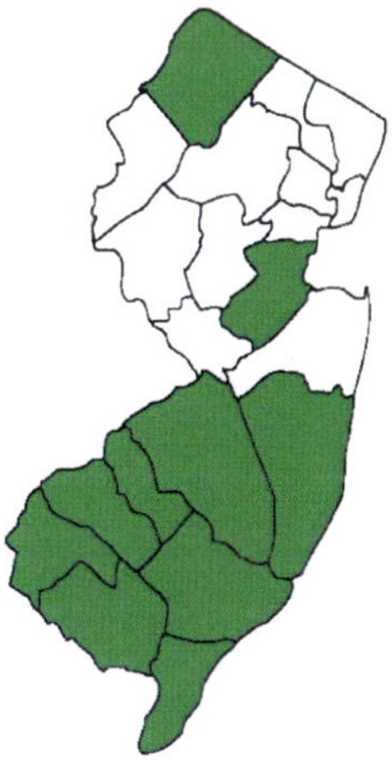

FLOATING BLADDERWORT *Utricularia radiata* Small

Floating bladderwort is a submersed, annual with slender, elongated stems. Submersed leaves (10–40 mm long) are alternate, repeatedly forked into thread-like segments, and bear many bladders on the sides. Uppermost leaves are whorled (4–7) around base of peduncle and noticeably inflated, floating at water surface. Floats (1–4 cm long, 2–4 mm wide) are spongy, mostly parallel-sided, with branching limited to tips. Flowers are dull yellow, stalked (10–20 mm long), spur pressed against the lower lip (8–10 mm long), and borne 1–7 (mostly 3–4) on an upright peduncle (3–5 cm tall). Turions are small (1 mm wide), roundish, and green.

HABITAT & DISTRIBUTION

Utricularia radiata is a native species of shallow, mostly acidic, ponds and lakes. It is **rare** in New Jersey, eligible for protection under the jurisdiction of the Highlands Preservation Area.

Notes: Similar to the more robust and bushier Swollen bladderwort (*U. inflata*) but with less densely branched leaves, smaller floats, shorter peduncles, and fewer flowers. Difficult to identify without floats and flowers.

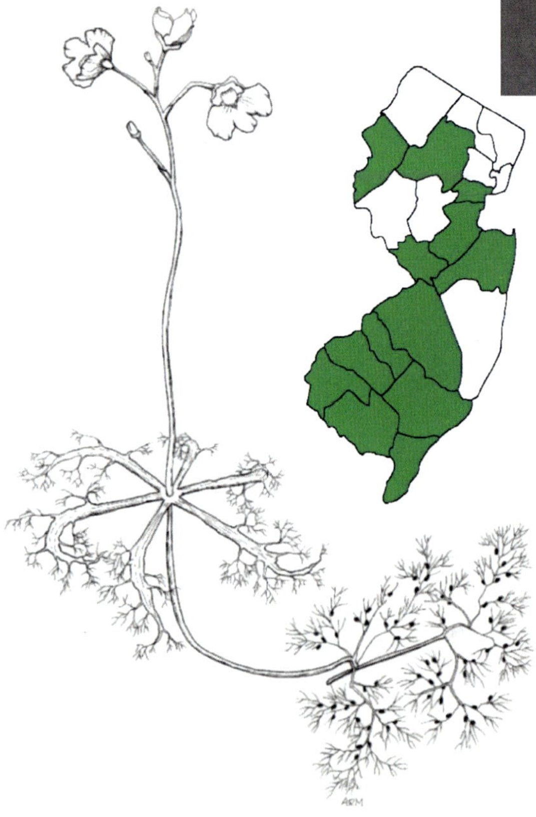

RESUPINATE BLADDERWORT *Utricularia resupinata* B.D. Greene

Resupinate bladderwort is an inconspicuous, delicate, perennial with horizontal, whitish, stems just below soil surface. Leaves are alternate, needle-like, unbranched, up to 3 cm long, with several transverse partitions. Leaves bear few, tiny (0.2–1.1 mm long) bladders often buried in the substrate. Flowers (1 cm) are purple, tipped backwards and facing upward, and borne singly at tip of an upright peduncle (2–10 cm tall) with a pair of scale-like bracts fused around peduncle. No turions are produced.

HABITAT & DISTRIBUTION

Utricularia resupinata is a native species occurring usually in sandy, very shallow (<15 cm), nutrient-poor ponds. It is rare and state-listed as ***endangered*** in New Jersey.

Note: One of the so-called "terrestrial" species of bladderwort, it is only apparent when flowering, which is sporadic in our region. It can form tangled mats in deep water which can dislodge and float.

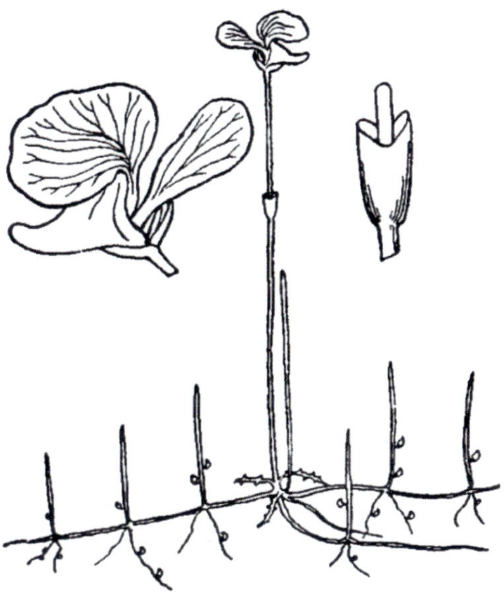

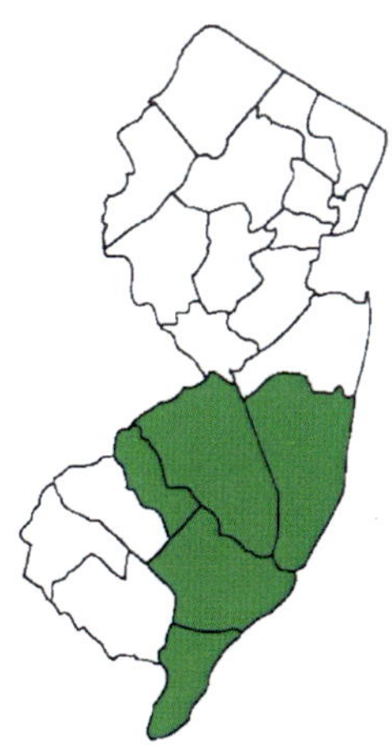

Striped bladderwort is a delicate, submersed (or creeping), perennial, with slender, intertwined, green stems radiating from the flowering stem. Above the substrate, leaf-like branches are green, forked 3 or 4 times, and bear few, if any, small (1–2.5 mm long), bladders on sides. Below the substrate, branches are whitish, forked 1–4 times, and bear many bladders. Flowers are pale yellow, with a spur about ¾ the length of the lower lip (8–10 mm long) and borne 1–6 on an upright flowering stem (15–30 cm tall). Capsules are 2–3 mm wide. Turions are not produced.

HABITAT & DISTRIBUTION

Utricularia striata is a native Coastal Plain species of acidic ponds and bogs. This southern species is reaching its northern limits in New Jersey.

Notes: It typically occurs in very shallow water (<10 cm) entangled in loose debris, but sometimes can be found in free-floating mats elsewhere. Similar to Creeping bladderwort (*U. gibba*).

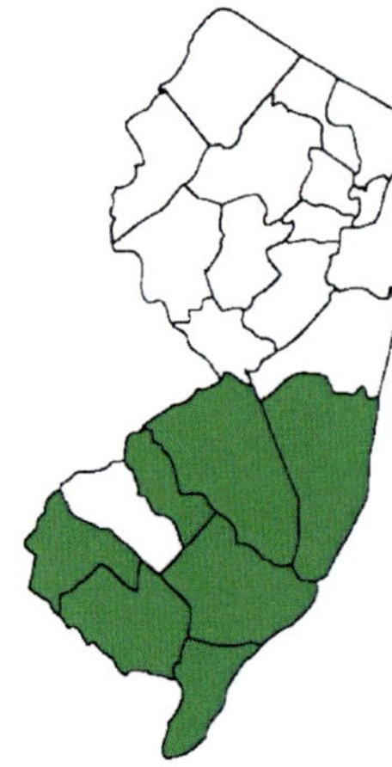

SLENDER BLADDERWORT *Utricularia subulata* L.

Slender bladderwort is an inconspicuous, delicate, annual species. Leaves (to 1 cm long) are alternate, slender, strap-like, unbranched, and mostly hidden within the surface of wet soil substrate. Leaves and stem branches can bear few, tiny (0.5 mm long), bladders also buried in the substrate. Flowers are yellow, each with an obvious stalk (4–15 mm long) and spur (2.5–5 mm) pressed against the lower lip (4–7 mm long). Flowers are borne 2–8 on an upright, zig-zagged, peduncle (3–20 cm tall) with a few, alternate, scale-like bracts. Sometimes plants have smaller, whitish, closed, self-pollinating flowers. Capsules are 1–1.5 mm long.

HABITAT & DISTRIBUTION

Utricularia subulata is a native, Coastal Plain species occurring on sandy, or peaty sands, of acidic pond shores or bogs. This species is approaching its northern limits in New Jersey, where it is most frequent in the Pine Barrens. One of the so-called "terrestrial" species of bladderwort, it is only apparent when flowering.

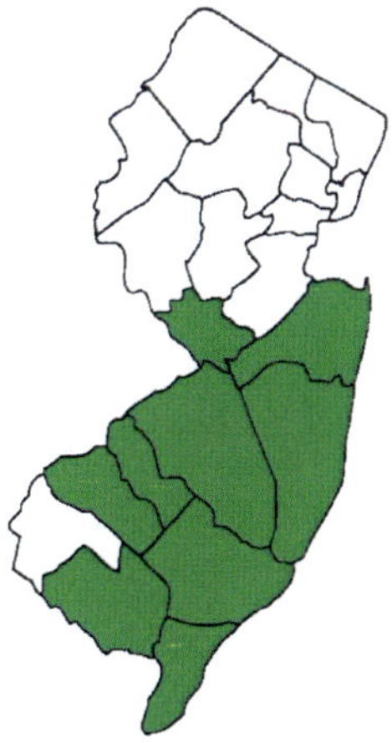

Common bladderwort, or Greater bladderwort, is a submersed, bushy, perennial with slender, elongated stems (30–100 cm long). Leaves are alternate, numerous, course (1.5–6.5 cm long), forked usually 6–17 times (and slightly zig-zagged) into narrow segments, with minute marginal spines. Leaves bear numerous, conspicuous, bladders (1–6 mm long). Flowers are yellow, spur tip curved upward, lower lip 1–2 cm long, and borne 6–14 on an upright peduncle (6–20 cm tall). Turions are large (1–2 cm long, 0.5–1.5 cm wide), rounded or elongated, abundantly haired, often mucilaginous, and green.

HABITAT & DISTRIBUTION

Utricularia vulgaris is a native species of ponds, lakes, and streams. It is common and widespread in New Jersey.

Notes: This species, suspended and free-floating in water, has broad ecological tolerances (e.g., indifferent to water chemistry, flow, and depth) and is usually abundant. After pollination, flower stalks recurve and bend so fruit development takes place under water. Our plants represent subsp. *macrorhiza* (Leconte) R.T. Clausen

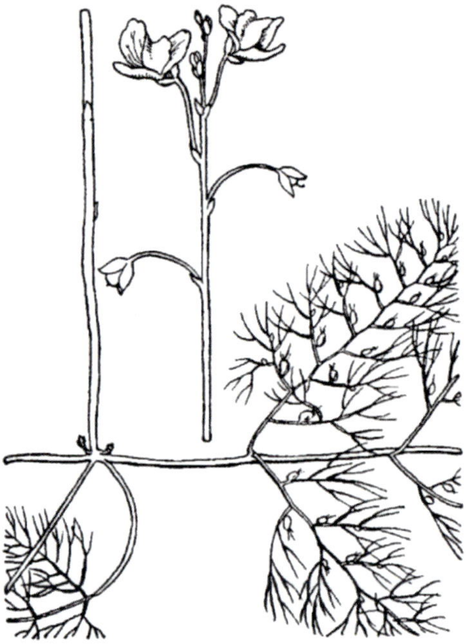

Turions

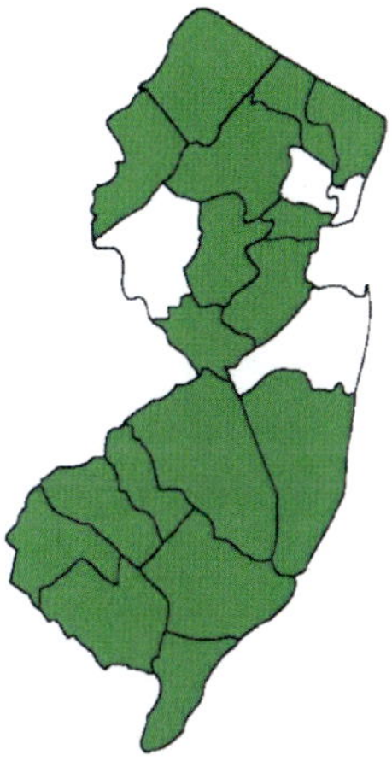

Vallisneria — Hydrocharitaceae
Tape-grass

AMERICAN EEL-GRASS *Valisneria americana* Michx.

American eel-grass, or Water-celery, is a rooted, perennial herb with long, submersed, ribbon-like leaves clustered along stolons. Leaves are basal, submersed (upper portions may be floating), flat, long (10–110 cm long, 0.5–1.5 cm wide), bluntly pointed, bright green, and somewhat translucent. The leaf midvein has 4–5 rows of lacunae on each side, giving the blade a 3-zone appearance (light-colored middle zone bordered by darker zone on sides). Flowers are unisexual (on separate plants) and small (2 mm wide) with transparent petals. Fruit is a cylindrical (50–120 mm long) capsule borne on end of an elongated, coiled stalk.

HABITAT & DISTRIBUTION

Vallisneria americana is a native species of fresh to brackish slow rivers, streams, or lakes. It is common and widespread in New Jersey. It is a colony-forming plant and a valuable waterfowl food.

Notes: Numerous male flowers detach from the plant and float to surface while single female flowers are projected to surface tethered by a long stalk. After pollination, the stalk coils and pulls the fruit underwater. It can appear very similar to non-flowering plants of *Sparganium* in deep waters.

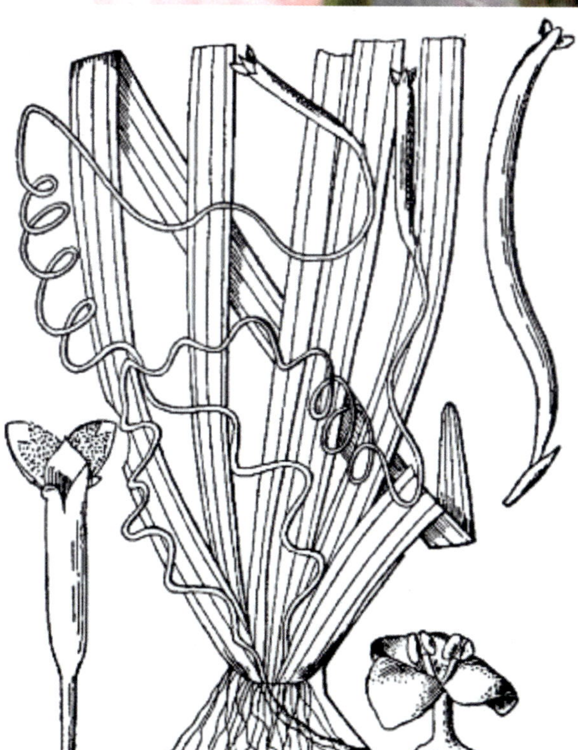

Wolffia — Araceae
Water-meal

The Water-meals are tiny (<1.5 mm long), green, rootless, perennials floating on surface of quiet waters. Plant body (called a thallus) is greatly reduced (not differentiated into stem and leaf), spherical, oval, or boat-shaped (i.e., flattened above and rounded below). Usually, two plants are connected. Flower and fruit are tiny, produced on upper surface, and rarely seen.

Three species occur in New Jersey. Identification is best when plants are fresh. Individuals reproduce vegetatively quickly and are usually very numerous, often intermixed with other duckweeds (*Lemna* and *Spirodela*). This genus contains the smallest known plant species in the world.

KEY TO SPECIES

1. Plants spherical, rounded in outline, largest individuals 0.5–0.8 (–1.2) mm wide .... *W. columbiana*
1. Plants oblong, longer than wide (or shaped somewhat like segments of an orange), seldom over 0.5 mm wide by 1 mm long, upper surface flattened 2
   2. Plants rounded at the ends (viewing from above); upper surface with a prominent, central, raised point in mature plant body .... *W. brasiliensis*
   2. Plants pointed at the ends; upper surface lacking a raised point..................... *W. borealis*

NORTHERN WATER-MEAL *Wolffia borealis* (Engelm.) Landolt

Northern water-meal is a tiny, rootless, free-floating perennial. Plants are oblong (0.7–1.5 mm long), longer than wide, and pointed at the ends with a minute upward bend. The upper surface is flattened, smooth, without a central, raised point.

HABITAT & DISTRIBUTION

Wolffia borealis is a native plant of nutrient-rich, quiet ponds and sluggish rivers. It is scattered in New Jersey, probably more common than indicated.

BRAZILIAN WATER-MEAL — *Wolffia brasiliensis* Weddell

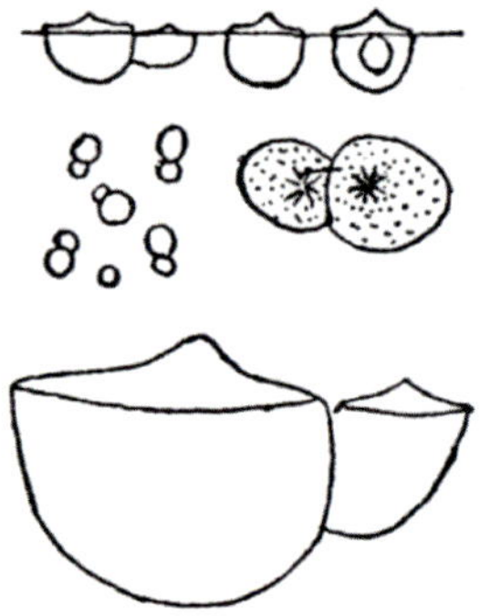

Brazilian water-meal is a tiny, rootless, free-floating perennial. Plants are oblong (0.5–1.6 mm long), longer than wide, and rounded at the ends. The upper surface is flattened marginally but raised in center with a prominent point.

HABITAT & DISTRIBUTION

Wolffia brasiliensis is a native plant of nutrient-rich, quiet ponds and sluggish rivers. It is somewhat widespread in New Jersey, probably more common than indicated.

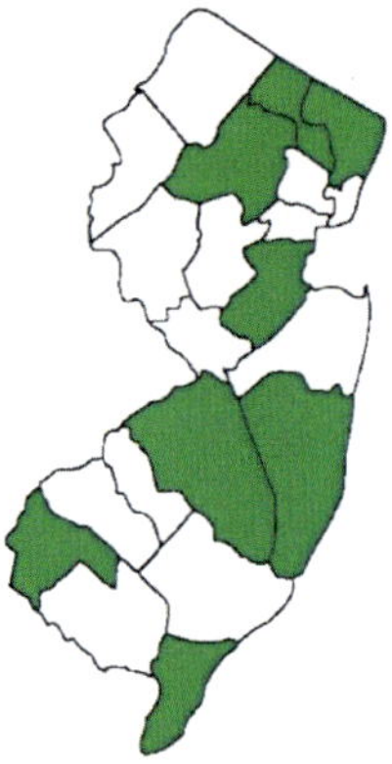

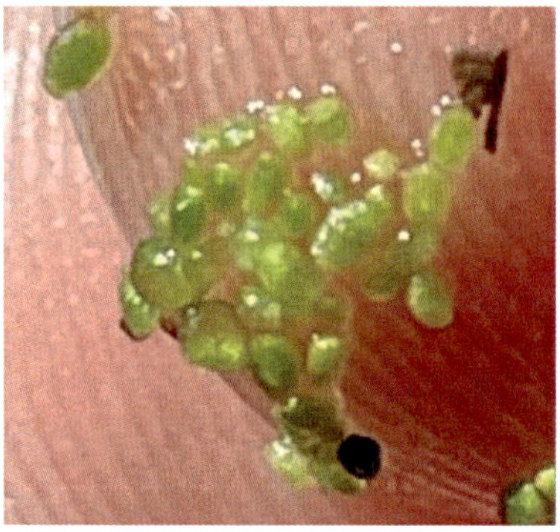

COLUMBIAN WATER-MEAL — *Wolffia columbiana* Karst.

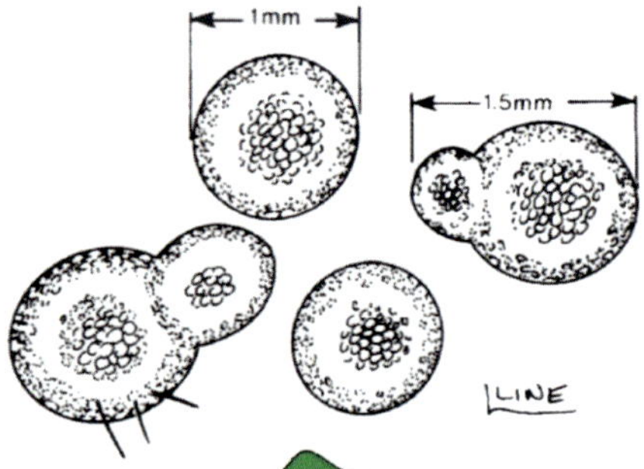

Columbian water-meal is a tiny, rootless, perennial, free-floating at water surface. Plants are spherical, rounded in outline. Largest individuals are 0.5–0.8 (–1.2) mm wide.

HABITAT & DISTRIBUTION

Wolffia columbiana is a native plant of nutrient-rich, quiet ponds and sluggish rivers. It is somewhat widespread in New Jersey, probably more common than indicated.

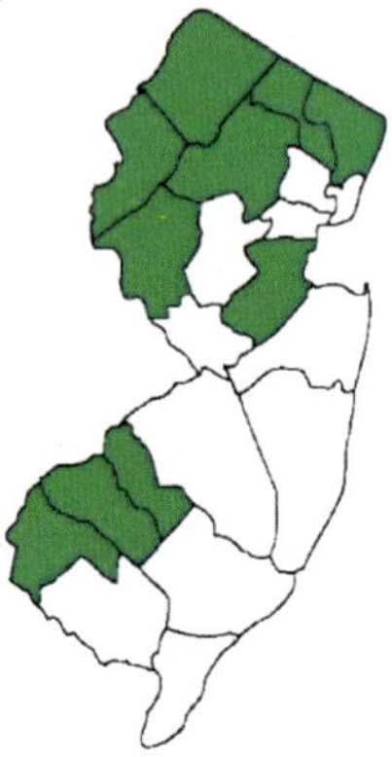

Wolffiella — Araceae
Bog-mat

SWORD-LIKE BOG-MAT — *Wolfiella gladiata* (Hegelm.) Hegelm.

Sword-like bog-mat, or Mud-midget, is a tiny, green, rootless, perennial, free-floating just below water surface. Plant body (or thallus) is greatly reduced (not differentiated into stem and leaf), linear and sword-shaped (6–8 mm long), curved, and hollow. Usually multiple plants are connected. Flower and fruit are tiny, rarely seen.

HABITAT & DISTRIBUTION

Wolffiella gladiata is a native, southern species of shallow still waters of ponds. It is critically imperiled and state-listed as ***endangered*** in New Jersey. Easy to overlook.

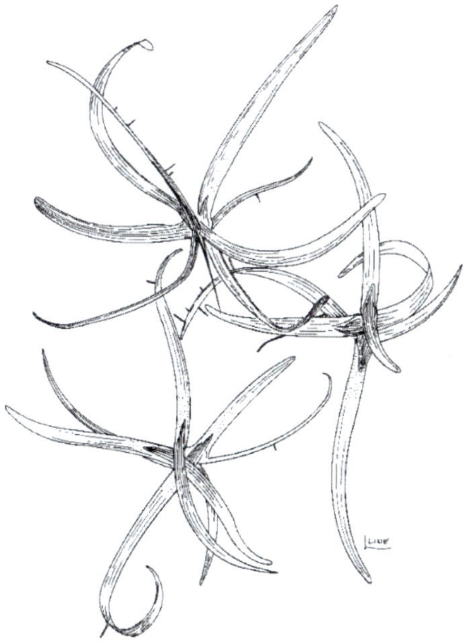

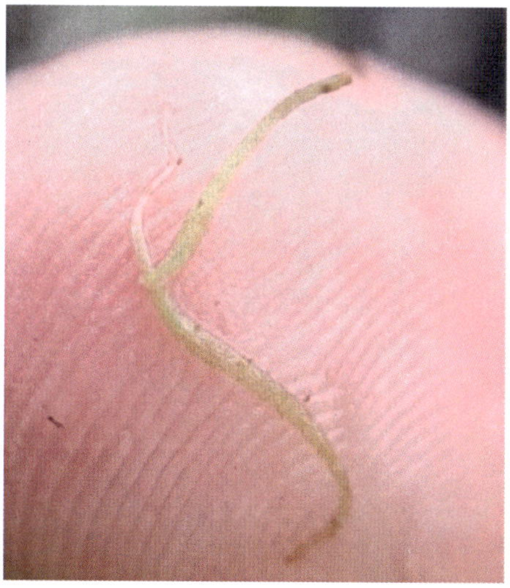

Zannichellia — Potamogetonaceae
Horned-pondweed

HORNED-PONDWEED *Zannichellia palustris* L.

Horned-pondweed is a delicate, rooted, annual plant, entirely submersed, with many, thin (0.5 mm wide) branching stems. Leaves are opposite (possibly obscured with smaller leaves in axils), green, linear (3.5–4 cm long, 0.2–1 mm wide) with sheathing stipules at their base, and pointed at tips. Flowers are unisexual and borne underwater in leaf axils. Fruit a cluster (2–5) of short-stalked (1 mm), flattened, achenes (2–3 mm long, 1 mm wide), slightly toothed on outer edge, with narrow extension (2 mm) at tip.

HABITAT & DISTRIBUTION

Zannichellia palustris is a native plant of freshwater lakes and tidal brackish waters. It is most common in hard waters near the coast but can be found more inland.

Note: Sometimes confused with Wigeon-grass (*Ruppia maritima*).

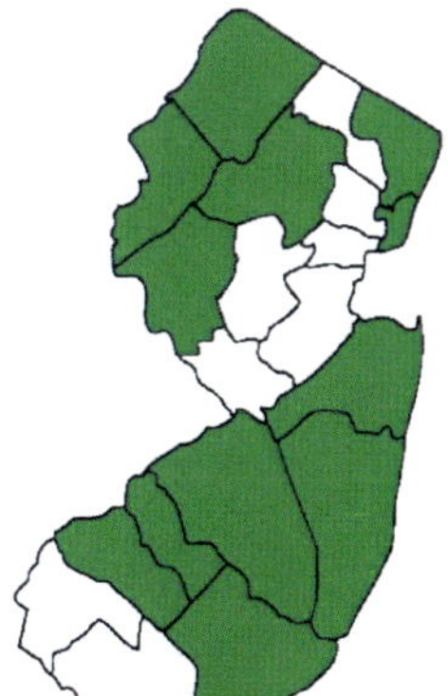

Zostera — Zosteraceae
Eel-grass

EEL-GRASS *Zostera marina* L.

Eel-grass, or Sea-wrack, is a grass-like, completely submersed, marine perennial with rooted, creeping rhizomes (2–6 mm thick) and flattened upright branches. Leaves are alternate, dark green, linear and ribbon-like (30–100 cm long, 2–12 mm wide), round-tipped, and sheathing the stem at base. Flowers are minute, submersed, unisexual (on same plant), lacking petals, in rows, enclosed within a leaf-like sheath (4–8 cm long) at end of a short (2–3 cm) stalk. Fruit a fleshy, oblong (2–5 mm long), beaked drupe.

HABITAT & DISTRIBUTION

Zostera marina is a native species most common in deeper subtidal (or less frequently in exposed intertidal areas) saline waters of sheltered ocean bays and inlets. It is ***rare*** in New Jersey, eligible for protection under the jurisdiction of the Highlands Preservation Area.

Notes: This is the only submersed flowering plant of marine waters in our region. It can form vast, dense colonies or eel-grass "beds". As a sea grass, it is an extremely vital component of estuaries regarding sediment stabilization, nitrogen-fixation, animal food, shelter, and nurseries.

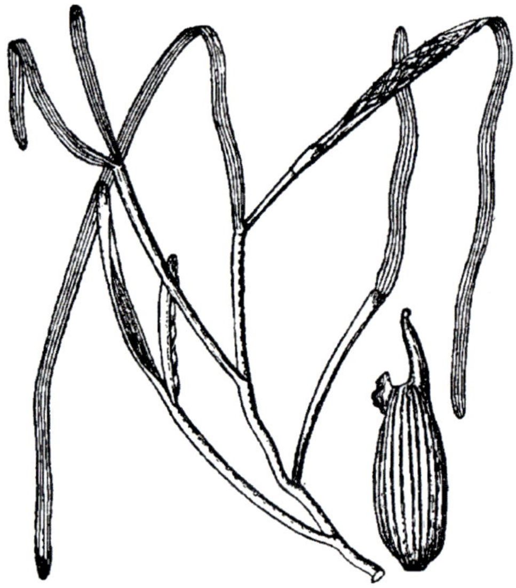

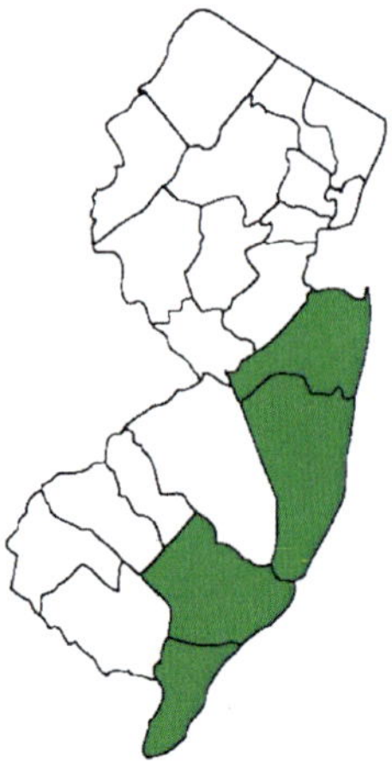

REFERENCES

Block, T.A. and A.F. Rhoads. 2011. Aquatic Plants of Pennsylvania: A Complete Reference Guide. University of Pennsylvania Press, Philadelphia.

Bowman, K. 2017. Field Guide to the Moss Genera in New Jersey With Coefficient of Conservation and Indicator Status. New Jersey Department of Environmental Protection, Trenton, New Jersey.

Collins, B.R. and K.H. Anderson. 1994. Plant Communities of New Jersey. Rutgers University Press, New Brunswick, New Jersey.

Crow, G.E. and C.B. Hellquist. 2023. Aquatic and Wetland Plants of Northeastern North America, 2nd ed. University of Wisconsin Press, Madison.

Fairbrothers, D.E., E.T. Moul, A.R. Essback, D.N. Riemer, and D.A. Schallock. 1965. Aquatic Vegetation of New Jersey, Extension Bulletin 382. Extension Service, Rutgers University, New Brunswick, New Jersey.

Flora of North America Editorial Committee, eds. 1993+. Flora of North America North of Mexico. 21+ vols. New York and Oxford.

Gleason, H.A. and A. Cronquist. 1991. Manual of Vascular Plants of Northeastern United States and Adjacent Canada. New York Botanical Garden, Bronx, New York.

Hough, M.Y. 1983. New Jersey Wild Plants. Harmony Press, Harmony, New Jersey.

Hutchinson, G.E. 1975. A Treatise on Limnology: Limnological Botany, Vol. 3. John Wiley & Sons, New York.

Les, D.H. 2017. Aquatic Dicotyledons of North America: Ecology, Life History, and Systematics. CRC Press, New York.

Les, D.H. 2020. Aquatic Monocotyledons of North America: Ecology, Life History, and Systematics. CRC Press, New York.

Les, D.H., E.L. Peredo, U.M. King, L.K. Benoit, N.P. Tippery, C.J. Ball, and R.K. Shannon. 2015. Through thick and thin: Cryptic sympatric speciation in the submersed genus *Najas* (Hydrocharitaceae). Molecular Phylogenetics and Evolution 82: 15-30.

Stone, W. 1911. The Plants of Southern New Jersey. Quarterman Publications, Inc., Boston.

Wolfe, P.E. 1977. The Geology and Landscapes of New Jersey. Crane, Russak & Co., New York.

ILLUSTRATION & PHOTOGRAPH CREDITS

Beyond my own photographs and illustrations, images were utilized either from the public domain, with permission from authors, or according to various Creative Commons licenses. Unless indicated otherwise, line drawings originated from N.L. Britton and A. Brown. 1913. *An illustrated flora of the northern United States, Canada, and the British Possessions. 3 vols.* Charles Scribner's Sons, New York (via USDA-NRCS PLANTS Database).

Photographs or drawings not listed with a credit below are either in the public domain or represent works of my own. For frequently cited sources, the following acronyms are used for brevity:

CBH © C. Barre Hellquist; Used with permission.
MIN © Katy Chayka/Peter M. Dziuk, www.minnesotawildflowers.info. Used with permission.
UFL © Univ. Florida, Center for Aquatic and Invasive Plants. Used with permission.
WF USDA-NRCS PLANTS Database / USDA NRCS. *Wetland flora: Field office illustrated guide to plant species.* USDA Nat. Resources Conservation Serv.

Page 2, A. Leahey, https://commons.wikimedia.org/wiki/File:Cranberry_Bog_Pine_Barrens,_NJ.jpg (CC-BY-SA-2.0)
Page 8, Figure 2, a-d: **UFL**
Page 9, Figure 3, a.: **UFL**; b.: **CBH**; d.: **UFL**; g.: **UFL**
Page 10, *Riccia*: C. Fischer, https://upload.wikimedia.org/wikipedia/commons/1/15/RicciaFluitansAgg.jpg (CC-BY-SA-3.0); *Ricciocarpus*, C. Fischer, https://upload.wikimedia.org/wikipedia/commons/3/37/RicciocarposNatans5.jpg (CC-BY-SA-3.0); *Fontinalis*, S. Pogacnik, https://www.inaturalist.org/observations/74473163 (CCO-1.0).
Page 11, *Chara vulgaris*, A. Митрошенкова, https://upload.wikimedia.org/wikipedia/commons/d/dd/Chara_vulgaris_161465805.jpg (CC BY 4.0); S. Lefnaer, https://upload.wikimedia.org/wikipedia/commons/5/59/Chara_vulgaris_sl18.jpg (CC-BY-SA-4.0); *Nitella flexilis*, S. Lefnaer, https://commons.wikimedia.org/wiki/File:Nitella_flexilis_sl24.jpg (CC-BY-SA-4.0).
Page 24, Photo: traps, S. Lefnaer, https://commons.wikimedia.org/wiki/File:Aldrovanda_vesiculosa_sl23.jpg (CC-BY-SA-4.0).
Page 25, Drawing: **UFL**; Photos: I. Taylar, https://commons.wikimedia.org/wiki/File:Azolla_caroliniana.jpg (CC-BY-2.0).
Page 27, Photos: R. Foster https://www.inaturalist.org/observations/92470784 (CC-BY-4.0); https://www.inaturalist.org/observations/31649871 (CC-BY-4.0).
Page 28, Photos: B. Michalek, https://www.inaturalist.org/observations/30476343 (CCO-1.0); S.L. Winterton, Aquarium and Pond Plants of the World, 3e, CDFA and USDA APHIS ITP.
Page 31, Photo: flowers, L.J. Mehrhoff, https://commons.wikimedia.org/wiki/File:Cabomba_caroliniana_5447098.jpg (CC-BY-3.0).
Page 32, Drawing: **WF**
Page 33, Photo: (*C. palustris*) R. Durand, https://www.inaturalist.org/observations/68629881 (CC-BY-4.0).
Page 34, Photos: (rosette) S. Kieschnick, https://www.inaturalist.org/observations/71669771 (CC-BY-4.0).
Page 35, Drawing: Coste and Flahault, *Flore descriptive et illustrée de la France, de la Corse et des contrées limitrophes*, 1901-1906 (Public Domain); Photo: R. Routledge, https://www.invasive.org/browse/detail.cfm?imgnum=5541152 (CC-BY-3.0).
Page 36, Drawing: Coste and Flahault, *Flore descriptive et illustrée de la France, de la Corse et des contrées limitrophes*, 1901-1906 (Public Domain); Photo: habit, L.J. Mehrhoff, https://www.invasive.org/browse/detail.cfm?imgnum=5447134 (CC-BY-3.0); rosette, J. Grundling, https://www.inaturalist.org/observations/47070337 (CC0).
Page 37, Drawing: **UFL**
Page 38, Drawing: C.F. Reed, *Selected weeds of the United States*. USDA Agric. Res. Ser. Agric. Handbook 336.
Page 39, Photo: D. Suitor, https://www.inaturalist.org/observations/84200597 (CC-BY-3.0).
Page 40, Photo: N. Aaron, https://www.inaturalist.org/observations/128239039 (CC BY 4.0).
Page 41, Drawing: **UFL**; Photo: J. Sullivan, https://www.inaturalist.org/observations/118995341 (CC BY 4.0).
Page 42, Photos: Lamiot, https://commons.wikimedia.org/w/index.php?curid=42528393 (CC BY-SA 4.0), G.A Baker, https://www.inaturalist.org/observations/86591697 (CC BY 4.0).
Page 43, Drawing: UFL; Photo: Amada44, https://commons.wikimedia.org/wiki/File:Eichhornia_crassipes_001.jpg (CC BY 3.0).
Page 44, Photo: R. Foster, https://www.inaturalist.org/observations/21099340 (CC BY 4.0).

Page 47, Photo: B. Knutsen, Norway.
Page 48, Photo: G. Grzejszczak, https://www.inaturalist.org/observations/14359941 (CC-BY-4.0).
Page 50, Photos: N. Martineau, https://www.inaturalist.org/observations/12871902 (CC-BY-4.0); Z. Wang, https://www.inaturalist.org/observations/97826547 (CC-BY-4.0).
Page 51, Photo: **MIN**
Page 52, Drawings: **UFL**
Page 53, Photo: C. Fischer, https://commons.wikimedia.org/wiki/File:ElodeaCanadensis.jpg (CC-BY-SA-3.0).
Page 56, Photo: Jomegat, https://commons.wikimedia.org/wiki/File:Eriocaulon_aquaticum_6884.jpg (CC-BY-SA-3.0).
Page 57, Photos: left, J. Horn, https://www.inaturalist.org/observations/101053036 (CC BY 4.0).
Page 61, Photo: **MIN**
Page 63, Photo: (*H. reniformis*) A. López Hernández, https://www.inaturalist.org/observations/155788236 (CC BY 4.0).
Page 64, Photos: top, Summit Metro Parks, https://www.inaturalist.org/observations/60029118 (CC BY 4.0); Plant, N. Aaron, https://www.inaturalist.org/observations/92236937 (CC BY 4.0).
Page 65, Photos: © Steve Turner (Missouriplants.com), with permission.
Page 66, Photo: bottom, B. Semmling, https://www.inaturalist.org/observations/57477122 (CC-BY-4.0).
Page 67, Photo: left, L. Allain, U.S. Geological Survey.
Page 68, Drawing: **UFL**; Photo: bottom, Darkmax, https://commons.wikimedia.org/wiki/File:Hydrilla_Verticillata_2.jpg (CC-BY-SA-3.0).
Page 70, Drawing: **UFL**
Page 71, Photo: A. Lindqvist, https://www.inaturalist.org/observations/134945995 (CC BY 4.0).
Page 72, Photos: top, Northcut, https://www.inaturalist.org/observations/109069450 (CC BY 4.0); bottom, L. Dasher, https://www.inaturalist.org/observations/104737332 (CC BY 4.0).
Page 73, Photo: bottom, mfeaver, https://www.inaturalist.org/observations/23244406 (CC BY 4.0).
Page 74, Photos: top, A. Penney, https://www.inaturalist.org/observations/1766660 (CC-BY-4.0); bottom, bobkennedy, https://www.inaturalist.org/observations/7688231 (CC-BY-SA-4.0).
Page 76, Drawing: C.A.M. Lindman, *Bilder ur Nordens Flora*; Photo: L. Gibson, https://www.inaturalist.org/observations/7595846 (CC-BY-4.0).
Page 77, Photo: J. Lee, https://upload.wikimedia.org/wikipedia/commons/b/b4/Isoetes_echinospora_%2820262801982%29.jpg (CC BY SA 2.0).
Page 78, Photos: top, N. Aaron, https://www.inaturalist.org/observations/73906882 (CC BY 4.0); bottom, D. Inozemtseva, https://upload.wikimedia.org/wikipedia/commons/a/a5/Isoetes_lacustris_rivnenskyi.jpg (CC BY SA 4.0).
Page 80, Photo: D. McCorquodale, https://www.inaturalist.org/observations/126730479 (CC BY 4.0).
Page 81, Photos: left, Q. Wiegersma, https://www.inaturalist.org/observations/59942968 (CC BY 4.0); right, B. Armstrong, https://www.inaturalist.org/observations/15396926 (CC BY 4.0).
Page 82, Photos: © Robert Wernerehl, with permission, https://www.inaturalist.org/observations/133611616 (CC BY-NC-SA 4.0); https://www.inaturalist.org/observations/99080698 (CC BY-NC 4.0).
Page 83, Photo: left, https://www.inaturalist.org/observations/30677513 (CC BY 4.0).
Page 84, Drawing: **WF**; Photo: right, J. Brew, https://www.inaturalist.org/observations/59348611 (CC-BY-4.0).
Page 85, Photos: M.J. Gras, https://www.inaturalist.org/observations/86536 (CC-BY-4.0).
Page 86, Drawing: **WF**; Photo: Z. Wang, https://www.inaturalist.org/observations/14888905 (CC-BY-4.0).
Page 87, Drawing: **WF**; Photo: left, C. Fischer, https://commons.wikimedia.org/wiki/Lemna_trisulca#/media/File:LemnaTrisulca.jpg (CC BY-SA 3.0).
Page 88, Drawing: **WF**; Photo: Z. Wang, https://www.inaturalist.org/observations/169668941 (CC-BY-4.0).
Page 90, Drawing: **UFL**
Page 91, Photo: right, M. Bedingfield, https://canberra.naturemapr.org/Community/Sightings/Details/3390212 (CC BY 3.0 AU).
Page 93, Drawing: **WF**
Page 94, Drawing: **WF**; Photo: left, J. Hollinger, https://commons.wikimedia.org/wiki/File:Water_Purslane_(1290675069).jpg (CC-BY-2.0).
Page 95, Photo: bottom, Summit Metro Parks, https://www.inaturalist.org/observations/20945297 (CC BY 4.0).
Page 96, Photo: bottom, S. Kieschnick, https://www.inaturalist.org/observations/3584949 (CC BY 4.0).
Page 97, Photo: K. Ziarnek, https://commons.wikimedia.org/wiki/File:Marsilea_quadrifolia_kz1.jpg (CC-BY-SA 4.0).
Page 99, Photos: top left, A. Fox, Univ. Florida, Bugwood.org (CC BY 3.0); top right, Y. Danilevsky, https://www.inaturalist.org/observations/19902829 (CY BY 4.0).
Page 100, Drawing: **UFL**; Photos: Sunny, https://www.inaturalist.org/observations/145869415 (CC0).
Page 101, Drawing: **UFL**
Page 105, Photos: turion, S. Johnson, https://www.inaturalist.org/observations/33406568 (CC-BY-4.0); flowers, O. Strickland https://www.inaturalist.org/observations/174715436 (CY BY 4.0).
Page 106, Drawing: **UFL**
Page 107, Photos: top, S. Lefnaer, https://commons.wikimedia.org/wiki/File:Myriophyllum_spicatum_sl5.jpg (CC-BY-SA-4.0); https://commons.wikimedia.org/wiki/File:Myriophyllum_spicatum_sl1.jpg (CC-BY-SA-4.0).
Page 109, Photos: left, C. Hohn, https://www.inaturalist.org/observations/12964590 (CC-BY-4.0); right, Y. Basov, https://www.inaturalist.org/observations/56117341 (CC-BY-4.0).
Page 110, Drawings: (*N. guadalupensis*) left, center **UFL**
Page 112, Photos: top, adapted from Les et al. (2015) Mol. Phylogen. Evol. 82: 15–30.

Page 114, Photo: Show_ryu, https://commons.wikimedia.org/wiki/File:Najas_gracillima.JPG (CC-BY-SA-3.0).
Page 115, Photos: J. Horn, https://www.inaturalist.org/observations/128925703 (CC-BY-4.0).
Page 116, Photo: R. Sorrells, https://www.inaturalist.org/observations/140335496 (CC-BY-4.0).
Page 117, Photo: bottom, E. Schmidt, https://www.inaturalist.org/observations/43036019 (CC-BY-4.0).
Page 119, Drawing: **UFL**
Page 122, Drawing: UFL; Photo: top, mfeaver https://www.inaturalist.org/observations/77833102 (CC BY 4.0).
Page 126, Photo: left, J. Hollinger, https://commons.wikimedia.org/wiki/File:Nymphaea_odorata_(2).jpg (CC BY 2.0).
Page 128, Photo: top, Gouwenaar, https://commons.wikimedia.org/wiki/File:18820180704_Dotterbloemen_Veersloot_Molensloot_langs_Pannepad.jpg (CC-BY-SA-4.0).
Page 129, Photos: top, mfeaver, https://www.inaturalist.org/observations/50188026 (CC BY 4.0); bottom, L. Gaudette, https://www.inaturalist.org/observations/13253962 (CC BY 4.0).
Page 130, Photo: top, J. Gallagher, https://www.inaturalist.org/observations/15660519 (CC BY 4.0).
Page 131, Photo: top, S.L. Winterton, Aquarium and Pond Plants of the World, 3e, CDFA and USDA APHIS ITP.
Page 133, Photo: right, C. Hohn, https://www.inaturalist.org/observations/13809078 (CC-BY-4.0).
Page 134, Drawing: **UFL**
Page 135, Photo: top, J. Shorma, https://www.inaturalist.org/observations/165840600 (CC-BY-4.0); top right, C. Fischer, https://commons.wikimedia.org/wiki/File:PotamogetonNatans2.jpg (CC-BY-SA-3.0); bottom left, A. Gunnar https://www.inaturalist.org/observations/15942868 (CC-BY-4.0).
Page 137, Photos: top left, J. Hollinger, https://commons.wikimedia.org/wiki/File:Potamogeton_gramineus_(3817604665).jpg (CC-BY-2.0); bottom right, K. Ziarnek, Kenraiz, https://commons.wikimedia.org/wiki/File:Potamogeton_obtusifolius_kz01.jpg (CC-BY-SA 4.0).
Page 138, Drawings: left, (*P. obtusifolius*) **CBH**; center, (*P. pusillus*) **UFL**; right, (*P. obtusifolius*) **CBH**
Page 141, Photos: top, L. Clark, https://www.inaturalist.org/observations/6611453 (CC-BY-4.0).
Page 142, Photo: right, https://www.inaturalist.org/photos/153685177 (CC BY 4.0).
Page 144, Photo: top, **MIN**
Page 145, Drawing: van de Weyer & Schmidt, https://commons.wikimedia.org/wiki/File:Potamogeton_berchtoldii_illustration_(01).png (CC-BY-SA-3.0); Photo:
Photo: H. TINGUY, https://commons.wikimedia.org/wiki/File:Potamogeton_berchtoldii_plant_(01).jpg (CC-BY-SA-2.0-FR).
Page 147, Drawing: **UFL**; Photos: top, N. Martineau, https://www.inaturalist.org/observations/15712219 (CC-BY-4.0); bottom, Q. Wiegersma, https://www.inaturalist.org/observations/94890555 (CC BY 4.0).
Page 150, Drawing: **UFL**
Page 151, Drawing: **WF**; Photo: S. Pogacnik. https://www.inaturalist.org/observations/170052070 (CC BY 4.0).
Page 152, Photo: N. Aaron, https://www.inaturalist.org/observations/184597192 (CC BY 4.0).
Page 154, Photos: (top) R. Foster, https://www.inaturalist.org/observations/20819808 (CC-BY-4.0); (center) Q. Wiegersma, https://www.inaturalist.org/observations/33730316 (CC-BY-4.0).
Page 156, Photos: (left) M. Bowser, https://www.inaturalist.org/observations/3642607 (CC-BY-4.0); (right) R. Foster, https://www.inaturalist.org/observations/20170344 (CC-BY-4.0).
Page 157, Drawing: Winterringer, *Aquatic plants of Illinois* (1966); Photos: (top) **MIN**
Page 158, Photo: left, **MIN**
Page 159, Drawing: **UFL**
Page 160, Photos: (top) S. Lefnaer, https://commons.wikimedia.org/wiki/File:Potamogeton_natans_sl22.jpg (CC-BY-SA-4.0); (bottom) I. Bashinskiy, https://www.inaturalist.org/observations/88367574 (CC-BY-4.0).
Page 162, Photos: (left) S. lefnaer, https://commons.wikimedia.org/wiki/File:Potamogeton_nodosus_sl3.jpg (CC-BY-SA-4.0); (right) M. Zappa, https://www.inaturalist.org/observations/51502409 (CC-BY-4.0).
Page 163, Photo: top, D. Frade https://www.inaturalist.org/observations/27900118 (CC BY 4.0).
Page 165, Photos: A. Hosper NL https://www.inaturalist.org/observations/15521384 (CC-BY-4.0).
Page 166, Photos: S. lefnaer https://commons.wikimedia.org/wiki/File:Potamogeton_perfoliatus_sl9.jpg, https://commons.wikimedia.org/wiki/File:Potamogeton_perfoliatus_sl10.jpg (CC-BY-SA-4.0).
Page 167, Photo: top, K. Ziarnek, https://commons.wikimedia.org/wiki/File:Potamogeton_perfoliatus_kz02.jpg (CC BY-SA 4.0).
Page 168, Photos: left, K. Peter, https://commons.wikimedia.org/wiki/File:Potamogeton_praelongus_bluete.jpeg; top, K. Peters, https://commons.wikimedia.org/wiki/File:Potamogeton_praelongus.jpeg (CC-BY-SA-3.0-migrated); bottom right, M. Садыкова, https://www.inaturalist.org/observations/99089458 (CC-BY-4.0).
Page 169, Photo: N. Aaron, https://www.inaturalist.org/observations/79811097 (CC-BY-4.0).
Page 171, Photo: N. Tippery, https://www.inaturalist.org/observations/51595046 (CC-BY-4.0).
Page 172, Drawing: **UFL**; Photo: Q. Wiegersma, https://www.inaturalist.org/observations/33154441 (CC BY 4.0).
Page 173, Photo: M. Bowser, https://www.inaturalist.org/observations/33453024 (CC BY 4.0).
Page 176, Photos: M. Bowser, https://www.inaturalist.org/observations/16033431 (CC BY 4.0).
Page 177, Drawings: **UFL**
Page 179, Photos: left, R. Watson, https://www.inaturalist.org/observations/16804436 (CC BY 4.0); right, L. Clark, https://www.inaturalist.org/observations/12889835 (CC BY 4.0).
Page 180, Photos: top, C. Fischer, https://commons.wikimedia.org/wiki/File:RanunculusTrichophyllus.jpg (CC BY SA 3.0).
Page 182, Photo: bottom, S.A. Schmid, https://www.inaturalist.org/observations/83165894 (CC BY 4.0).
Page 183, Photos: C. Catto, https://www.inaturalist.org/observations/86176938 (CC BY 4.0).

Page 184, Photos: left, bazwal, https://www.inaturalist.org/observations/18211442 (CC BY 4.0); right, H. Rose, https://commons.wikimedia.org/wiki/File:Ranunculus_sceleratus_leaf1_(14758147920).jpg (CC-BY-2.0).
Page 185, Photos: left, A. Moro, https://commons.wikimedia.org/wiki/File:Ranunculus_trichophyllus_leaf_(08).jpg (CC-BY-SA-4.0); right, L. Perrie, https://www.inaturalist.org/observations/19877727 (CC BY 4.0).
Page 187, Photo: bottom, J. Horn, https://www.inaturalist.org/observations/98553556 (CC-BY-4.0).
Page 189, Photos: top left, https://commons.wikimedia.org/wiki/File:Grassy_Arrowhead_(Sagittaria_graminea)_(38859446382).jpg (CC BY 2.0); bottom, R. Foster https://www.inaturalist.org/observations/31359039 (CC BY 4.0).
Page 190, Photo: **MIN**
Page 192, Photo: Specimen 57361, University of South Florida Herbarium (CC BY 3.0).
Page 194, Photo: bottom, I. Louque, https://www.inaturalist.org/observations/5129954 (CC-BY-4.0).
Page 195, Photo: right, **MIN**
Page 199, Drawing: **UFL**
Page 200, Photo: B. Semmling, https://www.inaturalist.org/observations/170738784 (CC-BY-4.0).
Page 201, Photos: top, Q. Wiegersma, https://www.inaturalist.org/observations/106989582 (CC-BY-4.0).
Page 202, Photo: top, K. Rossner, https://www.inaturalist.org/observations/90929760 (CC-BY-4.0).
Page 203, Photo: H. Hillewaert, https://commons.wikimedia.org/wiki/File:Sparganium_angustifolium.jpg (CC BY-SA 4.0).
Page 204, Photos: left, https://upload.wikimedia.org/wikipedia/commons/0/05/Sparganium_angustifolium.JPG (CC BY-SA 3.0); right, M. Vainu, https://commons.wikimedia.org/wiki/Category:Sparganium_angustifolium#/media/File:Sparganium_angustifolium_in_Estonia.jpg (CC BY-SA 4.0).
Page 205, Photos: top, R. Routledge, https://www.invasive.org/browse/detail.cfm?imgnum=5538795& (CC-BY-3.0).
Page 206, Photo: top, Jason Hollinger, https://commons.wikimedia.org/wiki/File:Small_Bur-Reed_(3818415894).jpg (CC-BY-2.0).
Page 207, Drawing: **UFL**; Photo: S.L. Winterton, Aquarium and Pond Plants of the World, 3e, CDFA and USDA APHIS ITP.
Page 208, Photos: left, E. Schmidt, https://www.inaturalist.org/observations/130072507 (CC-BY-4.0); right, Ljaž, https://www.inaturalist.org/observations/89444297 (CC BY 4.0).
Page 209, Photos: left, M. Bowser, https://www.inaturalist.org/observations/17159795 (CC BY 4.0); right, U. Magsar, https://www.inaturalist.org/observations/176937732 (CC BY 4.0).
Page 210, Photo: C. Fischer, https://commons.wikimedia.org/wiki/File:PotamogetonPectinatus2.jpg (CC-BY-SA-3.0).
Page 211, Photos: left, C. & T. Van Loon, https://www.inaturalist.org/observations/185859716 (CC BY 4.0); right, S. Lefnaer, https://commons.wikimedia.org/wiki/File:Potamogeton_pectinatus_subsp._pectinatus_sl31.jpg (CC-BY-SA-4.0).
Page 216, Photos: top left, C. Light, https://commons.wikimedia.org/wiki/File:Utricularia_geminiscapa_PinhookBog.jpg (CC-BY-SA-3.0); top right, Q. Wiegersma, https://www.inaturalist.org/observations/14405102 (CC BY 4.0); center left, Lauren, https://www.inaturalist.org/observations/81121943 (CC BY 4.0).
Page 217, Photos: left, S. Johnson, https://www.inaturalist.org/observations/30102530 (CC BY 4.0); right, M. Graziano, with permission.
Page 218, Photos: left, M. Graziano, with permission.
Page 220, Photo: right, M. Graziano, with permission.
Page 221, Photo: top, P. Skawinski, https://commons.wikimedia.org/wiki/File:Utricularia_intermedia_plant_(03).jpg (CC-BY-SA-3.0).
Page 222, Photo: bottom, M. Graziano, with permission
Page 223, Photos: right, L. McLaurin, https://www.inaturalist.org/observations/26647563 (CC BY 4.0).
Page 224, Photos: top, H. Bellat, https://commons.wikimedia.org/wiki/File:Utricularia_minor_flower_(01).JPG (CC-BY-SA-2.0-FR).
Page 225, Photo: R. Hammer, with permission.
Page 226, Drawing: **UFL**; Photos: top, MIN; bottom, N. Martineau, https://www.inaturalist.org/observations/15158860 (CC BY 4.0).
Page 227, Photo: M. Graziano, with permission.
Page 228, Drawing: **UFL**
Page 229, Photos: left, **MIN**; right, N. Martineau, https://www.inaturalist.org/observations/15712241 (CC BY 4.0).
Page 230, Photo: right, S. Keller https://www.inaturalist.org/observations/14302309 (CC-BY-4.0).
Page 231, Photos: left, N. Martineau, https://www.inaturalist.org/observations/19260491 (CC-BY-4.0); right, D. Loarie, https://www.inaturalist.org/observations/6827451 (CC-BY-4.0).
Page 232, Photo: right, N. Takebayashi, https://commons.wikimedia.org/wiki/File:Utricularia_macrorhiza_(29309016568).jpg (CC-BY-SA-2.0).
Page 236, Photo: C. Fischer, https://commons.wikimedia.org/wiki/File:WolffiaArrhiza2.jpg?fastcci_from=6316484&c1=6316484&d1=15&s=200&a=fqv (CC-BY-SA-3.0).
Page 237, Photos: top, A. Zharkikh, https://commons.wikimedia.org/wiki/File:2015.09.13_13.52.47_IMG_0449_-_Flickr_-_andrey_zharkikh.jpg (CC-BY-2.0); bottom, K. Burdick, https://www.inaturalist.org/observations/30397712 (CC BY 4.0).
Page 238, Drawing: bottom, **UFL**; Photos: top left, Z. Wang, https://www.inaturalist.org/observations/169677273 (CC BY 4.0); bottom, S..lefnaer, https://commons.wikimedia.org/wiki/File:Wolffia_columbiana_sl14.jpg (CC-BY-SA-4.0).
Page 239, Drawing: **UFL**; Photo: top, Summit Metro Parks, https://www.inaturalist.org/observations/33294085 (CC BY

4.0).
Page 256, Photo: Ashley McCabe, with permission.

GLOSSARY

Achene: A small, dry, non-opening, one-seeded fruit
Alternate: Applied to arrangement of leaves, whereby they arise singly at each node
Annual: Plants completing their life cycle in one year or growing season
Anther: The terminal portion of a stamen; bears pollen
Axil: As in leaf axil, the angle between a stem and a leaf
Basal: Applied to arrangement of leaves, whereby leaves are confined to the bottom or base of the plant
Bladders: small, sac-like structures specialized to capture prey
Blade: The expanded flat portion of a leaf
Bract: A much reduced leaf at the base of a flower stalk or flower cluster
Capsule: A dry fruit comprised of multiple divisions, normally opening to release seeds
Dimorphic: Having two forms, e.g., divided submersed leaves and undivided emergent leaves
Drupe: A fleshy fruit containing a seed(s) enclosed in a hard pit
Emergent: Existing above the surface of water, surrounded by air
Emersed: Projected above water surface
Flowering stem: The stalk of a flower cluster (i.e., a peduncle)
Follicle: A dry fruit which splits only along one side at maturity
Fragmentation: Process by which a plant body separates into multiple pieces, often with each detached section capable of rooting
Globose: Spherical in shape
Hydrophobic: Water-repellant
Leaf stalk: The stalk by which a leaf is attached to stem; a petiole
Ligule: a small projection of tissue towards tip of a stipule
Linear: Line-shaped; very long and narrow, with essentially parallel sides
Midrib: The central, linear, vein that runs along the length of a leaf blade from base to apex
Midvein: The thick central vein that runs along the length of a leaf blade
Node: A place on a stem where a leaf or leaf scar is attached
Nutlet: A diminutive nut; dry, non-opening, usually one-seeded, fruit with a hard shell
Obovate: Shaped like a section through a hen's egg but with the larger end toward the top
Opposite: Applied to arrangement of leaves, buds, or scars whereby they arise in pairs positioned across from each other, one pair at each node
Ovary: The usually swollen base of the female organ which contains the eventual seeds
Palmately divided: Arrangement of leaf segments or lobes, or veins, with these diverging from a common origin at the top of a leaf stalk
Peduncle: the stem or stalk holding up a flower cluster; a flowering stem
Perennial: A plant that lasts for more than two years
Petal: One of the inner floral leaves in a flower, usually brightly colored, which are whorled
Phyllodial: The condition of a leaf whereby the leaf stalk is expanded and functions as a leaf, i.e., a bladeless leaf
Pinnately divided: Arrangement of leaf segments or lobes, or veins, with these

displayed on either side of a central stalk or midrib, respectively

Receptacle: The expanded base of a flower

Recurved: Curved or bent downward

Rhizome: A horizontal underground stem with roots growing from it

Rosette: A circular cluster of tightly packed leaves, usually at ground level

Sepal: One of the outer floral leaves in a flower, usually greenish, which are whorled

Septate: With internal transverse partitions or walls called septa

Sinus: The space between two lobes of a leaf

Spike: An elongated, unbranched stem bearing flowers along it that lack stalks; youngest flowers at top

Spikelet: A very small spike consisting of several reduced flowers concealed behind scales; mostly in grasses and sedges

Stamen: The male, pollen-producing, organ of a flower comprising a stalk and the anther

Stipule: A leafy or linear structure at or near the base of the leaf stalk

Stolon: A horizontal aboveground stem with roots growing from it

Stomate: A leaf pore used for gas exchange

Submersed: Existing under the surface of water

Two-ranked: Where the leaves on a stem are arranged in two vertical columns on opposite sides of the stem, appearing as two rows of leaves

Tuber: A thickened portion of an underground stem serving as a storage organ, e.g., a potato

Tubercle: A low, round bump, e.g., on top of some *Eleocharis* fruits

Turion: A highly condensed vegetative organ specialized for overwintering, i.e., winterbud

Whorled: Applied to arrangement of leaves or flowers whereby they arise 3 or more at each node

Winterbud: See *turion*

INDEX

Aldrovanda vesiculosa 24
Algae 11
American frogbit 90
Arrowhead 188
  Awl-leaved 197
  Common 188
  Estuary 195
  Grass-leaved 193
  Hooded 195
  Narrow-leaved 192
  Northern 190
  Quill-leaved 198
  Sessile-fruited 196
  Spongy-leaved 195
Azolla 25
  caroliniana 25
  cristata 25
Beggar-ticks 26
  Beck's 26
Bidens beckii 26
Bladderwort 214
  Common 232
  Creeping 219
  Flat-leaved 221
  Floating 228
  Horned 217
  Lesser 224
  Mixed 218
  Piedmont 225
  Purple 226
  Pygmy 225
  Resupinate 229
  Swollen 220
  Two-flower 219
Bogbutton 202
  Pink 202
Bog-mat 239
  Sword-like 239
Brasenia schreberi 28
Bryophytes 10
Bulrush 200
  Water 200
Bur-reed 203
  Arctic 206
  Floating 205
  Narrow-leaved 204
  Simple-stemmed 204
Buttercups 180
Cabomba caroliniana 30
Callitriche 32
  heterophylla 34
  palustris 35
  stagnalis 36
Caltrop 212
Carex 1
Cattails 1
Ceratophyllum 37
  demersum 38
  echinatum 39
Chara 11
Charophytes 11
Coontails 37
Cow lily 124
  Tiny 124
Crowfoot 180
  Cursed 184
  White water 183, 185
  Yellow water 182
Ditch-grass 187
  Beaked 187
Duckweed 83
  Common 84
  Ivy-leaved 87
  Little 85
  Minute 86
  Pale 88
Duck-meal 207
  Common 207
  Spotted 207
Eel-grass 242
  American 234
Egeria densa 41
Eichhornia crassipes 43
Elatine 44
  ambigua 47
  americana 45
  minima 46
  triandra 47
Eleocharis 48
  acicularis 49
  obtusa 48
  palustris 48
  parvula 50
  robbinsii 51
  tuberculosa 48
Elodea 52
  Brazilian 41
Elodea 52
  canadensis 53
  nuttallii 54

Eriocaulon 55
  aquaticum 56
  compressum 57
  parkeri 58
Fanwort 30
  Carolina 30
Featherfoil 67
  American 67
Floating primrose-willow 96
Floating-heart 128
  Big 129
  Little 130
  Yellow 131
Fontinalis novae-angliae 10
Frog-bit 70
  European 70
Glyceria 61
  borealis 61
  septentrionalis 61
Golden
  club 132
  pert 62
Grasswort 89
  Eastern 89
Gratiola aurea 62
Guppy grass 115
Hatpins 55
Hedge-hyssop 62
  Golden 62
Heteranthera 63
  dubia 64
  multiflora 65
  reniformis 66
Hornwort 37
  Common 38
  Spineless 39
Horned-pondweed 240
Hottonia inflata 67
Hydrilla 68
Hydrilla verticillata 68
Hydrocharis morsus-ranae 70
Hydrocotyle 71
  americana 71
  prolifera 71
  ranunculoides 72
  umbellata 73
  verticillata 71
Hypericum boreale 74
Isoëtes 75
  acadiensis 75
  echinospora 77
  engelmannii 78
  lacustris 78
  melanopoda 75
  riparia 79
  tuckermanii 79
Juncus 80
  militaris 81
  pelocarpus 82
Lachnocaulon anceps 55
Lake cress 186
Landoltia punctata 207
Lemna 83
  minor 84
  obscura 85
  perpusilla 86
  trisulca 87
  valdiviana 88
Lilaeopsis chinensis 89
Limnobium spongia 90
Limosella australis 91
Liverworts 10
Lobelia 92
  Water 92
Lobelia dortmanna 92
Lotus 118
  American 119
  Indian 120
  Sacred 120
  Water 119
Ludwigia 93
  palustris 94
  peploides 96
Manna grass 61
  Eastern 61
  Northern 61
  Small Floating 61
Marsh pennywort 71
  Floating 72
  Many-flowered 73
  Swamp 72
  Whorled 73
Marsilea quadrifolia 97
Mermaid-weed 177
  Comb-leaved 179
  Marsh 178
Mosquito fern 25
  Eastern 25
Mosses 10
Mudwort 91
  Atlantic 91
  Awl-leaf 91
Mud-midget 239
Mud-plantain 63
  Bouquet 65
  Grass-leaved 63
  Kidney-leaved 66
Myriophyllum 98
  aquaticum 100
  heterophyllum 101
  humile 103
  pinnatum 104
  sibiricum 105
  spicatum 106
  tenellum 108
  verticillatum 109

Naiad 110
  Brittle 116
Najas 110
  canadensis 112
  flexilis 112
  gracillima 114
  guadalupensis 115
  minor 116
  muenscheri 112
Nasturtium officinale 117
Nelumbo 118
  lutea 119
  nucifera 120
Nitella 11
Nuphar 121
  advena 122
  lutea 121
  microphylla 124
  ×*rubrodisca* 124
  variegata 125
Nymphaea odorata 126
Nymphoides 128
  aquatica 129
  cordata 130
  peltata 131
Orontium aquaticum 132
Persicaria 133
  amphibia 133
  coccinea 133
Pickerelweed 136
Pipewort 55
  Hairy 55
  Estuary 58
  Flattened 57
  Parker's 58
  Seven-angled 56
  Ten-angled 57
Pistia stratiotes 134
Podostemum ceratophyllum 135
Polygonum amphibium 133
Pondweed 137
  Alga 148
  Alpine 142
  Berchtold's 145
  Big-leaved 143
  Blunt-leaved 165
  Clasping-leaved 166
  Curly 149
  False 208
  Fern 173
  Flat-stem 176
  Floating 160
  Grassy 156
  Illinois 158
  Leafy 155
  Long-leaf 162
  Northern snail-seed 174
  Oakes' 164
  Red 142
  Ribbonleaf 153
  Richardson's 172
  Robbins' 173
  Small 171
  Snail-seed 147
  Spotted 169
  Water-thread 151
  White-stemmed 168
Pond lily 121
  Immigrant 122
  Small-leaved 124
  Yellow 125
Pontederia cordata 136
Potamogeton 137
  alpinus 142
  amplifolius 143
  berchtoldii 145
  bicupulatus 147
  confervoides 148
  crispus 149
  diversifolius 151
  epihydrus 153
  filiformis 209
  foliosus 155
  gramineus 156
  illinoensis 158
  natans 160
  nodosus 162
  oakesianus 164
  obtusifolius 165
  perfoliatus 166
  praelongus 168
  pulcher 169
  pusillus 171
  richardsonii 172
  robbinsii 173
  spirillus 174
  zosteriformis 176
Primrose-willow 96
Proserpinaca 177
  palustris 178
  pectinata 179
Quillwort 75
  Acadian 75
  Black spored 75
  Engelmann's 78
  Lake 78
  Riverbank 79
  Spiny-spored 77
  Tuckerman's 79
Ranunculus 180
  aquatilis 183, 185
  flabellaris 182
  hispidus 180
  longirostris 183
  recurvatus 180
  repens 180

sceleratus 184
trichophyllus 185
Riccia fluitans 10
Ricciocarpus natans 10
Riverweed 135
Horn-leaved 135
Rorippa aquatica 186
Rotala ramosior 94
Ruppia maritima 187
Rush 80
Bayonet 81
Brownfruit 82
Sagittaria 188
australis 188
calycina 195
cuneata 190
engelmanniana 188
filiformis 192
graminea 193
latifolia 188
montevidensis 195
rigida 196
subulata 197
teres 198
Sago false pondweed 210
Salvinia minima 199
Schoenoplectus subterminalis 200
Sclerolepis uniflora 202
Sea-wrack 242
Sedges 1
Smartweed 133
Scarlet 133
Water 133
Sparganium 203
americanum 203
androcladum 203
angustifolium 204
emersum 203
eurycarpum 203
fluctuans 205
minimum 206
natans 206
Spatterdock 121
Spikerush 48
Spikesedge 48
Little-headed 50
Needle 49
Robbins' 51
Spirodela polyrhiza 207
Spongeplant 90
American 90
St. John's-wort 74
Northern 74
Stuckenia 208
filiformis 209
pectinata 210
Tape-grass 234
Threadfoot 135
Thread-leaf false pondweed 209
Toothcup 94
Trapa natans 212
Tropical duckweed 134
Typha 1
Utricularia 214
biflora 219
cornuta 217
geminiscapa 218
gibba 219
inflata 220
intermedia 221
juncea 223
macrorhiza 232
minor 224
olivácea 225
purpurea 226
radiata 228
resupinata 229
striata 230
subulata 231
vulgaris 232
Vallisneria americana 234
Water bulrush 200
Water cress 117
Water hyacinth 43
Common 43
Water lettuce 134
Water lily 126
Fragrant 126
Water lobelia 91
Water lotus 119
Water marigold 26
Water pennywort 71
Water purslane 94
Water spangles 199
Water starwort 32
Greater 34
Pond 36
Two-headed 34
Vernal 35
Water star-grass 64
Watermoss 199
Waternymph 110
Canadian 112
Brittle 116
Northern 112
Slender 114
Southern 115
Watershield 28
Waterweed 52
Brazilian 41
Common 53
Free-flowered 54
South American 41
Waterwheel plant 24
Waterwort 44
American 45

Asian 47
Long-stem 47
Small 46
Water-celery 234
Water-chestnut 212
Water-clover 97
European 97
Water-meal 236
Brazilian 238
Columbian 238
Northern 237
Water-milfoil 98
Cut-leaved 104
Eurasian 106
Low water 103
Northern 105
Parrot's-feather 100
Slender 108
Variable-leaved 101
Whorled 109
Water-primrose 93
Common 94
Creeping 96
Water-shamrock 97
Water-thyme 68
Wigeon-grass 187
Wild rice 1
Wolffia 236
borealis 237
brasiliensis 238
columbiana 238
Wolffiella gladiate 239
Yellow cress 186
Lake 186
Zannichellia palustris 240
Zizania 1
Zostera marina 242

ABOUT THE AUTHOR

Donald J. Padgett is a native of northeast Philadelphia with fond memories of nearby New Jersey, especially the Jersey Shore. He earned a B.S. in Biology from Susquehanna University, Selinsgrove, Pennsylvania, and an M.S. and Ph.D. in Plant Biology at the University of New Hampshire, Durham. Under the direction of Garrett E. Crow, his doctoral dissertation examined the taxonomy and evolution of Pondlilies (*Nuphar*).

As Professor of Biological Sciences since 1999 at Bridgewater State University, Bridgewater, Massachusetts, he regularly teaches courses on plant identification, wetland ecology, invasion ecology, and general biology. His research focuses on the ecology of aquatic and wetland plants, most recently examining the role of aquatic turtles in hydrophyte dispersal. He has authored numerous research articles and published several regional field guides on plant identification.

Dr. Padgett has also been an environmental consultant for over 20 years mostly dealing with rare and endangered hydrophytes and their management. He currently serves as managing editor of the *Northeastern Naturalist*.

Other field guides by Donald Padgett:

Wetland Plants of New England: A Guide to Trees, Shrubs, and Lianas

Aquatic Plants of Massachusetts

Aquatic Flora of Connecticut & Rhode Island

Aquatic Flora of Northern New England